Composing Drama
for
Stage and Screen

Stanley Vincent Longman
University of Georgia

Allyn and Bacon, Inc.

Boston   London   Sydney   Toronto

Library of Congress Cataloging-in-Publication Data

Longman, Stanley Vincent.
  Composing drama for stage and screen.

  Includes index.
  1. Playwriting. 2. Moving-picture authorship.
I. Title.
PN1661.L6 1986   808.2   85-30798
ISBN 0-205-08737-X

Printed in the United States of America

10 9 8 7 6 5 4 3 2 1 91 90 89 88 87 86

Contents

Preface

Some years ago, when Jeremy Soldevilla, then of Allyn and Bacon, suggested writing a new book on playwriting, I initially resisted the idea of adding yet another treatise on the topic. As I considered the matter over the next two years, however, I concluded that there is a book on the subject worth writing: one that is not prescriptive, listing the "rules" of what one had to do as a playwright, but rather descriptive, addressing the possibilities, the sorts of things one could do. By and large, what interests me and, I think, the better playwrights who have worked with me, are the conditions implied by the stage or screen as dramatic media. There are multiple ways of dealing with these conditions and a dramatist must be willing to grapple with them. I know of no book that quietly and directly deals with these conditions. Certainly none does so for all three dramatic media used most frequently in the contemporary world: stage, film, and television. A new book should also emphasize that dramatic writing is not simply writing, but rather composing an experience made up of actions to be witnessed. This book is the result of both convictions.

Many people have directly or indirectly contributed to this book, reaching back to the time playwriting first began to exert a fascination over me and extending through the work of writing the manuscript. Studying and writing under the guidance of Curtis Harnack, William Reardon, James Hatch, and Howard Stein influenced me greatly, and I express my gratitude to each of them. I also thank the many colleagues with whom I have worked in the theatre and specifically in the development of new plays, in connection with the Drama Department at the University of Georgia, the New Play Project of the Southeastern Theatre Conference, and the Play-writing Awards Program of the American College Theatre Festival. These include, among many others of course, William Wolak, Faye Head, Charles Eidsvik, Leighton Ballew, and August Staub, all at the University of Georgia; Marian Gallaway, Douglas Young, and Roland Reed with the New Play Project; and David Young, Michael Kanin, Jerry Crawford, Sam Smiley, Ronald Willis, Christian Moe, John Kirk, Roger Cornish, John Cauble, William Gibson, and Larry Divine associated with the American College Theatre Festival. In addition, several others have worked with me and no doubt influenced me in other connections related to playwriting, including Virginia Scott, Louis Giannetti, George Savage, Corinne Jacker, Lloyd Richards, and Franco Sandrelli. Perhaps some of the strongest influences have come from students, among whom I would list Mohammed ben Abdallah, Nancie Allen, Stewart Bankhead, Tom Boeker, Kathleen Campbell, Ethel Chaffin, Angela Elam, Thomas Fuller, William Goulet, Jimmy Grier, Frank Hall, Larry Hembree, Regina Hicks, Paul Holmberg, Lee Holston, Linda Duck Hyde, Don Massa, Michael O'Brien, Cary Parker, Muriel Pritchett, Kenneth Robbins, Dennis Scott, Rory Sullivan, Leslie Wade, Elliot Wasserman, Robert Watson, John Wilson, Jen Kai Yang, and Michael Yoder.

Finally, in the actual work of bringing together the manuscript for this book, I must thank several people, and first among them Ruth Longman for her help and support. She read and criticized the writing as it went forward and patiently endured the whole process. My friend and colleague August Staub also was encouraging, sometimes to the point of prodding or even nagging. I owe a debt, too, to Charles Eidsvik who carefully reviewed the material on screenwriting and made many valuable suggestions, and to Barry Sherman who did the same for the material on television writing. Now as the book enters its final phases of editing, I must thank Hiram Howard of Allyn and Bacon for his support and Elydia Siegel of Superscript Associates for her attention to the spirit of the book and its finer details.

A word about pronouns: they, you, and he. "They" is used in virtually all references to the audience, for the presence of so many people makes "it" seems weak and impersonal. "You" refers to the reader. "He" is used as a generic third person regardless of gender. He might well be a she, but constructs like "he or she" or "he/she" become very awkward.

Stanley Vincent Longman

Introduction

This book is intended for readers seriously interested in composing drama. The word "composing" is carefully and calculatedly chosen. Plays are not so much written as composed, for they consist not just of words to be spoken by actors but of actions accomplished in some sort of space. We are used to the idea of composition in music and see the composer as one who calls for the creation and duration of tones. A playwright composes exchanges of energies among performers who embody fictional characters. Both composer and dramatist use paper as an intermediate medium for describing their work in its ultimate medium. Writing words on paper serves to signal other people what to do, much as the scoring of music alerts musicians when and how long to sound what notes. "Scoring" a play is not as precise an activity, but it is of the same order.

As an aspiring dramatist, you can find many guidelines for playwriting written by playwrights, teachers, journalists, and critics, especially between 1920 and 1960. Not many of these books are still on the market and most were written out the conviction that certain rules and regulations could help anyone write a play. Rules are rules, after all, and no matter what play you thought you were writing, you would do it better if you knew them. The success George Pearce Baker had early in the century teaching playwrights at Harvard and later at Yale provided some of the inspiration behind that conviction. Baker himself contributed to the proliferation of books on playwriting. Many of these primers on playwriting religiously catalogued do's and don'ts. Do write the play on the basis of conflict, don't resort to description; do show the characters in action, don't let them talk to us; do set the play in one locale, don't shift locales constantly; do write about interesting people with whom we can identify, don't write about failures who fully deserve to fail. Above all, write a play that will engage an audience, don't bore them. Only the last "rule" applies universally, but it is scarcely worth enunciating because anyone who knows at once how to engage an audience can do without a book on the subject. As for the other rules, there are any number of plays that violate one or another of them and yet succeed. These are not just plays by such "strange" playwrights as Samuel Beckett or Peter Handke. Many are written by Chekhov, Molière, or even Shakespeare.

A look at the theatre of the late fifties, however, reveals a spirit of experimentation setting in, determined to challenge any and every "rule" of dramatic writing. Absurdists were fond of breaking the bonds that normally hold a play within a determined form. Environmental theatre enthusiasts sought to pull down all traditional barriers between spectacle and spectators. Playwrights often dispensed with "plot" in the generally understood sense of the word. All the playwriting books seemed addressed to a theatre that was dying, if not virtually dead—the theatre of the "Well-Made Play." Such books certainly had little relevance for anyone wishing to write for the theatre of today, much less tomorrow. Many argued that there were no rules, nor even principles. A playwright had to make his own way, profiting by his own life and artistic experience. No book could do that work for him.

Both views, that there are rules and regulations and that the only principles are those that apply to the individual artist, are in some measure wrong. There is no rule that cannot be profitably broken. At the same time, if there were no principles cutting across drama in all its individual works, we would not know how to deal with the theatrical or the cinematic experience at all. We would be at sea every time we encountered a new work. No play is absolutely unique, a law unto itself. Certainly it is remarkable how wide a spectrum the stage will accommodate and the effort to describe and define drama has never yielded a final statement. Every time a principle seems universally valid, some playwright will prove it less than universal. This should not, however, prevent us from exploring the dramatic experience for what we may be able to discover useful to the composition of future plays.

This book proposes to deal with the conditions inherent in the drama and in its several media, particularly the stage, the big screen (cinema) and the small screen (television.) Drama by its nature imposes certain conditions. The stage and the screen as dramatic media also impose conditions. These conditions imply certain principles, and understanding these principles shortens the time spent adapting to the conditions. Drama works by a carefully defined separation of its own realm from that of everyday actuality. It makes deliberate use of overt visual and oral suggestions to imply a richer imagined existence. It resorts always to action, in the sense of effecting change and affecting others. These conditions cannot be expressed as rules, but anyone who would write a play has to deal with them. To be sure, as a screenwriter or playwright you do have the right to choose your public, but the public is equally free to choose its plays. If you are not sensitive to the nature of the dramatic encounter between the public and the play, you may well end up writing plays for an audience of one: yourself. Of course, that may satisfy you. If it does, this book is not for you.

Plays naturally and normally are to be shared. The extent to which your play can be shared depends ultimately on your willingness to grapple with the material, the medium, and the dramatic mode. This book attempts to address these matters. Rather than impose rules or regulations, and so stultify creativity, it attempts to develop a sense for the dramatic and a relish for its potentials. Hopefully, too, it will inspire you to take on the challenge of composing a play.

The book also explores the dramatic experience in the forms in which it most commonly appears in the contemporary world. Despite the deep traditions and rich understandings pertinent to stage plays, the fact is that most new plays appear on screen. Certainly the likelihood of gainful employment is higher there than in the so-called "legitimate theatre." The appetite for new material has become voracious, thanks mostly to television. No doubt for that very reason, much of the material seen on television, even if smoothly produced, is relatively empty, inane, and poorly written. Nevertheless, the basic principles by which drama works apply here as well as they do on stage. Indeed, the stage reminds us always of the economy of means that enriches any dramatic work. It is probably the best training ground for any dramatist, no matter the ultimate medium in which plays appear. For this reason, Part I of this book deals with the dramatic mode in general, regardless of medium, Part II with the stage medium, and Part III with the screen media—film and television. The final section, Part IV, deals with the "post-partem" phase of the dramatist's work, as the script receives its final polishing and goes out into the world to be manipulated, exploited, undermined, ruined, or, perhaps, beautifully realized by others.

The structure of this book grows out of an effort to acquaint you with the conditions of the dramatic mode—the creation of a pretense of life through a spectacle of action. One such condition is the simultaneous existence of two levels of reality in a play: the physical reality of actors upon a stage or images upon a screen and the virtual reality of characters in their world. All drama consists of an act of presentation to a gathered audience. This act creates at once a sense of tension, a line of energy running between the spectacle and the spectators. Tension also characterizes the levels of reality as well. In fact, it is a basic motif to drama. Dramatic composition consists of handling, focusing, and controlling lines of tension. We are used to seeing drama as being rooted in conflict—tension created by the opposition of characters one to another. That certainly is one source of dramatic tension, indeed the most reliable, but it is not the only one. It can take other forms as well: tragic irony, comic incongruity, intriguing disparity, mysterious contrast. All of these are at the disposal of the dramatist. You owe it to yourself to be sensitive to them.

It is not enough, however, to be sensitive to the conditions; they are inherently abstract. Theory can serve good purpose, but a work of art needs the stuff of life. Without that, it rings hollow, dull. Creativity calls for three elements: the vibrancy of life in its big and little dimensions, a perspective or point of view that lends interest, and a capacity to render both in the chosen mode and medium. One of the paradoxes of dramatic composition is that it strives to *be* life while deliberately *not being* life. Another is that it assumes universality through the particular: only those plays that seize a sense of life being lived in a vivid present moment can hope to appeal to people living at diverse times and places. Of course, there is no way to give a dramatist a sense for life, but there are habits of thought and discipline that can sharpen awareness of the life that swirls around us all. These can help you to grapple successfully with the challenge of composing drama.

Any book on dramatic composition ought nowadays to take into account the new-found open structures of plays and movies. Such freedom requires a keener sense for the essence of drama, for it lacks the usual comfortable structuring devices such as protagonist, reversals and discoveries, or major dramatic questions. This is a time of great challenge for a dramatist, and the future may well entail a gross mismanagement of such freedom, producing theatrical or cinematic counterparts of "minimal art" and "found objects"—reductions of art to its simplest level. Indeed, such instances already exist. On the other hand, the present day climate offers the opportunity to rediscover dramatic art in new modes, new styles, with new arrangements of tensions, and new uses of medium. The best contemporary dramatists, such as Tom Stoppard, Harold Pinter, Ronald Ribman, Sam Shepard, David Mamet, Dario Fo, Friedrich Duerrenmatt, attempt just that. At the same time, our world has a seemingly insatiable appetite for entertainment. On that score alone, having a sense for the dramatic and how it operates is valuable. In neither case can we simply repeat "tried and true" formulas and expect them to work indefinitely. After awhile they grow tired and their bones show. Formulas work only so long as audiences do not recognize them, and even when they do work, they diminish the stature of art.

The structure of the book attempts to strike a balance between theory and practice. The hope is that you may continually sense relationships between the conditions of drama and your own perceptions and attitudes of life and so become eager to translate your material into drama. Theoretical insights can open up possibilities not otherwise glimpsed. Meanwhile, drama is intensely personal. Composing it calls for meshing your personality with the material of the play and with the potentials drama offers. It is a struggle, but it can be exhilarating because no other form of writing gives back a more palpable sense of reward when everything meshes. The audience rises in a standing ovation.

PART I

The Dramatic Mode

1

Drama
and Life

All art, drama included, is first and foremost an experience shaped by using the stuff of life for a specific purpose. An artist takes experience and recasts it in the form of a new experience. The materials which the artist manipulates vary considerably from one art form to another: pigments applied to a canvas, photographic images projected on a cinema screen, musical notes sounded in sequence, chiseled stone, or a series of dance steps. All of these provide distinct experiences by virtue of the materials used, but they are all capable of reflecting common human experience. This is the source of their power. We encounter a work of art with the anticipation of entering a new realm, somehow removed, different, unusual, or special. This is the appeal of art. We may also emerge from the experience somewhat changed, seeing life in a new, slightly different way. Looking at a painting, listening to a jazz combo, reading a comic strip, watching a movie, attending a play—all are occasions to move away from life and to see it from a new perspective.

In all these respects, drama is like any other art; it differs from other arts in the materials it uses, the nature of its experience, and its way of reflecting life. The dramatist sees things in terms of action, builds the audience's experience through encounters and confrontations, and reflects life through the interplay of action and spectacle with the imagination of the gathered audience.

This chapter investigates the special province of drama, how it relates to life and how it acts on experience by recasting it rather than simply copying it. To use the stuff of life and the materials of a particular art form is to create a new and distinctive experience.

The Dramatic in Everyday Life

The term "art" conjures up the vision of some exalted and rarefied offering intended for a connoisseur or a coterie of knowledgeable viewers. Only the initiated have access to it. "I don't know much about art, but I know what I like," as the not-so-old saying has it. The same response can happen at the mention of "the Theatre." Very special, mysterious, profound things happen in the Theatre. Very special people go to the Theatre.

Whatever truth in this view, it is equally true that art and theatre are a part of life. To call something an "art" is merely to recognize in it the effort to manipulate specific materials for the enjoyment of other people. The work could be an opera or a "rock" session, a marble statue or a piece of wood whittling, a five-act tragedy or a stand-up comedy routine, a woodcut or a comic strip. All of these are pieces of art. An art work is simply a type of endeavor in which the artist uses certain materials to shape an experience for others. The operatic composer, the rock musician, the sculptor, the whittler, the cartoonist, indeed all artists, do this. Few people have trouble recognizing a comic strip as a part of life, but many find it hard to find life in a symphony.

Paradoxically, the ease with which we grant a comic strip a place in life grows from our recognition that it exists outside life. We do not question its right to occupy its own ground, shape its characters on its own terms, use balloons for speech, or frames for segments of action. The first step in creating a work of art—comic strip, painting, or drama—is to remove it from the world around. This consists of somehow framing it, setting it apart, and establishing conventions by which an illusion of life may be sustained.

This description is as true of a play as of any other art work. The dramatist first separates an experience from its actual context in life (even if it is an entirely imagined experience), then recasts it in the medium of the stage or the screen. In the audience, we become engaged, even enthralled, with this new experience in proportion to the opportunity it affords us to reflect on life itself. A truly powerful play causes us to see ourselves as we had never quite done before, and with a leisure life itself never allows us.

The mere act of extracting an experience from its normal context throws emphasis upon it. Imagine that you are approaching two people on the street who are conversing animatedly. As you pass, you hear only this much: "Of course, there's no excuse for putting a bag over it, but there is not much use in it either. The bag will burst before long." The other replies, "Burst? I'm going to rip it open this afternoon." You have no idea what the conversation is about. That short exchange, however, holds fascination partly because it is out of context. That itself makes it provocative. The two speakers might very well forget their words, but the eavesdropper has trouble forgetting them. The same happens in a play as it opens on a group engaged in some activity and closes when they are engaged in another. Simply isolating action in this way gives it impact. It prompts us to see the closing activity as related to the opening and to recognize all the intervening activities as contributing to the final moment. We do not respond in this way to life itself, but we delight in doing so in the theatre.

Having isolated a segment of life, a dramatist must take advantage of the impact it creates and manipulate the material to make it as fully compelling as possible. This requires seizing the qualities in the medium, in the composition of the audience and in the action represented that might in combination create fascination, wonder, amusement, compassion, or whatever suits the purpose. On this score, drama does not differ from life in kind, only in degree. We encounter things in life that are dramatic. We all know people who are distinctly dramatic. We all remember events in our lives for their sheer dramatic power. Moreover, we all possess that instinct that causes us to behave for effect when we encounter others — the instinct for drama.

Consider the number of times in the course of a single day you find yourself confronting other people. Whenever we encounter others, we are always in some measure aware of the act of presenting ourselves and almost as often conscious of the effect we are having (or wish we were having). This everyday experience contains the very essence of the dramatic: *the encounter*. The prime ingredient in drama is the encounter that occurs when we come together to witness the spectacle of people encountering each other, their fates, or perhaps an absurd circumstance. The encounter is the basic motif of drama. Encounters in real life, however, have varying degrees of effect on those who participate in them. The more striking or profound the effect, the closer to drama. Naturally, it is possible to control the effect and this too happens in everyday life. When the encounter is formalized, as in the theatre, it becomes crucial that the effects be carefully shaped. This is the first and most fundamental duty of the dramatist.

It can be useful to examine some instances in real life that produce dramatic effect. Some events, by their very nature, spellbind the onlooker. Without any contriving, a palpable tension causes one to sit up and take notice. A man standing on a window ledge twenty stories above the street is dramatic in this sense. Assuming that he is genuinely committed to suicide, his purpose has nothing to do with affecting the casual passerby. He may wish to create guilt or compassion in the person who pushed him to this extreme, but, if he is really serious, his struggle is with himself. And that struggle, graphically apparent in his perching on that ledge, creates the compelling stuff of drama.

Other instances of the dramatic in real life involve the deliberate effort to work an effect. Social or political protest, of the sort America, France, and other countries witnessed in the late sixties and early seventies, often took on dramatic qualities. Protestors organized and manipulated events to affect others. The Catonsville Nine carried files from the offices of a draft board to the street, where they poured blood on them. The spectacle was hard to ignore. The sit-ins, marches, rallies, demonstrations were quasi-dramatic events—not fully dramatic because they took place in the context of actual life. Occasionally in those days, to heighten awareness of issues, actions were fine-tuned into the form of "guerrilla theatre." Those were times of "consciousness raising"—a phrase which, however cumbersome, holds rich dramatic connotation. Such "contriving" does not belong to protestors alone; those in power also resort to the dramatic. Public appearances of leading figures are often elaborately planned affairs, calculated to make a leader appear larger than life, a person of formidable dimensions.

Whether or not someone intends to create effect, no event is really dramatic unless it is "played" to a gathered audience. There is an old philosophical conundrum: "When a tree falls in the forest, does it make a sound if no one is there to hear it?" The "dramatic" answer is "No." All the drama evaporates if a suicide ledge is above an empty street or if no one is out front of the draft board offices when the blood is poured. The same is true of a play. If no one is "out front," there is no drama. Naturally, everyone involved in the creation of a play, the dramatist first of all, is intensely interested in the crowd "out front." Every task—writing the play, planning the production, rehearsing the actors—contributes to producing an effect on an audience. Although the best effects are those the audience feels happen spontaneously, without contrivance, such effects require the most work. They also require that someone be "out front."

The dramatic then is a part of life; we see it daily. We encounter it when we meet a friend, when we witness a planned event, or when we suddenly come upon an intriguing act. Naturally, we look for it when we go to the theatre or the cinema and we are badly disappointed if it is not there. A dramatist therefore must understand the essence of a drama—an encounter with a spectacle of human action—and recognize the elements that make for drama. Five elements can be identified:

1. The first and most basic ingredient in the dramatic mode is *the encounter*. It occurs on the most fundamental level when spectator meets spectacle. This moment produces an immediate polarity, a palpable tension, which prompts the spectator to watch, to listen, and to attend the event. The dramatist seeks to play on this tension, to create and sustain effects and responses.

2. *Polarity and tension* provide the fundamental motif of the dramatic mode. Any onlooker becomes more or less involved in proportion to how much seems to be at stake. Tension may take multiple forms: conflict, incongruity, irony, disparity, contrast, anticipation. A play may be seen as an energy system of lines of tension; the basic tension inherent in the act of encounter is multiplied in a myriad of other poles of tension.

3. The dramatic mode depends upon *action*, action that we may directly see and hear. Drama occurs. When it ceases to occur, it ceases to exist. In this respect, drama is perhaps more lifelike than any other art. Life, too, ceases to exist when it ceases to happen. It cannot be encapsulated, contained, or frozen without destroying it. Moreover, one senses drama in much the same way one senses life: by observing the actions of others. Just as we come to know other people by seeing them and hearing them, so we become involved in a play and its characters. The objective experience of our eyes and ears lets us translate action into inner life.

4. The dramatic mode depends upon a *sense of immediacy*. It appears to be happening *now*. This is the source of the old adage that "The theatre dies every night only to be reborn when the curtain rises the next night." Dramatic action resides in what Thornton Wilder has called a "perpetual present time." A novel, on the other hand, is a story of something that appears over and done with. A play carries with it the "illusion of the first time," the sense that it is occurring now, before our eyes, spontaneously, without plan or contrivance. Paradoxically, only careful planning and contrivance, and continual repetition and practice can produce this illusion.

5. As a result of all of these conditions, the dramatic mode employs a *driving force*, an impetus that moves action forward against odds of one sort or another. The spirit of encounter, the use of poles of tension, the reliance on action, and the sense of immediacy all play into the emergence of a driving force. Typically, what keeps a spectator's attention is the sense of something pending, something about to happen, something acting against resistance, all in the immediate present.

Throughout this book we will be exploring the rich implications of these five elements. No matter what medium is used for dramatic purposes, these elements are present in some measure. The screenwriter will tap them every bit as much as the playwright.

Mode vs. Medium

Thus far we have been discussing the dramatic mode without regard to the medium in which it may appear. "Mode" is significantly different from "medium." Mode refers to a manner or manifestation of experience. The dramatic mode is experience manifested through the spectacle of human action. There are other modes besides the dramatic: the musical mode employing tone and rhythm; the graphic mode, using line, color, or mass in two-dimensional space; the lyrical mode using the play of words; the narrative mode using words for storytelling. Medium refers to the context, conditions, and materials of an art form in which experience is re-created. Thus painting is a medium using pigments applied to a two-dimensional surface. The cartoon and the comic strip use ink drawn on paper, but they tap the graphic mode as much as painting. Some experiences lend themselves to re-creation better in one medium than another. The glory of a stupendous sunset, for example, can be caught in painting, but would be difficult in a cartoon and virtually impossible in bas-relief sculpture.

Through the ages, the dramatic mode has found its medium in the theatre, in the actual encounter of performers and spectators. Our age has produced new media that each provide a home for the dramatic: radio, television, and cinema. All of these—the stage, the speaker box, the tube, and the silver screen—have the capacity to present the spectacle of human life through action, and this of course is the dramatic mode. Just as in the contrast between the painting, cartoon, and bas-relief sculpture, all of which are visual media, one dramatic medium may reflect a certain human experience more vividly than another. A movie, for example, may convincingly portray the agony of loneliness through the interplay of images, but a stage play attempting the same thing would produce unendurable tedium.

What differentiates the dramatic media is the essential material they employ. In the confined space of the stage, performers present themselves to a gathered audience. Television and cinema present the interplay of moving images upon a two-dimensional screen. Radio presents suggestive sound. These media may all serve purposes other than dramatic ones. The stage could be the arena for acrobatic tricks, magic acts, or dances. Film may be used for recording actual events as documentaries or for rendering visual designs in motion (what some call "pure cinema"). Television can be used for journalistic reporting, for game shows, sports, or advertisements, and indeed these take up the majority of program time. When, however, they use the images or sounds of performers to create a spectacle of imagined human action, they become dramatic. It is this ingredient of *imagined* human action that makes the difference. Whenever imagined activity accompanies the actual presentation of performances, images, or sounds, "the magic" of drama can emerge. The relationship can be graphically represented as a set of interlocking circles, as shown on page 9.

Watching a drama, we translate what we actually see into an imagined life that is not really there. We take a succession of moving images passing across a movie screen (perhaps the image of a coffin being lowered into a grave followed by one of an eye shedding a tear) and create in our minds an imagined experience that was never really there at all (death and grief). On stage, a Shakespearean soliloquy presents us with an actor speaking alone and we translate it into a character ruminating in his mind. There

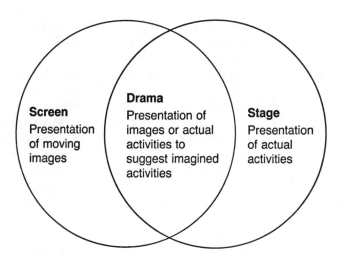

is always a degree of disparity between the actual experience of the stage or screen and the imagined experience it summons up in our mind's eye. Living actors performing before us on stage create characters living their lives in our imagination. Images of faces, bodies, hands on screen and voices on a sound track also prod into life a set of characters in our imagination. Characters exist only in our minds as products of the signals provided by actors or their images before us. In this sense, no matter what medium, the dramatic is always double-edged. The actual and the imagined exist side by side.

Actuality vs. Reality

Drama works by deliberately setting itself apart from surrounding life by such devices as the proscenium arch, the platform stage, pools of light set against darkness. All arts do this: painting by way of the picture frame, sculpture by way of the pedestal, music by themes and codas. In short, art tends to separate itself from actuality in order to reflect upon reality. Drama in particular, due to its double-edged nature, points up the difference between actuality and reality. Drama makes use of the stuff of actuality (human activity) and recasts it in a new actuality (performers or images before an audience) in order to reflect upon reality.

What is the distinction between the two? Actuality refers to the physical phenomena of our day-to-day existence. Reality is the meaning we attribute to experience. It is this distinction that makes drama possible, for we can witness events on stage or screen that would be patently impossible in the "real world," and find in them vibrant expression of our reality. Masses of people, for example, do not transform themselves into rhinoceroses, as they do in Eugene Ionesco's *Rhinoceros*, and yet we can recognize in the mutation a kind of reality: figuratively, the masses can and sometimes do change into blind, unthinking, thick-skinned, beady-eyed, compassionless monsters.

The dramatic mode entails that wonderfully ironic experience Samuel Coleridge called the "willing suspension of disbelief." It is a calculated phrase. We do not in fact believe the illusion projected from the stage or from the screen, but we do, for the time being agree to suspend our disbelief—agree, that is, to accept the illusion for the sake of whatever it may show us about human reality. We know full well that we are witnessing a stage over a span of time, say from eight in the evening until ten. But we are also willing to accept for the duration that much more time has elapsed and that the stage is also somewhere else, perhaps far removed from where we presently sit. The opening scene of *Hamlet* illustrates this well. For the duration of the scene—some 175 lines (about twenty minutes' playing time)—we are on the ramparts of the castle at Elsinore from midnight until the cock's crow at dawn. Nights in Denmark may be short, but not that short. We know that, but for the sake of the illusion and the play as a whole, we accept passing the night in Denmark.

This is the double existence of drama referred to earlier. Watching the performers move before us (or their images on a screen), we create our own illusion of the lives of the characters in collaboration with the artists. The first of these artists, chronologically if in no other way, is the dramatist who shapes the outlines of the illusion by playing upon the double levels of the dramatic mode and developing a compelling tension to hold the audience. The dramatist must attend to actors as well as characters; to the actual passage of time for the audience and the virtual time of the characters; to the stage or the screen and the world of the play.

On our part, as audience members, we are continually torn between two contrary mental impulses: empathy and aesthetic distance. Empathy is the vicarious sharing of the lives of the imagined characters. In the full throes of empathy, we feel as if we were ourselves undergoing the characters' experience. Aesthetic distance checks the power of empathy. It is a state of detached contemplation, recognizing the play as a contrivance, a pretense, and knowing it will somehow round out and conclude. In that spirit, we wait in anticipation of what the contrivance will produce, what it is all about. Too much aesthetic distance and drama evaporates. It needs imagination and illusion to succeed. Too much empathy is equally stultifying, for then the play merges with life and so loses form and meaning. The two forces need to strike a balance, checking the power of each other. That balancing act produces "willing suspension of disbelief."

Out of all this, the manipulation of illusion, the balancing of empathy and aesthetic distance, and the interplay of the actual and the imagined, drama reflects reality. It separates itself from actuality and creates an illusion in order to produce some new insight into the age-old question of what it means to be human; and that is a matter of reality.

The Play as a Game

Play is a fundamental human instinct and it is probably no accident that our word for drama is "play." Johan Huizinga has suggested that the distinguishing factor of our humanity may be the instinct for play, and he calls both his book and the human animal *Homo Ludens* (playing man) rather than the familiar *Homo Sapiens* (knowing man). Play calls for assuming roles, establishing rules and boundaries, and deliberately setting play apart from ordinary, mundane activity. This instinct has given us games, religious rituals, formal ceremonies, and, of course, drama. The term need not imply frivolity. Play is one of the important ways we have of knowing or understanding our condition as humans; it also serves as a reminder of the sense of delight in such discovery.

Like games, plays work on pretense, based on their own rules and regulations. Moreover, plays have their own domain, their own playing field. Note the many references Shakespeare makes to this condition: "All the world's a stage," we are simple players "who strut our hour upon the stage," "What you will," "As you like it," "To hold as 'twere, the mirror up to reality," "Suppose within this wooden O are two mighty monarchies." All of these suggest the delight of play as well as its power to reflect human life. Like a game, a play first sets itself apart within its own space and time, and, for the duration, new rules substitute for the usual, mundane conditions. Plays and games are both conducted through actions, reactions, and interactions, all based on some pretense. Moreover, plays and games both develop tension by pitting a will against resistance, usually in the form of obstacles or opposing wills. A major difference lies in the contribution of the spectator, who is not crucial to the game, but who is integral to a play.

Twenty-three centuries ago, the philosopher Aristotle sought to describe the premise upon which drama rests. He asserted that drama creates its own world with each play, a world operating on its own probability. What is probable or believable in a play is not necessarily probable in the actual world. The dramatist has the option, the artistic license, to establish a unique world. This does not mean that a play avoids dealing with reality, only that it is free to do so on its own terms. Like any freedom, Aristotle's "probability" carries with it an obligation. Once the realm of the play is established, what becomes probable must remain so. Moreover, the mere fact that something is possible in the real world does not render it the more believable in the play's world. It still has to be made probable in terms of the play. Although *Alice in Wonderland* and *Through the Looking Glass* are not plays, they provide good illustrations. They are riddled with impossibilities that are nevertheless probable on their own terms. People do not have to run fast in order to stay in the same place, as Alice and the Red Queen must do on the chess board. The realm beyond the looking glass is not our realm. The impossible becomes possible, even probable.

With this new probability, the work of fiction may provide novel and intriguing insights into our existence; while we may never literally run fast in order to stay in the same place, we have all had experiences that might aptly be described that way.

Like a game, a play also sets up goals, and with them a driving force striving toward them. The tension between combatting teams in a sporting event has a rich sense of the dramatic. A play too builds upon tension. It derives from a force operating against resistance until at last it overcomes it or is itself defeated.

Composing a play, then, may be likened to inventing and conducting a game with the following phases:

1. It sets up its own realm isolated from actuality in time and space.
2. It establishes a form of pretense conducted through action.
3. It creates its own rules, its own kind of expectation and probability.
4. It moves forward by a will exerting itself against resistance or obstacles.

Unlike a game, however, a play takes on its unique nature by the act of presentation. It is not complete until it encounters its audience.

A Play Finally Defined

We have now laid sufficient groundwork to hazard a definition of a play: a play is a spectacle of human life based on pretense and conducted through action. Because it calls both for spectacle and for action, a play naturally resorts to creating, sustaining, and varying tensions. About a century ago, the French critic and theorist, Ferdinand Brunetière, defined a play as "The spectacle of a will striving toward a goal and conscious of the means it employs." The definition is still apt, even if some of the conclusions Brunetière drew from it are today questionable. Since a play is a presentation communicating by observable actions to an audience, it is naturally a spectacle. Brunetière's "will" refers us to the play's driving force, which creates a forward motion; the word "striving" implies obstacles or contrary wills working as resistance against the driving force. Most intriguing in Brunetière's definition is his insistence on the will's being aware of "the means it employs." Inasmuch as drama is spectacle and action its means, it makes sense that the "will" acts by knowing what it is doing. We can sense the will only through what it does. So, while it is conceivable that the central character might not know exactly what his goal may be, he must be aware of the means he employs.

Since drama relies on observation, it requires that the will and its obstacles or contrary wills be observable. Brunetière takes this requirement literally and insists that they be embodied in characters whose interaction naturally becomes conflict. According to this requirement, one character must be the central character, the "protagonist" (from "pro" meaning "for" and "agon" meaning "act" or "struggle"). Conflict, Brunetière argued, is the very essence of drama.

There are, however, many plays not based on conflict, plays that nevertheless hold audiences in rapt attention. Anton Chekhov's *The Three Sisters* and Thornton Wilder's *Our Town* are two plays in which the will is not embodied in a character. Neither play has a protagonist. The will, the driving force, moves outside the characters, as the passage of time exerting pressure on the characters. This is not to say that the will is disembodied. In Chekhov's play, we become aware of it first through sound effects, then by the glancing blows time deals to the sisters as they dream of going to Moscow; in Wilder's play, the stage context and the Stage Manager himself help us sense the force at work. While some plays lack protagonists, even more lack antagonists. Melodramas almost invariably have them, but more subtle plays may rely on contrary forces within the protagonist, or in adverse circumstance, or in concrete obstacles. Moreover, the audience always exerts a certain force in any play, sometimes strongly enough to be reckoned with. A brilliant example of this occurs in Molière's *Tartuffe*, where the audience in its superior wisdom invades the stage by proxy in the character of the King's Officer to put Orgon's world to rights.

Instead of "conflict" as the essential ingredient in the drama, "tension" may be more apt and all-inclusive. Tension begins with the polarity between spectacle and spectator and elaborates in a variety of other forms: contrasts, disparities, incongruities, ironies, as well as conflicts. Here drama is clearly distinct from actuality. Life itself may from time to time exhibit all these forms of tension, but drama is infused with them as a means of catching and holding audience attention. Life, of course, cares not a whit if we sit up and take notice, nor that it "mean" anything. Drama derives its core purpose from its audience, so it must care: someone must watch and it must mean something on some level. The dramatist, as the one who makes the play "care," does so chiefly by manipulating lines of tension.

To revise Brunetière, tension is the essence of drama. It begins with the encounter of spectator with the spectacle and develops in the encounter of a driving force with resistance in the forms of obstacles, uncertainties, and contrary forces. The tension may produce conflict, and most often it does; but it may also take other forms, such as contrast, irony, incongruity, and imbalance.

A Slice of Life: An Illustration

The phrase "slice of life" was coined in the 1880s when Naturalism was in vogue. The Naturalists dedicated themselves to portraying life in all its detail, exactly as we see and hear it. In the theatre the ideal was to present a "slice of life," cut right out of the organism of life and transplanted on stage. The Naturalists were satisfied that they accomplished a wonderfully scientific service to the world by allowing us to examine life so closely in the laboratory of the theatre. Naturalism was a short-lived movement, for its playwrights did nothing beyond isolating a piece of reality for presentation in the theatre, trying deliberately to avoid creating effect. Although the movement is long dead, the attempts at duplicating life have never altogether ceased. During the early 1970s, a couple lived together for several days in a store display window in New York City as a spectacle for passersby. Andy Warhol has made several films that look at an object or person for hours.

Nevertheless, one way more readily to understand the work of the dramatist is to examine a slice of life. Such a scene has a "wet noodle" effect, lacking any tension or interest. It should be a challenge to the dramatist in you to locate and develop a tension that could arouse an audience's interest in the scene. The scene below is a simple recording of the events of a few minutes in a bus station; it is a slice of life.

> The scene is a bus station in the dead of night. A CLERK sits behind the counter, reading an issue of *Police Gazette* and occasionally whistling through his teeth. A JANITOR is lackadaisically picking up bits of trash: wrappers, cigarette butts, old newspapers, and used ticket stubs, and placing them one by one in the trash can. A middle-aged man, half asleep and bedraggled from his journey, is seated on one of the benches. This is SAM.

(AS THE CURTAIN RISES, enter BELLE from the main entrance of the terminal. She carries three suitcases awkwardly, and plops down on the same bench with SAM.)

BELLE
Whew! That was rough going. Boy, does it feel good to take a load off.

(The telephone on the ticket counter rings. CLERK answers.)

CLERK
Hello, bus terminal . . . . . . 4:40 and 8:30 . . . . . . No, they both go straight through. . . . . . . Yeah. You're welcome

SAM

That's a lot of luggage you got there.

BELLE

Yeah. Like I said, it feels good to sit down for once. I carted it all the way from Hapgood Avenue. You know Hapgood Avenue? Where it is, I mean?

SAM

No. I don't live here. I'm from out of town.

BELLE

No kidding? I'm going out of town.

SAM

Yeah. Well, that's where I came from—out of town.

BELLE

I'm going out of town, over to Elwood. You know Elwood, about seventy miles east of here? Hey, I guess I oughta buy a ticket.
      (She goes to the ticket counter.)
Hey, can I buy a ticket to Elwood?

CLERK

One-way or round trip?

BELLE

Gee, I don't know. See, I'm not sure how long I'm going to stay over in Elwood. Maybe I oughta buy a one-way, and buy one for coming back when I know better when I'm coming back. Whaddya think?

CLERK

Fine with me. That'll be $4.95.

BELLE

How much is a round trip?

CLERK

$9.90.

BELLE

Well, that settles it. I better just take the one-way.
      (She pays for the ticket, takes it and returns to the bench.)
See, I don't want to use up all my money right away.

SAM

Yeah. Round trip costs twice as much.

BELLE

Still, I'm gonna havta have busfare back, I suppose.

SAM

I suppose so.

BELLE

You come from Elwood?

SAM

No.

BELLE

See, I thought maybe, since you come from out of town, you maybe come from Elwood.

SAM

Well, I don't. I come from Burnam.

BELLE

Burnam? Gee, that's a long way. You come from there today? You been traveling all day or something? You look kinda tired.

SAM

Yeah, well, I am tired.

BELLE

It's no wonder, traveling all that way. I would be, too. And here I am complaining about carting all my stuff from Hapgood Avenue. Here you are, been on a bus most all day, I expect. You gotta right to complain.

SAM

I'm too tired to complain.

BELLE

Yeah. Well, I get that way sometimes, too—too tired to complain, you know. I mean, it takes energy to complain.
            (She takes a pack of cigarettes out of her purse.)
You wanna smoke?

SAM

No, thanks.

BELLE

Mind if I do?

SAM

No. Go ahead.

BELLE

Thanks. Calms the nerves, you know. When I go on a trip like this, I like to have my smoke.
            (She lights up.)
You going to Elwood?

SAM

No. Fact is I never heard of Elwood.

BELLE

Never heard of it? Oh, it's a real nice town. My sister lives there. That's who I'm going to see, my sister, Beulah. She's lived in Elwood the past ten years. Likes it, I guess, or she wouldn't stay there, don't you suppose?

SAM

I expect you're right.
            (The telephone rings on the ticket counter.)

CLERK

Hello, bus terminal. . . . . . . Next bus leaves at 4:40. . . . . You're welcome. Good night.

(JANITOR is satisfied he has finished the waiting room and goes into the men's room.)

BELLE

Yeah, I think she must like it. Whenever I get a chance to get away, I like to go over to Elwood myself.

SAM

Yeah, I guess it must be a nice town.

BELLE

It is. Real nice. You'd like it.

And so on. Obviously, the scene could go on and on, and it is threatening to do so. It will be a toss-up between Sam and us as to who will fall asleep first. No lines of tension are drawn. The result is that there seems to be no good reason for us to be watching the play at all. Belle appears ready to carry on until the 4:40 bus arrives. The only tension present, and it is a faint one, is the growing exasperation of Sam. One might play it up in order to make the scene stage-worthy. We might also create tension out of the very inanity of the whole conversation, pushing it until the audience's exasperation turns into amusement at the idiotic repetition. Still other lines of tension could be drawn, although they are presently untapped: the Janitor and his ritual of examining the trash he picks up, and the Clerk and his *Police Gazette*. Either one, or both, of them could provide a new source of interest if we wished. Moreover, the limbo-like atmosphere of the bus terminal in the dead of night could provide a source of interest, as could the outside worlds of Hapgood Avenue and Burnam. All these could contrast with the domain on stage and so produce a sense of tension. Belle or Sam might be trying to avoid the one or the other of these offstage places. Objects could also provide interest: the trash, the magazine, the telephone, the luggage, and Belle's purse. Right now, none of these provides any dramatic interest, but any of them could.

The Three Paradoxes of Dramatic Creation

By way of summary, three paradoxes embody most of the observations we have made of the dramatic mode. The "slice of life" scene helps illustrate all of them, especially the first.

1. *Drama is life and is not life.* Drama uses the stuff of life for its own purposes; its basic motif, the encounter, is borrowed from life itself. An audience encounters and comes to know the characters of a play much as we do in life. Life is full of situations that become spellbinding and fascinating (in other words—spectacular) due to their inherent tensions. These are moments that attract and so create an audience, even if it is a single enthralled onlooker. Drama also uses the motif of the encounter for its material. It comes in the forms of confrontations between characters, of struggles against circumstances or of discoveries of other forces. Unlike life, however, drama operates in its own imagined domain, according to its own rules and probability. It need not, and indeed it should not, imitate life. It resorts to action as its particular way of reflecting reality. Paradoxically, how closely these actions match actual human activities is no measure of how well they reflect reality. Outrageous distortions of the "real world" may produce a vibrant and meaningful depiction of "reality."

2. *Only contrivance can create believability.* A play must be deliberately distinct from actuality. Even the most Realistic play, one that appears very much like actuality, requires a playwright to contrive the material convincingly. It is not enough that such-and-such an event is possible or even likely in the real world; it must be believable within the imagined world of the play. The first duty of a dramatist is to ensure that no one would prefer to leave the theatre. That means composing lines of tension that arouse interest and anticipation. Only then do events in the play appear natural and convincing, however unnatural and incredible they might be outside the play. All this requires careful contrivance. The most natural play is the one that is most carefully contrived.

3. *Universality can only be achieved through the particular.* Like any artist, a dramatist is prompted to create a work relevant to all people in all times. This is the prime ingredient in the great works of the past, the "classics," which have guaranteed their authors immortality. Who would not like the same guarantee? And yet, to give in to this impulse may yield a play that is so abstract as to be thoroughly lifeless. The more conscious you are of Grand Themes, Important Ideas, and Deep Meanings, the more surely your play will die aborning. So, far from giving you immortality, it may even mortify you before your friends. What most accounts for drama in any human experience, on stage, on screen or in life itself, is the presence of those details, those specific little moments, objects, qualities that provoke a vision of a life being lived. The immediacy of the dramatic moment, the sense that it all is happening now before us, requires the sort of detail that absorbs our attention and deepens the experience. Drama calls for particular people caught up in particular circumstances. The audience can give them imaginative extension into life in general, but if a play starts on that level, it will go dead—never inviting the audience to make these extensions.

This third paradox is a natural result of the first two. That drama *is* life and is *not* life means that it takes the materials of life and uses them for its own purposes. That only contrivance can create believability requires the dramatist to manipulate material in such a way as to make it not only believable in terms of the play, but also richly suggestive in terms of the life experience of the audience. Together, these paradoxes lead to the third one, for they create the necessity for details that vivify characters' lives and elicit a palpable response. Only then can the audience identify with the characters, recognize their condition, and find parallels in life that expand the play beyond its own boundaries. That is true universality.

Exercises

Note: The Sam-Belle scene above is printed in the generally accepted format for a stage play. The format has these characteristics:

1. It is single-spaced except a) between speeches and b) between stage directions that refer to the actions of others besides the speaker of the preceding line. Then it is double-spaced.

2. Characters' names appear CAPITALIZED, centered above each speech and in the stage directions.

3. A quarter margin (a quarter of the way into the page) is used for all stage directions. The first of these, describing the opening action, is usually introduced by the phrase "AS THE CURTAIN RISES," or "AS THE LIGHTS COME UP," all CAPITALIZED.

4. Stage directions are also set off in parentheses.

5. The set description at the outset of the script is set off the half-margin, without parentheses.

Use this format in writing your exercises and plays for the stage. One may as well get used to it. It is a format that commands a certain respect, giving an agent or a producer an initial impression of professionalism.

1. Rewrite the Sam-Belle scene to develop a line of tension. In other words, make the scene interesting.

2. Write down a sequence of conversation you overhear. Analyze your transcription for potential dramatic material. Write it now as drama.

3. Scan the newspapers for stories with dramatic potential. Select one such story and use it as the basis for a scene.

4. Take the following circumstance and develop a scene out of it: An envelope arrives bearing the outside notation: "URGENT: STRICTLY CONFIDENTIAL."

5. Write a brief autobiography. You may treat your whole life, a sequence of events, or a single episode. Write it in whatever form strikes your fancy: as a first-person narrative, a third-person narrative, as a dramatic dialogue, or in any other form. Do it quickly without much reflection. Afterwards, notice the tone you take, the form you select, the way it uses emphasis and subordination. What does it tell you about your tendencies as a writer?

2

The Dramatist's Involvement

Every play has two more characters than indicated in the cast: the audience and the dramatist. Although neither is actually present on the stage or the screen, each significantly influences the drama. Each has a personality which alters the world of the play. The characters and their behavior are different because of the power of these two personalities. The audience may begin as an amorphous entity, but it assumes character as members become involved in the play. More will be said about this "character" later; the dramatist is our present concern.

Drama consists of a three-way intrigue among the dramatist, the experience represented in the play, and the audience gathered to share it. First the dramatist and later the audience struggle, hopefully with fascination and full absorption, to catch the values and meaning in the play. The dramatist's involvement gives the characters, their story and their world a distinct quality. The audience is always at least vaguely aware of the presence of the dramatist, that conniver and contriver operating behind the scenes. In the process, the dramatist naturally considers the audience. So, when we watch a play, we tend to watch it with the eyes of its creator—provided it is a successful play. This is so much the case that a scene that seems trivial and inconsequential in the hands of one dramatist can become poignant and moving in the hands of another. A comparison of Shakespeare's plays with their sources can be very revealing on this score. The personality of the dramatist is a telling factor in any play.

This does not mean that you must now busy yourself making over your personality into a "dramatist's personality." Probably no such thing exists. No one could declare beforehand that this person has a dramatist's personality and that one does not. What it does mean, however, is that an important part of a dramatist's work lies in discovering how his personality may engage with the dramatic mode. History offers many examples of dramatists whose personalities would not appear well suited to the profession. George Bernard Shaw, Luigi Pirandello, and Anton Chekhov are among them. Shaw would seem too caught up in himself and too given to abstract ideas ever to be able to handle the demands of drama. In fact, William Archer attempted to work with him on his first play and gave up, urging him to do the same. Pirandello delighted in philosophizing and storytelling; he considered essays, short stories, and novels perfectly appropriate outlets until he was almost fifty, when he discovered the apt way the stage could embody his unique vision. Anton Chekhov placed such demands on the theatre that it took the genius of Konstantin Stanislavsky to ferret out the distinct ways in which the stage could convey the effects, and even then the demands were not entirely met. At the opposite extreme, writers such as Henry James and Thomas Wolfe might seem potentially fine dramatists. Their fiction is full of rich, imaginative, provocative pictures of humanity. How much more powerful might they be if we encountered them on stage? In fact, both James and Wolfe did write for the theatre, and both without notable success. What happened for Shaw, Pirandello, and Chekhov, but did not for James or Wolfe, was the discovery of how their personalities could engage with the dramatic.

Actors often remark that playwrights are most peculiar people. As soon as they figure out one playwright, the next one presents an entirely new puzzle. Indeed they are peculiar, thank goodness. The delight we take in encountering a new play is partly the delight in seeing the world in a new way. Even in the case of a new play by a familiar playwright—perhaps especially then—we enjoy witnessing how this new material is treated by a familiar sensibility. So, the work of the dramatist is highly personal in nature. Your first struggle as a dramatist is in a sense a struggle with yourself. To win it you need to find answers to such questions as: How do I relate to my material? What's my point of view? How do I make it *my* material? How can I make drama work for me?

This chapter deals with such questions. The answers, of course, you must find within yourself, for there are no right answers, only those that suit one playwright as an individual creator. Playwriting, they say, cannot be taught. This is true insofar as one cannot teach a dull person to be interesting—which is of course what any dramatist chiefly wants. But there are two areas in which one may learn: one is the nature of drama's demands, limitations and challenges, and the other is a set of personal habits of thought and practice valuable in creating drama. Chapter 1 dealt primarily with the first of these; this chapter takes up the second.

The Cycle of Dramatic Creation

A drama begins in the mind of the dramatist and ultimately comes to rest in the minds of its audience members. In between, the dialogue in the script, the director's approach, the actors' interpretations, the nature of the setting, costumes, lighting, all serve to prod the audience members' imaginations to give life to the performance. Thus a play may be seen as a means of kindling life in the imaginations of others. This involves a "cycle of dramatic creation," beginning with a vision, passing through the medium of the stage or screen, and coming to rest in a vision now shared with others.

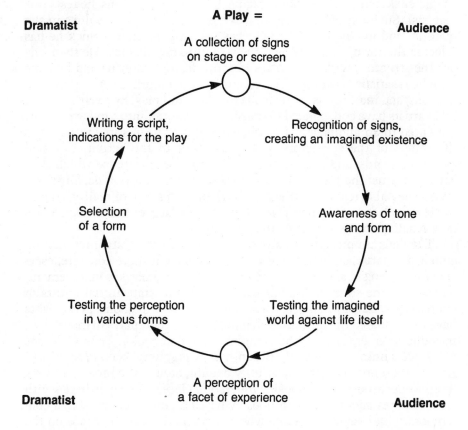

Dramatist

Audience

A Play =
A collection of signs
on stage or screen

Writing a script,
indications for the play

Recognition of signs,
creating an imagined existence

Selection
of a form

Awareness of tone
and form

Testing the perception
in various forms

Testing the imagined
world against life itself

A perception of
a facet of experience

Dramatist

Audience

Suppose you observe or undergo an experience that strikes you as dramatic. You see it as having potential as a spectacle for others. You test this potential by writing out various approaches you think might enhance its interest. Finally, you settle on a tone and a presentation that lets you write the script. The director and collaborating artists fill out the suggestions in the script, giving them full life on stage or screen. There the audience encounters it. They take the images presented and translate them into an imagined existence. They set it against their own experiences, and recognize in it some correspondence with reality, and accordingly it becomes more or less engaging. If it is a strong correspondence, the play is successful. Hopefully the response coincides reasonably closely to the dramatist's vision. The cycle might be graphically presented as a circle, which should be read from six o'clock up to twelve and back down to six again, as shown in the diagram on page 23.

Initially, at six o'clock, a particular facet of human life strikes the dramatist's interest. He undergoes, observes, or invents (which is usually some combination of the other two) an experience that seems to have dramatic potential. By writing out trial scenes, snatches of dialogue, character sketches, notes about staging or shooting locations, he tests this material. Such experimentation gives him a sense for the values in the material and for the form it might best assume. By nine o'clock he has selected the form, the style, and the structure for the play. He then fills out the structure with particulars in script format, altering and revising until he is satisfied that the script contains the appropriate details, rhythm, tensions, and indications for its realization as a full play. By twelve o'clock, other artists have collaborated in translating the script into a full experience presented to an audience. After twelve, the play begins its journey into the minds of the spectators, who create out of the activities, visual elements, words, and other elements an imagined existence which they balance against their awareness of the aesthetic factors of tone, form, and style. They also test all of this against their own sense of reality, so that by six o'clock there is again a perception of some facet of human experience now residing in the minds of the spectators.

The diagram presents an abstract version of the creative interaction among dramatist, audience, and reality. To make it more concrete, especially between six and twelve, the period of the dramatist's involvement, let us examine some particular cases which illustrate initial efforts of dramatists to transform perceptions or insights to script. Some playwrights have freely shared the process of shaping some of their plays in interviews, introductions, essays, and portions of their notebooks. Toby Cole has published a number of these in the anthology *Playwrights on Playwriting*. Among these, perhaps the most fully documented is the process Henrik Ibsen went through in composing his *Hedda Gabler*. The play began with a set of notes about a woman (loosely based on an actual person, a contemporary Norwegian novelist) who felt such a lack of influence on the lives of others that she set out to create a sensational past for herself that would be sure to have impact. Ibsen added to these notes some ideas concerning a mutual suicide pact she might have with a friend who carries through her end of the bargain, and about a lost manuscript belonging to a man she hates because of his enviable sense of mission in life. These were notes along with others for a play Ibsen abandoned, but they re-emerged later when he began planning *Hedda Gabler*. There they appear in altered form. The lost manuscript still belongs to that man of mission, Eilert Lovborg, but the mutual suicide pact transforms into Hedda's special instructions to Eilert for his romantic suicide. The triangle of Hedda-Eilert-Tesman was initially the center of this new play in the making, to which Ibsen added Eilert's new love, Thea, and Hedda's scarcely disinterested friend Judge Brack, both of whom serve to push Hedda's character into relief and to balance the structure of the play. The burning of the "lost manuscript" was one of the great inventions of this new play in the making. Other notes have been preserved for us, and out of them we can sense the gradual emergence of the now-familiar spectacle of Hedda, the self-hating manipulator of the destinies of others.

In writing the play *Six Characters in Search of an Author*, Luigi Pirandello dramatized the playwright's struggle to create. Pirandello himself had encountered a newspaper story that intrigued him. It was essentially the story of a family that had split up, to be reunited years later in a bizarre, unwitting encounter between the father and his wife's daughter in a brothel. He decided to try to make a play from the material, but it refused to take shape for him. Nevertheless, the characters he created assumed such passion that they would not let him alone. He first wrote about this struggle in a short story entitled "A Character in Search of an Author," describing the stepdaughter's haunting of the writer in his study. Then came the famous play, a play about a play that refuses to take shape. In it, six characters (the father, the mother, the stepdaughter, the legitimate son, and two small stepchildren) appear at a rehearsal one day insisting that the director and his actors do their play. The theatre artists at first regard these interlopers as an outrageous joke, but they gradually become intrigued with their story and finally agree to stage it. The more they try to do it, however, the more awkward and cumbersome the task becomes, for the characters' views of things are too contradictory and the stage too confining to permit the play to come to life. Yet the passion does come to life and it assumes greater depth because of the whimsicality of the framework. So this play about a play trying and failing to be a play becomes one of the great serious plays of the modern theatre.

You might now try this experiment, which perhaps would work better if you do not happen to know the plays just discussed. Test the material of these stories for yourself. How does each story strike you? What possibilities do they offer you? What would happen if you treat them comically, or if you shift focus from one character to another? What if you dramatize only certain parts of the story or combine the stories in some way? Testing material consists of applying as many "what if's" to it as you can. If you were to carry through and complete a play, the uniqueness of your personality insures that the result would be very different from Ibsen's or Pirandello's. Here the old adage "There is nothing new under the sun" has its saving grace, for each person sees things differently and each personality can give new life to the old material of living. One delight of dramatic creation is that it can spark and vivify stories that have been told a thousand ways. Carlo Gozzi once declared that there were only thirty-six dramatic situations, and that every play is simply a variation on one of them. This so intrigued Georges Polti in the nineteenth century that he wrote a book entitled *The Thirty-six Dramatic Situations*, systematizing, describing, and giving examples of each one. The notion is absurd in one sense, but it is certain that the number of possibilities is finite. Novelty and invention come with the perspective applied to material, not in the material itself.

A productive relationship between personality and creation has a double edge: it is both instinctual and intensely disciplined. On the instinctual side, it means that creativity depends on your adhering to your own natural bent, or, as Polonius put it, you must "To thine own self be true." Disaster could well occur if you try to pattern yourself after some dramatist whose personality is far from your own. Suppose Eugene O'Neill wanted desperately to be George S. Kaufman, who in turn wanted to be Maxwell Anderson, who gnashed his teeth because he wasn't Thornton Wilder, who meanwhile was struggling to write like Eugene O'Neill. Imagine the results if James Thurber had taken the notion to write deep, ponderous tragedies about the dark and bestial side of man. He would probably have faced unbearable frustration and the world would be the poorer for it. You need make no apologies for who you are. If your instinct tells you that a situation involving a man's loss of a cherished manuscript is comic, let it be comic. It may seem a horribly inhumane reaction, and in real life it would be. But we are not dealing with real life here. Putting a character on stage or screen puts distance between him and us. He now occupies his own fictional world. In this new context things that would otherwise seem horrible or disgusting may suddenly appear charming or amusing, provided we can accept the dramatist's tone. So one ought to indulge one's own natural reactions. One might make a case, as Samson Raphaelson does in *The Human Nature of Playwriting*, for a dramatist's obligation to give vent to his secret vices when creating a play. Secret vices are a great deal more interesting than public virtues. If you have a fascination for manipulation and exploitation, or for duplicity and connivance, or for murder and revenge, you had best restrain yourself in real life, but in creating drama you should indulge yourself fully. If you tend to be flippant, witty, uncaring, and detached, people will tend to find you irritating when something serious is called for, but in the world of your plays, again, you should indulge yourself.

An excellent illustration comes from the British playwright Harold Pinter. In his plays a surface realism and decorum is ruffled by intruding, mysterious, ominous forces that eventually shatter the surface. Plays such as *Birthday Party, Homecoming,* or *Old Times* baffle many viewers, and people often ask Pinter what they mean. On one such occasion, after a public lecture, someone rose in the audience and asked the familiar question: "Really, Mr. Pinter, what *are* your plays *about?*" Feeling impish and just a little tired of the old question, Pinter replied, "They are about the weasel under the coffee table." As Pinter tells this story, he meant nothing by the remark, only to provoke. Later he was surprised to learn how provoking he had been, when several scholarly articles appeared applying the image of the weasel under the coffee table to the plays of Harold Pinter. The story makes the scholars sound absurd. On the other hand, impish and off-handed as the remark was, it sprang spontaneously to Pinter's mind, much as the strange worlds of his plays had done. The image is in perfect keeping with the disturbing, ominous forces that arise in those worlds.

Now for that other edge of the personality-creation relationship: discipline. Indulging yourself is no way to write a play. It may get you started; it may rekindle a dying enthusiasm. But something else is needed if you are going to write a full and compelling play. Despite the supremely personal nature of creativity, it requires that you bring your personality, your instincts and insights, into accord with the demands of your medium. That is a matter of discipline. However interesting you may think you are, others will have to be persuaded. People are perverse that way, especially when they are gathered together in a crowd as in a theatre. You cannot appear before them and declare, "Look at me; how interesting I am!" (even if someone such as Woody Allen can occasionally get away with it). As a dramatist, your charge is to demonstrate your artistry through the surrogates of your characters and their world. To be blunt, your audience is not interested in you as a personality. Aside from your friends and your relations, no one cares particularly *who* wrote the play. In fact, in a successful play, the audience is oblivious to the fact that *anybody* wrote it. But an audience cares very much that the play engage their interest, and that means they must feel they can enter into the tone of the play, taking the dramatist's personality for their own. They will not tolerate so much as a minute of boredom. After two or three of those minutes, they will start finding their ways to the exit. Then they will remember who wrote it, and remember next time to stay away.

To keep them there and bring them back the next time, you do need to respond to the world around you in a genuine manner; but you must also contrive the dramatic experience in a convincing enough way that the audience too responds genuinely. It all calls for honesty and humility and craft: honesty with yourself, humility before your characters and your audience, and craft in the face of the demands of your medium.

Humility and honesty are personal questions you will have to deal with your own way. Craft, however, we can discuss, for it involves discipline and practice. It is a matter of bringing your personality into accord with your medium. Comic strips provide a vivid illustration of this. Examine the evolution of any well-known comic strip, such as *Donald Duck, Pogo,* or *Peanuts.* Contrast the earliest versions of Charles Schulz's *Peanuts* with

the most recent and notice how much more comfortably the characters
have come to live in their world as the style is honed, the tone sharpened,
and the form refined over the years. It is a long and laborious process. No
one should expect that a medium—theatre, novel, or cartoon—will respond at once to the sheer charm of one's personality. Still, working at it
can be a joy, and if you find that to be the case, you have won half the battle.

Finding Material

The initial question you very logically might ask yourself is "What shall
I write about?" Despite the logic of it, it is the wrong question to ask. Obviously, it will have to be answered if anything is to be written at all, but
it is not the *first* question to answer. This perhaps is a chicken-and-egg
paradox. One might suppose that creation begins with inspiration. Inspira-
tions, however, generally do not appear out of the blue. If you are bent
on awaiting that moment of inspiration, chances are the golden moment will never arrive. But, if you channel your thoughts, energies, and
ideas into constantly working with dramatic materials, inspiration will
come. Winnie-the-Pooh, that bear of little brain in A. A. Milne's books,
has some words of wisdom to offer on this score. Speaking to Piglet about
inventing "hums" (his word for poems), he remarks: "But it isn't easy,
because Poetry and Hums aren't things which you get, they're things which
get you. And all you can do is go where they can find you." In other words,
you find material by working with it. Just as an artist continually sketches
and so measures his ideas, a dramatist writes snatches of dialogue, pieces
of action, character descriptions, and other possibilities to test their value
for fuller treatment. This is what Pooh might mean by "going where they
can find you."

Still this sounds contradictory. After all, what material can you work
with until you find it? What you experience day in and day out, what you
observe, what you go through, what you think of, and what you remember—all these give you ample material. They are all fair game. At this stage,
maintaining a commonplace book can be very useful to you. This is a
writer's notebook which serves as a repository of all manner of material
that strikes you as potentially useful. In fact anything can go into it so
long as it interests you; that is the source of the term "commonplace." The
commonplace book serves at least four good purposes: 1. it is a record of
ideas, 2. it encourages the habit of observation, 3. it reinforces the discipline
of writing, and 4. it provides a place for experimenting, sketching, and
testing material. By setting aside a particular hour of every day in which
you promise yourself to work on the commonplace book, you shortly will
find that your problem is not one of finding material for the next play you
write, but rather one of choosing which play you will write next.

This process will tell you what material is distinctly your material. You will find yourself at ease with and intrigued by it. You know at once that you could work with it. The familiar word of wisdom to the writer is "to write about what you know." To follow that advice rigorously would lead you into obvious absurdities. It would mean only an ancient person with rich experience could ever write more than a few plays — and that person is probably too tired to do it. Even at that, as Bernard Grebanier points out in *Playwriting:* "A man could never write about women, never having been one, or a woman about men; no one could write about death, never having died, etc." The advice is probably the product of the Realist prejudice that only direct, objective experience counts. Somewhere between that advice and the Romantic idea that the source of material is in inspiration lies a middle road that leads more reliably to your material.

To find that road, we need to understand something about human invention. Here are a couple of examples. Mythical beasts, such as unicorns, griffins, mermaids, and dragons, seem at first glance to be pure inventions. On closer examination, they all prove to be clever combinations of features of other animals: the unicorn derives from a horse and a single horn borrowed from an antelope; the griffin from an eagle and a lion; the mermaid from a woman and a fish; and the dragon from various lizards, bats, and birds. André Breton, the "dean" of Surrealism, once remarked that when we attempted to imitate walking we invented the wheel. The wheel form is available in nature, but it is human invention that saw that it could do the work of moving us about. As the mythical beasts and the wheel suggest, there is no such thing as pure invention. No one invents anything absolutely new, only new combinations of the familiar.

The "familiar" covers wide territory. It consists of all you have experienced directly, all you have witnessed, and even all you have encountered in books, short stories, movies, and stage plays. How inventive you can be in combining these in new forms has most of all to do with *how* you view them. In other words, the perspective you bring to the material bears directly on how interesting it may be to someone else, such as an audience. We all undergo a wide variety of experiences in the course of a single day. Some leave vivid impressions behind, others fade almost at once. Paradoxically, what makes an experience vivid is not really the experience, but the way we look at it. Having a rich, varied, adventurous life is no guarantee of material appropriate for presentation on stage or screen, because it cannot of itself make you interesting. You may very well lead what most would regard as a dull existence, but, if your response to the life around you is interesting, invention is possible. The novelist Donald Windham once remarked that one does not write about what one knows so much as about "what one *must* know." If something has a profound effect on you, you want to know why. You want to explore it further. Writing is a way of doing that. No two persons have identical responses to the same experience, and this is the wonder of creativity. It is the very lifeblood of art. So your perspective, your way of looking at things, matters very much. Do not apologize for it; cultivate it. In this sense, writing "about what you know" makes sense, for it calls on you to write about *your* reactions, *your* views, *your* sense of life.

If you record the basic events of a single day, yesterday for example, they may well seem dull, but there is always variety and the possibility of taking a point of view on them that lends interest. Here is a sort of log of a day in the life of a college student. Upon waking, she encounters her roommate who has been up all night writing a paper. It is no wonder sleep was so fitful, and she wishes the roommate would organize her life to prevent such last-minute marathons; then she realizes that she herself must turn in a paper on Henry James in two days — a paper she has scarcely begun to write. Over breakfast she hears about a friend's escapade of the night before. Then she is off to class where she learns about the events leading to the signing of the Magna Carta, and afterwards she goes to the library to find some books about Henry James. There some friends prevail on her to go for coffee and they spend an hour arguing politics. The next class deals with the life cycle of certain metamorphic animals. After a quick lunch, she goes to her room, planning to work on her paper. She ends up sound asleep. She dreams she is transformed into a giant queen insect forced by workers to sign a document relinquishing powers to them. To her chagrin, she awakens to discover that she had missed her afternoon class. She decides to make the best of it all and sample a few chapters of Henry James's *The American*. She becomes engrossed in the book, reading chapter after chapter until dinner time. Discussion at dinner deals with various movies playing in town and that leads to a group forming to go to the cinema, including our friend. The film is an entertaining adventure story. Afterwards, she happens to meet a young man she admires. She had always enjoyed talking with him, but this time she says something foolish and she leaves him abruptly. She returns to her room. Now at last she starts writing her paper, but after a while she finds she cannot concentrate. She finishes the day chatting with the roommate who turned in her paper that morning. And so on.

There is nothing very remarkable here. It is the story of a day largely wasted, a story scarcely worth telling. Still, there are possibilities in it. They exist, for example, in the irony of her resentment against the roommate and her own disorganized day, in the poignancy of having said the wrong thing to the young man, the glimpses she had had of the lives of others in dining hall conversations, reflections afforded by James's novel, the movie, the class lectures, and her dream. They all could provide material if we can discover an interesting angle on them. And yet it was a dull day.

In addition to direct experience, you have a wealth of material at hand in the form of reported or observed experience. Newspapers are full of provocative material, especially the so-called "human interest" stories. Gossip always presents possibilities, sometimes a wonderful invention in itself. Stories people tell about themselves, activities you see others doing, chance remarks that suddenly take on interest, jokes and stories you hear or read, all these and many more are sources for your material. It all depends on how they strike you.

Gaining Distance and Perspective

If point of view is important in making material interesting, then distance is important. You cannot take a point of view on anything without standing away from it. For that reason, direct, personal experience is frequently not useful to you as a dramatist. You are too close to it. To tell the story of your break from mother and father, of your first love, of the bewilderment of objectives in your life, or the pain of some disillusionment you had will awaken the beast of self-justification, unless enough time intervenes to give you distance. Otherwise, you turn writing into mere therapy. Making peace with yourself is your personal, private business. A public theatre is no place to battle it out. An audience is not apt to care. No doubt there are therapeutic values in writing, but they cannot be your first concern. Your life may yield some fine material—but only those events and relationships of your life with which you have come to terms. Dramatic writing calls for imagination to lift experience out of the mundane into a realm that challenges and provokes. And this requires a certain detachment. With distance, you may well sense the ironies, meanings, humor, or tragedy inherent in the material. Then you can go to work.

As you do so, consider the weight and feel of the material. Think of it as something you might take in your hand and sense the life within. Some material will seem heavy, slow, ponderous, surrounded with an aura of ominousness perhaps; other material may seem light, airy, warm, and friendly; still other, staccato, nervous, and fitful. Whatever the feel it gives you, respect it. It will indicate the direction you should take with it. Naturally the material will have no particular feel at all if it does not mean something to you; in this case the direction you should take is to throw it out. On the other hand, anything that produces an immediate and reasonably strong reaction in you probably has a potential worth considering, for it certainly has meaning for you.

Below are five brief tales. They are told in as neutral a way as possible to keep them at the level of "raw material." They have no emotional content and no meaning. One or another of them, however, might strike a chord for you. You might see it from a point of view that makes it promising. To do so you need to give each one a chance by considering the various ways it could take form and gain an audience's interest.

1. A young man arrives in a strange town. Feeling lonely, he takes up with a group of people he encounters in a tavern. They treat him kindly, buying his dinner, and indulging him by listening to his stories. Then they offer to show him their town and take him off in a car. After touring about, they reach the outskirts of town, take his wallet and valuables, put him out of the car, and drive off.

2. Two women, living together in a small apartment, receive a visit from a third woman whom one had known years before. The visitor takes her old friend aside and persuades her to leave her present way of life and to join a new enterprise. When the old friend informs her housemate of her decision, the housemate flies into a rage and attacks the visitor viciously.

3. During a heavy rainstorm, a man stumbles into a seaside boarding house to gain shelter. He finds the occupants engaged in a table-top game, which they invite him to play. Playing the game, he discovers that it is intended to determine his own fate at the hands of the boarders.

4. A woman visits her brother in another city. She has long harbored a deep resentment of his wife, who is fully aware of it. The wife leads a vigorous, rewarding life as an executive for a manufacturing firm, a life that the sister regards with suspicion and envy. She insists that it undermines the wife's duty to the brother. Meanwhile, she begins to behave toward her brother as she feels a wife should, short of incest. The brother becomes insufferable and the sister more and more irritating, until the wife can take it no longer. She leaves them to their own devices.

5. A middle-aged man returns home at his usual hour to find his wife entertaining an earnest young woman whom he does not recognize. She claims to be his illegitimate daughter. This astonishes him, for he can think of no circumstance that could account for it. For some reason, his wife finds the whole business highly amusing and entertains the guest through dinner and well into the evening. After the guest's departure, however, she turns on him, and no amount of disclaiming can convince her that the guest's story was untrue. The next day, he finds the same young woman at his office, where she offers, for a certain sum of money, to clear the air for him.

·   Potentially, all five tales could be plays or movies. Some of them, perhaps all of them, may mean little to you. If so, you could not fill them out profitably and they should be left alone. One or two may actually have struck a responsive chord. Something in your background, in your sense of humor, of drama, of irony corresponds to the qualities implicit in the tale. Whatever it is, it is almost certainly different from the response of another person. No two people could take the same thumbnail sketch and turn out the same play; the law of averages would prevent it. Not only would it be impossible for the same words in the same order to emerge from two people working independently, the very idea of the play would vary considerably. Imagine, for example, how differently various dramatists would approach any one of these tales—Arthur Miller, Luigi Pirandello, Neil Simon, Bertolt Brecht, or Jean Anouilh. Feel free therefore to take one of the tales and claim it for your own. No one could challenge you.

We might almost say that any material is fair game so long as it has vibrancy and meaning for you and prompts you at once to take a point of view. This is not an argument for plagiarism, which occurs when you take material, meaning, *and* point of view from someone else. Greek myths have been treated again and again, but always with new meanings and new points of view. Compare the story of Phaedra and Hippolytus in Euripides's *Hippolytus*, Jean Racine's *Phaedra*, and Eugene O'Neill's *Desire Under the Elms*. If material has a special meaning for you, your treatment of it is apt to be original.

It is not enough for the material to be interesting and appropriate for you. If you are to use it for dramatic purposes, it must also be appropriate to the dramatic mode and to one of its media. This may require some special study and experimentation. If you like the material, but do not see at once how it might be treated dramatically, you should not give up on the spot. It is worth exploring. Working the material into the medium may tell you a great deal about it. It may even suggest new ideas, new material. Nevertheless, the dramatic mode is limited, and it does not lend itself equally well to all material.

The dramatic mode, as we have seen, calls for the presentation of an action involving the motif of encounter and the use of tensions. Some material will not fit, material for example deriving from a sense of inward, subjective serenity. A play might create that effect in the end, but it would be hard pressed to use it as its material.

Because of the nature of the dramatic mode, you generally find it more useful to begin with an idea rooted in a human situation. To start with a theme or an abstract message, such as "resentment may breed evil," or "pretending to be what one is not leads to absurdity," or "love has redemptive powers," tends to inhibit creativity. Such statements usher in no rich sense of immediacy, no urgency, and no action. The resulting play is likely to remain flat. To start with a character can also be unproductive. However spectacular and dramatic the character may be, a play virtually demands other characters, circumstances, and even objects in order to produce action. Although it may be difficult to provide all these things to surround the character, it can be done. Still, the play is apt to appear as an excuse for the display of that one character. A situation, however, may be dramatic from the start, tending to imply simultaneously theme, character, and action. It is much more likely to contain the seeds of a full drama.

Wherever you start your work, you have one more source of material available beyond life, observation, and your imagination—the form you use. Drama itself poses conditions that can become richly suggestive as you work with them. Again, the gospel according to Pooh: Winnie-the-Pooh comes upon a fallen tree and decides to make a poem about it without any idea where it will go, saying, "Well, I shall begin 'Here lies a tree' because it does, and then I'll see what happens." He has a form of poetry in mind (iambic tetrameter with a rhyme scheme of abbaa), and this together with the fallen tree produces the poem. By the same token, drama, the stage, the screen may all suggest things to you. You may find that an opening line, a stage setting, a film location, a moment of encounter, may all prompt in your imagination material that you would otherwise not have thought of. A man sits down at the dinner table and announces, "After we have dined, I want to tell you something that will fascinate you, but also cause each of you discomfort. Bon appetit!" That is provocative enough to launch a play, although what it is about is anybody's guess at the moment. Or: a man comes on stage, sees a rope lying on the ground and extending off into the wings. Unable to make out where it leads, he picks it up and begins to pull against the weight at the other end. Or: a woman pulls back the curtain on a window and looks out, saying, "Do you know that there is a man across the street studiously not looking at this house?" All of these could lead to clichés, but if they engage imagination they might lead on to a very compelling play. At least they do imply action, the use of space, and an anticipation of some future discovery. In that is the stuff of drama.

Some of the five tales told above may lend themselves more readily to narrative treatment; others have clear dramatic potential. Some suit the screen better than they do the stage. All of them nevertheless could be given a satisfying dramatic treatment. Any situation that suggests action within time and space and implies a tension to provoke audience anticipation has dramatic potential. Drafting the script on the basis of selected material will itself produce more material, for the act of drafting continually engages the imagination.

Composing vs. Writing

Drafting dramatic material is different from any other form of writing. Throughout we have been using the word "composing" in preference to "writing" to describe the work of the dramatist. There is good reason for this. While a dramatist does indeed write a script, the writing itself is only a means to the end of a full play in performance. The script is really a tool, a blueprint for that full play. Ultimately, the dramatist is attempting to control actions, not words (although words may themselves be actions). Many of the terms we use in connection with drama carry suggestions of building, constructing, putting together—terms such as "dramatic structure," "dramaturgy," "scenario," "storyboard," and "playwright." "Dramaturgy" means the putting together of drama and "playwright" means builder of plays. All these terms suggest that a play is not so much written as put together—built. A dramatist does indeed write the dialogue for a play, but does so only as one indication of the interactions of the characters. The playwright ultimately attempts to control the lines of energy exchanged among actors and audience in the three-dimensional space of a theatre. The screenwriter tries to work out such exchanges between two-dimensional screen images and the audience. In either case, the play script or the screenplay are complete works of art only in the sense that they attempt to account for the total experience of the play; otherwise they are mere guides to a full work of art to take place later with the help of many other people. From start to finish, plays are put together, constructed, wrought, or built. The relationship between script and play is analogous to that between score and symphony. Since it is rather easier to read a play script than a musical score, we sometimes lose sight of this. In any event, this prompts us to use the word "compose" for the work of the dramatist.

Seen this way, the challenge for a dramatist lies in an empty space (in the form of a stage or a screen) set before an audience and available for a span of time. He must ask himself how to fill that space and spend that time to best engage the audience's imagination. Space, time, and imagination—these are the basic building blocks. Words typed on a page are merely indications of how the blocks will be arranged.

This is an exciting challenge. Those little ciphers you put on paper may one day blossom into a full world occupied by living, breathing characters. Even though actors do the breathing; and designers, carpenters, painters, electricians, seamstresses, and others fill out their world; and everything happens in that familiar meeting ground called a "theatre." You yourself describe this event first. The audience's encounter with the world you first described in your script can assume an immediacy and power unattainable in any other form of fiction. The theatre event can be truly stunning. Such a level of compelling power is denied the novelist, whose readership is vague and amorphous. A novel assumes its richest life only in the minds of distant readers. The dramatist's audience is assembled at the moment of encounter, experiencing the fictional world the moment it happens. This is the excitement of drama.

This excitement has its obverse side, however. The dramatist has far less control over the experience he creates than the novelist. If the dramatist is lucky enough to secure a production, others will be involved in the process of creation. Moreover, in the process of composing the play, the dramatist must rely on guesswork, for he cannot see the results of his decisions. Unlike the novelist who can see his work in its intended medium as he writes or the painter who can stand back and judge his painting's effect any time he chooses, the dramatist must write the script "with the theatre in his head," to use Kenneth Thorpe Rowe's phrase. He puts down on paper descriptions, dialogue, and instructions that he guesses might work in a movie theatre or a playhouse. Composing drama is isolated and uncertain work. It is even more isolated than composing music, for the composer has a much more exact way of giving instructions, of designating intentions, than the dramatist and that gives the composer a very good idea of the sound of the music in performance. The dramatist can only guess at the final outcome.

This also means that the dramatist must "depend on the kindness of strangers," as much as Blanche DuBois had to do. The composer may be reasonably assured that musicians will play the notes and intervals as he instructs them. The dramatist may only be assured that the actors will speak the words, more or less. He cannot count on the atmosphere being right, the tensions being focused, the actors behaving appropriately, the design giving the right appearance, or the director even understanding the play. So while composing the play may be lonely and the long wait while the script sits on various desks even lonelier, once production begins the dramatist suddenly finds a crowd pressing in upon him, everyone jostling everyone else to present new ideas about the script. In the welter of talk, drawings, rehearsals, and more talk, the play can get lost. Men in white coats may come to take the dramatist off.

If he can avoid the men in white and survive the mayhem, he may find the play that emerges works after all. It may even assume values he did not know were there. He may catch himself wondering, "Did I write that?"—not necessarily with chagrin. This can happen if the play is good to start with, if the artistic collaborators understand and care about it, and if the dramatist does not lose his head and so can capitalize on new ideas and discoveries through the rehearsal process.

The opposite can also happen. The opening of the play becomes the climax of a long nightmare. Its closing is actually a relief. Assuming that the script and fellow artists are at least decent, this agony can be avoided by recognizing at the outset what "composing" the play means.

Composing consists of controlling tensions by focusing, varying, vivifying, and channeling them. The dialogue is only one symptom of these tensions. In fact, the most important part of the dramatist's work is not writing the dialogue. It is instead the charting of energies through action that can engage audience interest. Words spoken are only one kind of action that energy can take. Outside forces, the past, objects, atmosphere, rhythm and tempo, visual effects can also convey action. Composing a play requires you to keep them all in mind. The first and most fundamental tension is drawn between spectacle and spectator. The play strives to be hypnotic, or awe inspiring, or stupefying, or amusing, but always entertaining. The etymological meaning of the word "entertain" is "to hold between," which suggests that your main task is to hold your audience. And indeed it is your first order of business. If you can do that, your pay "works," as they say, and you need adhere to no other rule. No one can tell you exactly how to do that, but it does involve tapping the tensions available in the story, the characters, their world, the stage or screen medium— wherever you can find them—and giving them focus.

The more familiar you are with drama and its media, the more quickly you find useful tensions. A tension requires a polarity, two opposites to set up lines of energy. The motif of the encounter has a polarity built into it. So does conflict. So do foreboding, comic incongruity, tragic irony, and dramatic contrast. Within the story, love, hate, fear, anxiety, envy, wonder, cruelty can each set up a polarity between characters or between a character and circumstance. The stage medium, as we shall see, possesses its own sets of polarities, such as onstage versus offstage, and the screen medium its own too. This is not a matter of "the more the merrier." You do not want to be using every tension available, but rather isolating and defining tensions to channel energy and focus attention. Naturally, this also calls for varying the tensions, shifting them as the play progresses, to keep attention.

If the dramatist is alert to the polarities available in the material and the medium, he can draw meaningful tensions and control them more effectively. The resulting play will be genuinely composed—not just written—and it stands a better chance against the vicissitudes of the production process.

"The Courage to Create"

This phrase is borrowed from the title of an inspiring and insightful book by Rollo May. May argues that courage is the most basic virtue, for it liberates the others. One cannot love without courage, nor be charitable, have hope, take faith, be patient. All these are acts of courage. Courage is the assertion of the self without any assurance of reward. It is a leap into the unknown. May catalogues four kinds of courage: physical, moral, social, and creative. Of these, he declares, the last is the most difficult and perhaps ultimately the most important.

The creative act is courageous. It requires a commitment of one's total self without any objective, reliable evidence that the endeavor will work or be even vaguely worthwhile. It is a frightening prospect. One may well be literally "laughed off the stage." The world is full of people who have perfectly wonderful plays in their heads. At cocktail parties, such a person might regale new acquaintances with stunning ideas for a play, just a few tantalizing tidbits you understand, and then go home smug in the conviction that this glimpse of a creative mind struck awe in all who listened. Years go by, and you might well hear the same story from the same person at another cocktail party. The play never got written. Fear prevented it. It was always easier to chat about it casually than to do it, especially since the result might fall far short of the vision. Admittedly, in ninety-nine cases out of a hundred, the fear is justified. Still, one would think it healthier to quit talking and either do it or put it away. To do neither will create a sense of emptiness, incompleteness, even despair. It amounts to an act of cowardice.

Beyond this fear and cowardice is what we might call the "Pooh Syndrome," in honor of Winnie-the-Pooh, who sometimes despairs of being able to create new "hums." He complains that when a beautiful idea gets out in the open for all to see, it does not always look so good any more. Of course, Winnie-the-Pooh went right on making hums just the same. There is no way to test an idea but by getting it out in the open. More often than not it will be disappointing, and almost certainly frightening, but no good ideas will come otherwise. Even the most seasoned, the most experienced dramatist must repeat this act of courage again and again,for every new play undertaken poses a new set of challenges and threats of failure.

Dramatic composition calls for perhaps a greater courage than other art forms. The dramatist always works at a step removed from the piece of art he is creating. The piece of paper he writes on bears no resemblance to the stage or the screen that is to be the real medium. Words put down on paper are merely indications of what is to happen later, much later, if at all, among a group of actors. A final production will require the full-spirited commitment and sensitive understanding of several other artists. It will even require luck, for things on stage or on screen never correspond exactly to the initial vision. Chance may reveal weaknesses and potentials never considered until the script fell into the hands of director, designers, actors, and others. It can produce paranoia in the dramatist and convince him that everyone and nature herself conspired against him. Eventually the audience, and certainly the critics, become co-conspirators. There is a certain adversary quality to the relationship between dramatists and everyone else. Fundamentally, however, it must be one of mutual understanding and commitment: understanding and commitment to what is most crucial in the dramatic experience they all prepare together. They then all share in a purpose. That, too, amounts to courage.

This courage must be seasoned with a healthy dash of doubt. None of this is to imply that the courage to create entails self-righteous certainty. One could be wrong. "People," says Rollo May, "who claim to be *absolutely* convinced that their stand is the only right one are dangerous. Such conviction is the essence not only of dogmaticism, but also of its more destructive cousin fanaticism. It blocks off the user from learning new truth." And a dramatist can always learn a new truth, even (perhaps especially) about his own work.

Seen this way, creativity takes on value as a faculty essential to our mutual search into truth. Creativity employed by artists and audiences alike can produce insights otherwise unavailable. For the lonely artist at work, that ideal of a shared vision can keep him going. Creating a play is more than an act of ego-satisfaction (although it surely is that, too). It is an act of sharing, of charity, that one does ultimately out of love for others. And that renders creativity important for society at large, which requires it in order to reexamine itself and move forward.

Exercises

1. Examine the five tales outlined in this chapter.
   Write a scene appropriate to one of them. Describe how two contrasting playwrights might handle one of these stories.

2. Begin the practice of maintaining your own "commonplace book." Let it be a free-form notebook in which you write ideas, observations, snatches of dialogue, character sketches, experimental scenes, possible play titles, newspaper clippings, or notes on other people's plays, stories, movies, novels. It is your personal collection of things that interest you as a dramatist. Keep at it as a regular habit, adding something every day at a particular time when you know you can stick with it if a good idea emerges you really want to work with.

3. Below are nineteen dramatic situations. Select one and write an opening scene for a play script or screenplay:
   1. One Sunday morning, an old couple receive an unexpected visit—an undertaker's assistant.
   2. One man tries to get another to help him play a trick on his son.
   3. A spinster hears on the radio that a lion has escaped from the zoo and is thought to be in her neighborhood.
   4. Two hitchhikers attempt to cross a busy highway.
   5. A young couple staying overnight in a motel finds a baby on their doorstep—on their honeymoon.
   6. A young misogynist hermit finds an attractive girl in his house.
   7. An old woman with a mattress full of money is confronted by a charming but persistent thief.
   8. An established politician learns that his earlier career as an embezzler is known by one of his lieutenants.
   9. An old religious crank is pressured to sell one of his dearest idols recently purchased from a thief.
   10. Two spinsters decide to go slumming.
   11. A Mother-Superior in charge of a correctional institution discovers that one of her wayward girls has had a vision.
   12. Four longtime friends, all women, disappear from their homes one Tuesday afternoon.
   13. A group of boarders, who have never had much to do with each other, find themselves confronted by a mystifying new boarder who seems to threaten their well-being.
   14. A woman is left for a period of time by her husband who has given her a plain box not to be opened unless he does not return.
   15. A respectable, middle-aged man of some power is accused of rape by one of his employees, a young woman of questionable repute. (Depending on whether the charge is true, the two might exchange reputations.)
   16. A self-reliant, egocentric, domineering person is stricken with an incapacitating illness and becomes unwillingly dependent on others.

17. A wealthy, elderly woman finds herself without means when her son takes over her finances and places her in a home.
18. After an unsuccessful revolt, a group of prisoners turn on each other in retaliation for the failure.
19. A young wife refuses her much older husband any physical contact until he fulfills a promise he made to her years ago.

3

Involving
the Audience

At the outset of the last chapter, we suggested that there are two more characters in any drama beyond those in the cast: the dramatist and the audience. Surely it would be difficult to say much about the latter: an audience is simply a collection of people who happen to be in the theatre of a certain evening. Who they are and how they will behave would seem beyond our guessing. And yet, they are a powerful presence. No play is complete without them. Somehow, we must know something about the audience if we are to compose a play. Failing to take them into account would be the undoing of a dramatist.

This is not as difficult as it seems. Every dramatist implicitly chooses an audience. That collection of individuals that flock to a play by Neil Simon is clearly not the same as the audience attending the latest Harold Pinter play, and neither group is quite the same as the crowd jostling to see the newest installment of George Lucas's *Star Wars*. "Implicitly choosing one's audience" is tantamount to "characterizing one's audience." Every play promises a certain sort of audience involvement and that promise already begins to characterize the play's audience.

Each of the three audiences listed above might contain some of the same individuals. Nevertheless, even they change in some measure by virtue of the dramatic experience they encounter and share with the others. Becoming involved, the audience assumes a collective character. Every audience is willing to do so, but only the dramatist (with his artistic collaborators) can make it happen. The greatest danger would lie in treating the audience as some amorphous mass of receptive but passive humanity. It is not only insulting; it cripples drama. Drama is drama only when it engages the creative collaboration of its audience.

Drama and the Crowd

Drama depends upon a crowd—it may be an intimate crowd, but a crowd nevertheless. Without it, potential dramatic effects ring hollow and false. Drama requires a sense of occasion, of festival, and of sharing. Anyone who has ever acted knows the empty feeling that comes about the time of dress rehearsal when a play seems "to hunger for an audience." The play is literally only half there. Without its better half, it is dead. It might seem that this applies only to live, stage drama. Certainly, the need for an audience is more intense in that medium simply because of its immediacy. Yet, watching a movie as a solitary spectator in a huge cinema house or in the loneliness of one's car at a drive-in is fundamentally unsatisfying, too. Without the combustion of the crowd, there is no drama. Thornton Wilder, in his essay "Some Thoughts on Playwriting," offers some valuable insights into this condition:

> The theatre partakes of the nature of festival. Life imitated is life raised to a higher power. In the case of comedy, the vitality of these pretended surprises, deceptions, and *contretemps* becomes so lively that before a spectator, solitary or regarding himself as solitary, the structure of so much event would inevitably expose the artificiality of the attempt and ring hollow and unjustified; and in the case of tragedy, the accumulation of woe and apprehension would soon fall short of conviction.

There is something fundamentally different about an individual who joins a theatre audience and that same individual alone with a novel. The occasion, the confinement in an auditorium for the duration with fellow spectators, create a quiet sense of anonymity. One identifies with the group, ceasing in some measure to be an individual. Unlike the novel reader, the spectator cannot put the play down for a while if it becomes tedious or skip uninteresting passages in pursuit of something more enticing. The novelist might never be wiser, provided he can still count on a faithful coterie of some respectable size. The dramatist, on the other hand, must respect the fact that the people in his audience have given themselves to the play for the duration. If they choose to "put the play down" by the only act possible—walking out of the theatre—the dramatist has lost not only them, but his play in the bargain. No audience, no play.

Drama as Aesthetic and Social Event

Put another way, drama is both a social and an aesthetic event. Two kinds of reality exist side by side. One is the reality of the theatrical environment: the playhouse auditorium and its stage, the cinema house and its screen, or the living room and its television screen. The other is the reality of the play's imagined world. One might, romantically, imagine the second annihilating the first. In truth, they hold each other in suspension, complementing each other, and adding dimensions to the experience of both. It may be, as Robert Benedetti argues in *The Actor at Work*, that we should "abandon the distinction between reality and illusion, and instead speak of various *levels* or kinds of reality that co-exist within the theatre, each of which contacts the audience in its own way and for its own purpose, but interacts with the other realities." This is the real source of dramatic excitement: the interplay of levels of reality. And the first of these is the interplay of the social and the aesthetic levels.

Seen in this way, the audience is anything but a passive, receptive mass of humanity; they are part of the play. They interact with each other and with the performance. More than that, their imaginations collectively shape the imagined world of the characters. Thus, even on the aesthetic level, the theatre experience is also a social one. The successful dramatist knows how to engage the audience's collaboration. He finds the means to inspire it, sustain it, and make it rewarding. Audiences generally are self-respecting enough to resist a play that does not engage their creative energies.

On this score, we can discuss the audience as "a character" in a play. We may not be able to describe the specific individuals who compose an audience, but we can describe the audience of a particular play. The play is built to involve, arouse, move, and compel its audience, who thereby assume character.

Here are two contrasting examples of the engagement of the audience's creative energies—the first comes from a highly theatrical play and the other from a realistic play. Dario Fo, one of Italy's leading dramatists, has written a delicious satire on the exploits of Christopher Columbus, a play entitled *Isabella, Three Ships and a Tall-tale Teller* (*Isabella, tre caravelle e un cacciaballe*). Fo calls for a setting consisting of a bare platform set upon the stage in the midst of a Renaissance, false-perspective cityscape. The platform becomes the playing area of a group of players who transform the platform first into the courtroom of Ferdinand and Isabella by hanging heraldic banners from staffs; later into a gallows by flipping down the tops of the staffs and hanging nooses; and later still into Columbus's ship by suspending sails from the staffs. When Christopher Columbus puts out to sea, he and his sailors stand on the platfom waving to the lords and ladies of court, who stand on a rolling platform in front of the "ship." As the ship leaves, stagehands pull the rolling platform offstage by means of a large rope, while the lords and ladies wave their handkerchiefs to Christopher. Once at sea, a great storm erupts. Lights flash, and the sailors bounce about on the platform/ship. Stagehands run across in front of the platform carrying a huge sheet which they unfold and shake to create great billowing waves. Some sailors fall from the platform and "drown," crawling offstage on hands and knees under the billowing sheet. Never for a moment does the audience forget the "social reality" of the platform, the rope, the sheet, the actors, and stagehands; but they also create with them another reality, in its own way just as real, of a dockside farewell and a great storm at sea.

It might seem that such audience engagement would not happen in a realistic play. It can; in fact, it must. The opening of Anton Chekhov's *The Three Sisters* provides a fine illustration. Chekhov calls for a setting with a drawing room downstage and a dining room alcove upstage. When the play begins, the sisters, Olga, Irina, and Masha, are in the downstage area; moments later three men, Tusenbach, Chebutykin, and Soliony, enter the alcove, sit at the table, and engage in their own conversation. Downstage, two of the sisters talk about Moscow:

OLGA

Eleven years have gone by, but I remember everything as if we'd only left there yesterday. Oh, my goodness! I woke this morning, the sun was blazing. I could feel that spring was here. And I did so long to be home again.

CHEBUTYKIN

You've gone out of your mind.

TUSENBACH

It's all nonsense, of course.

(MASHA, engrossed in her book, quietly humming.)

OLGA

Masha. Don't hum. How can you! (Pause) School all day, private lessons all evening, so I have headaches all the time. I'm beginning to feel quite old. Shall I tell you something? Every single day of the four years at the high school, minute by minute, I have felt my strength and my youth draining away. And only one dream kept growing stronger and stronger.

IRINA

To go to Moscow! To sell the house, make an end of everything here, and . . . Moscow.

(CHEBUTYKIN and TUSENBACH laugh.)

IRINA

Brother will be a professor most likely, so he won't be staying here. The one thing in the way is poor Masha.

OLGA

Masha will spend the whole summer in Moscow every year.

(MASHA whistles.)

IRINA

It will all be arranged, if God wills.

In this sequence, the laughter and remarks of the men, and, for that matter, the humming and whistling of Masha, have nothing to do with the conversation between Olga and Irina. Yet, by punctuating the conversation in this way, Chekhov invites the audience to make their own conclusion: all the talk of Moscow will never actually lead the sisters there. Chekhov did not say so. Not even the three men say so. The interplay of the two levels of action implies it. We the audience say so. The rest of the play will bear us out and we can congratulate ourselves on having been so perceptive. The audience is collaborating as creatively with Chekhov here as they are with Fo in the previous example.

Nor should it be thought that this collaboration of the audience in creating a play is the special province of the stage. It occurs as well in the screen media. Indeed the very basis of the screen lies in the capacity of the imagination to make leaps and fill in gaps that literally exist between one image and another, and between one shot and another. A movie depends upon the imaginative capacity of its audience to provide a context for each image. A classic example is the riot scene in Sergei Eisenstein's *Potemkin*. The first shot establishes the context: a view of the Odessa Steps waterfront with the mob encountering the Czarist soldiers. Each succeeding shot is a detail which the audience transposes into that same context. Film shots may be taken in any order and in any number of different places, but the order they assume in editing depends upon the audience's imagination. Similarly, within shots, the interplay of planes frequently provides the audience with the means to grasp implicit meanings. This is the case, for example, in a famous shot from Orson Welles's *Citizen Kane*, in which a pill bottle is seen in the foreground, Mrs. Kane lying in bed in the middle ground, and Mr. Kane standing in the bedroom door in the background. An audience may readily seize the implication: she has taken poison because of him. Shortly viewers will congratulate themselves on their perceptiveness.

While it is true that the dramatist must manipulate and control an audience, there must be no condescension about it. An audience will resist assuming a character, or even an attitude, if it seems to be imposed on them. They want, and deserve, to feel they share in the creation of the world of the play. Their interaction on the "social level" serves to create the "aesthetic level." if the audience genuinely feels that the dramatist has invited them to join in exploring the world of the play, they will willingly enter into the drama, suspend disbelief, and respond creatively to the suggestions laid before them. The least hint of contrivance and manipulation interfering with their involvement will alienate and drive them away. The condition is the source of the age-old truism "Great art conceals art." Art is, by definition, a contrivance; great art, however, conceals the fact by inviting the audience to collaborate.

Polarity as the Basic Dramatic Device

All this implies that an audience becomes involved through an intriguing interplay of levels: their own reality versus the reality of the play; one character's reality versus another's; the world onstage versus the world beyond, and the reality of the present versus that of the past. Contrasts, opposites, disparities, incongruities, ironies, and conflicts—these are the stuff of drama, the source of fascination. The common denominator among all of them is polarity. Polarity is the basic dramatic device and the creation and variation of polarities the work of a dramatist. It derives from the moment of theatrical encounter (spectator meeting spectacle) and it enlarges and varies at every level thereafter.

In Chapter 1, five characteristics of the dramatic mode were listed. The first two are of special interest here:

1. The first and most basic ingredient in the dramatic mode is *the encounter*. It occurs on the most fundamental level when spectator meets spectacle. This moment produces an immediate polarity, a palpable tension, which prompts the spectator to watch, to listen, and to attend the event. The dramatist seeks to play on this tension to create and sustain effects and responses.

2. *Polarity and tension* provide the fundamental motif of the dramatic mode. Any onlooker becomes more or less involved in proportion to how much seems to be at stake. Tension may take multiple forms: incongruity, irony, disparity, contrast, anticipation. A play may be seen as an energy system of lines of tension; the basic tension inherent in the act of encounter is multiplied in a myriad of other poles of tension.

A play is an encounter between two worlds: the world of the play itself and the world of the audience. When an audience gathers and individuals take their seats facing a closed curtain or blank screen, they bring with them all the mundane concerns that colored the day each has just passed. Some have had problems at the office, others with their automobiles, others with a friend or lover, others with their children, and still others with their bankbook. Some arrive as individuals, others in couples or in parties of friends. Yet, they all bring a generally shared understanding of the world we live in. More than that, by virtue of their common humanity, they bring with them the concerns that color all of human life: fear, uncertainty, love, joy, despair, hope. With the dimming of the lights, a hush falls on the audience. The conversations cease; all attention is riveted on the blankness before them. The curtain rises or the projection light strikes the screen. It is one of those exciting moments everyone relishes. In a bad play, it is the most exciting moment. A good play, however, builds upon that initial tension.

What makes this moment exciting is the wonderful promise; anything is possible. A wholly new world is about to unfold. These screen images or live actors are about to induce in us a vision of another life. Herein lies the key for multiplying tensions. The first source is simply the act of presentation. The next is the delightful disparity between the actual world of the audience, actors, and images and the virtual or imagined world of the characters. Neither one ever ceases to exist. They maintain themselves in a state of suspension throughout the play.

No dramatist can afford to forget that the play ultimately resides in the imagination of the audience. The play passes through three phases of existence: the script, the performance, and the imagined experience. Neither of the first two is complete. The play completes itself in confronting its audience, for there stage actions or screen images take on their full meaning. The total effect is indeed greater than the sum of the parts. Taken singly, the lines and actions of a play are relatively empty. They remain flat, idle, and opaque until they engage an audience's imagination. There they assume dimension, a rich context, a sense for the world at large—in short, meaning.

Three Stages of Creation

In this connection, the three stages of creation outlined in Suzanne Langer's book *Feeling and Form* are enlightening. First, the art work seeks to divorce itself from actuality. By various formal means, the audience is alerted not to mistake the realm of the art work for the real world. The pedestal for sculpture, the picture frame for painting, the coda for music, the proscenium for stage drama, the screen for film—all are formal reminders of this. Should an artist take a greasy differential from a junkyard, place it on a pedestal, and label it "The Modern World," he has accomplished this first step of creation—but not the other two. He has asked us to regard the differential in a new way. Andy Warhol has done much the same thing with the Empire State Building in his film *Empire*—some eight hours of viewing the building. All art starts there: it asks us to regard something in a new way simply by divorcing it from life.

The second step consists of manipulating the illusion. Langer refers here to the materials of the medium. The dabbing and stroking of pigments upon a canvas, the arrangement of tones and durations, the chipping away of stone, the performance of actions upon a stage—all these are manipulations. They are determined by the materials of the medium selected. Certain works of art stop at this second step: Abstract Expressionism and "Action Painting" both concentrate attention on the act of manipulating the medium. In theatre, various forms of communal environmental theatre celebrate the spirit of encounter and the act of moving in space, and so tend to be "second step" works of art.

The complete work of art goes one step further, to what Langer calls the "emergence of transparency." At this point, at last, the audience is fully engaged. Imagination lets them see through the manipulations of the medium to catch an insight into reality itself. The separation of the art work from actuality and the manipulating of the medium are formal and technical matters, but when successful they provoke the audience to see their own world in a new light. Opacity fades; the work of art becomes a sort of lens for viewing the world as they never had before. The emergence of transparency requires that the audience be reasonably comfortable with the terms of the art work and that the handling of its materials is effective. If we are unfamiliar with the form or conventions of an art work (as in the case of a Japanese Noh Drama for most Westerners or a heavy-handed avant-garde piece for an ordinary spectator), we cannot transcend our awareness of the art work as art to experience any reality beyond it. But when we are comfortable with the nature and terms of the art work, a vivid sense of human experience shines through. This does not mean that we forget the nature and terms of the art work. We may be very alive to them and still see beyond them.

When you come to know an excellent play well, it is always a surprise to discover how little in the script inspired so much. Seemingly few words and little activity summon up a rich experience. The gap is filled by the contributions you yourself gave the experience. The storm scene in *King Lear* is a case in point. It is vivid, exciting, and memorable, yet also surprisingly brief. The secret of the successful dramatist is knowing how to spark such visions in an audience, how to prod into life a vibrant sense of reality.

The audience, then, is your collaborator. Through the medium of performer in space, your imagination engages theirs. On this score alone they deserve your respect. When the lights go out in the auditorium, they are very nearly as anxious as you that your play engage, fascinate, and compel attention. They, too, have invested time and money. For the duration, they have given themselves to the play. The play that then does not deliver is a vast disappointment—and most audiences know it in the first few minutes.

The question then is: once you have their attention, how do you keep it? By what means does the dramatist engage the audience's imagination?

Histrionic Sensibility

Drama, in all its forms, is objective; it plays directly upon the senses of sight and sound. The audience can only glimpse the inner lives of the characters by what they see and hear them do. The dramatist has to provide the most telling signs and they must occur in time and space. He does not have the novelist's freedom to explore the subjective mind directly. He cannot stop the play, explain a character, and then carry on. To be sure, a playwright might resort to a soliloquy or a screenwriter to a dream sequence, but such devices can ring hollow. An audience does not believe anything unless reinforced by action. In the final analysis, only action convinces.

This might seem a severe restriction, and it is. Yet, as in all matters creative, such restrictions fire the imagination. Moreover, an audience is happy to make up the difference. "Reading" the action, discovering the drive or motivation behind it, is a pleasure. Our "histrionic sensibility" lets us indulge it.

This term, coined by Francis Fergusson and described in his book *The Idea of a Theatre*, refers to that innate human faculty to grasp the meanings of the acts of others. "Histrionic" derives from the Etruscan word for action or performance and "sensibility" of course means awareness: hence "awareness of performance." Were it not that we all possess this faculty, drama would not be possible.

Suppose you are in the grandstands when a runner slides into third base. You see the umpire's thumb fly up, the runner jump to his feet and stand nose-to-nose with the umpire, his jaw working. You cannot hear a word, yet you know very well what is transpiring; your histrionic sensibility tells you. In private conversation with a friend, you understand each other far more by intonations, "body language," facial expressions, eye contact, and other such sources than by the words. In the act of living, our histrionic sensibility is constantly engaged. Sometimes our survival depends on it. Drama depends on it, too, for it is the first link binding the spectacle and the spectator.

Histrionic sensibility works through two sources: the context and the tone of the action. In the example of the baseball runner, you sense the action partly through context—the circumstance surrounding the event, and partly through the tone—the manner in which it is done. Both are required. If the audience is unclear about the context, the tone alone will not convey meaning, and vice versa. Psychologists have shown that a close-up photograph of a face expressing extreme emotion cannot be identified as any specific emotion, because without the context one emotion may easily be mistaken for another—ecstasy for pain, for example.

Three examples from stage plays illustrate these points. In the very last scene of Shakespeare's *King Lear*, Lear enters carrying the body of his daughter Cordelia. From the context, we know he is distraught, clinging to every last shred of hope that she may yet be alive. He tells us so, as well; but that is not enough. Shakespeare adds these "histrionic" details:

LEAR

Howl, howl, howl, howl! O, you are men of stones!
Had I your tongues and eyes, I'd use them so
That heaven's vault should crack. She's gone forever!
I know when one is dead, and when one lives;
She's dead as earth. Lend me a looking-glass;
If that her breath will mist or stain the stone,
Why, then she lives.

KENT

Is this the promised end?

EDGAR

Or image of that horror?

ALBANY

Fall and cease.

LEAR

This feather stirs; she lives! If it be so,
It is a chance which does redeem all sorrows
That ever I have felt.

KENT

(Kneeling)
O my good master!

LEAR

Prithee, away.

EDGAR

'Tis noble Kent, your friend.

LEAR

A plague upon you, murderers, traitors, all!
Cordelia, Cordelia! Stay a little. Ha!
What is't thou say'st? Her voice was ever soft,
Gentle, and low, an excellent thing in woman.

As the scene progresses, Lear becomes distracted with other news, but he returns to Cordelia with his last speech:

LEAR

Why should a dog, a horse, a rat, have life,
And thou no breath at all? Thou'lt come no more,
Never, never, never, never, never!
Pray you, undo this button. Thank you, sir.
Do you see this? Look on her, look, her lips,
Look there, look there! (Dies.)

In these passages, there are only two stage directions: "Kneeling" and "Dies." Yet, there is a wealth of action implicit in all that is said. One can picture his entrance carrying her and see in his face the rage he feels at everyone he sees, everyone left living, for each is guilty at the least of outliving her. He moves from rage with "Howl, howl, howl, howl!" to grief with "She's dead as earth," when he must be placing her on the ground, and then on to hope as he asks for a looking-glass. He receives a feather instead. Then he must be kneeling beside her as he thinks he sees it stir and hears her speak. Finally, in his grief, he loses all control and must ask someone else to undo his button, which someone does: "Thank you, sir." All these are actions, histrionic suggestions that round out and complete the effect of the alternating states of Lear's mind. The audience not only senses these alternating states the more vividly, they also believe them.

The same principle applies to comic effects. In Molière's *Tartuffe*, perhaps the two most famous sequences are the entrance of Tartuffe and the so-called "table scene," both justly renowned for their economy of effect attained by resorting to the audience's histrionic sensibility. In the first instance, Tartuffe has been mentioned for more than two acts before he finally appears. We have seen the effects he has had on the members of Orgon's household. Some have argued that he is a pious, upright man, others that he is a hypocritical, lecherous scoundrel. As the evidence piles up, the latter group seems to be right. When he finally enters, we know they are right. As he comes through the door, he sees Dorine and turns to call back to his servant Laurent—putting on this performance just for her:

TARTUFFE
(Seeing DORINE.)

Laurent, put away my hair shirt and my scourge and continue to pray Heaven to send you grace. If anyone asks for me, I'll be with the prisoners distributing alms.

DORINE

The impudent hypocrite!

TARTUFFE

What do you want?

DORINE

I'm to tell you . . .

TARTUFFE

For Heaven's sake! Before you speak, I pray you take this handkerchief.
(Takes handkerchief from his pocket.)

DORINE

Whatever do you mean?

TARTUFFE

Cover your bosom. I can't bear to see it. Such pernicious sights give rise to sinful thoughts.

DORINE

You're mighty susceptible to temptation then! The flesh must make a great impression on you! I really don't know why you should get so excited. I can't say that I'm so easily roused. I could see you naked from head to foot and your whole carcass wouldn't tempt me in the least.

Any doubts that Tartuffe was a hypocritical, lecherous scoundrel are dispelled within moments of his arrival on stage. The two actions of calling offstage to Laurent with the obvious purpose of impressing Dorine and extending the handkerchief to her clinch his true nature.

Nor is the playing on histrionic sensibility the special province of the old masters. In Friedrich Duerrenmatt's *The Visit*, Anton Schill (or Alfred Ill, depending on the translation) finds that Claire Zachanasian—once his beloved whom he betrayed years ago and now the richest woman in the world—has put a price on his head. She returns to her old hometown of Gullen, which has deteriorated into a doleful pocket of poverty, to promise the townspeople a billion marks in exchange for the death of Anton Schill. They are horrified. The mayor proudly rejects her offer, "in the name of humanity." Her reply is, "I can wait." She takes up residence in town to do just that. The grotesque success of her scheme is demonstrated in the ensuing scene. It takes place in Schill's grocery shop, as various townspeople arrive, order goods, and then charge them. When the fourth one does so, Schill suddenly looks down at the man's feet:

SCHILL

Helmesberger, are those new shoes you're wearing?

SECOND MAN

Yes, what about it?

SCHILL

You, too, Hofbauer. Yellow shoes!

FIRST MAN

So?

SCHILL

(To the women.)
And you. You all have new shoes! New shoes!

FIRST WOMAN

A person can't go around forever in the same old shoes.

SECOND WOMAN

Shoes wear out.

SCHILL
And the money? Where does the money come from?

FIRST MAN
We got them on credit.

SCHILL
On credit? And where all of a sudden do you get credit?

SECOND MAN
Everybody gives credit now.

FIRST WOMAN
You gave us credit yourself.

SCHILL
And what are you going to pay with? Eh?

(They are all silent. SCHILL advances on them threateningly.)

With what? Eh? With what? With what?

(Suddenly he understands. He takes off his apron quickly, gets his jacket, and walks off with an air of determination.)

The new yellow shoes become virtually an act of betrayal. No amount of talk could possibly be as convincing. Of course, the townspeople cannot bring themselves to believe that Mme. Zachanasian means what she says. In any event, their deprivation has rendered them all desperate. They will grasp at any straw in their misery. Meanwhile, the audience retains the image of Mme. Zachanasian from their first encounter with her. She arrived in Gullen in a sedan chair, borne by two muscle-bound former convicts whom she bought out of prison, and followed by a retinue consisting of a caged live panther, a butler (the judge who once condemned her, whom she also bought), and two eunuchs (the false witnesses who informed against her, whom she has had castrated and blinded). All of that should persuade the audience of the seriousness of her offer to the town.

In film or television, the reliance on action and the audience's recognition of it is in some respects even more important. Since the screen media depend on the play of images, they are more visually oriented. If the screen image does not reinforce the action, believability is at once sacrificed (unless of course a deliberate and well-charted irony is at work). In a well-made film, virtually every moment depends on image and action. Athough decisions as to what the film audience will see belong to the director, who plans the actual shots the camera will take, the screenwriter needs to provide the impetus for action and images that communicate. Here are two vivid examples. In *The Pawnbroker*, a 1964 film directed by Sidney Lumet, the spindle on the pawnbroker's counter becomes more and more important as the pawnbroker himself becomes more and more obsessed with his guilt—until he drives it through his hand. Similarly, in Alfred Hitchcock's *Frenzy*, the strangulation scene ends not just with the death of the victim, but with the murderer picking up an apple and biting into it. Both tell us more about the characters than any amount of dialogue, explanation, or exposition could possibly do.

Making a Scene an Action: An Example

The mode of action is so important to the dramatic experience that not only is nothing convincing unless rendered in action, but nothing seems worth watching. Dialogue itself is much more than the exchange of words; it is the interplay of actions. Many people who like to resort to dialogue in writing narrative fiction fancy themselves potential playwrights—until they discover there is more to dramatic dialogue than speeches. Only when a speech is an action is it dramatic.

To be an action, dialogue needs a sense of direction, of forward movement. It does not need to be violent or riddled with invective; it may even be quiet and subtle and pleasant. But it must appear to be moving. A gathered audience needs and deserves a sense of anticipation, which comes of a scene's seeming to move forward toward some moment of heightened tension. One action leads to another and together they create a vector, a perceptible direction which the action of the entire scene or play will pursue. Actions, reactions, and interactions bind together to establish a coherent action overarching them all and characterizing the scene. The great Russian stage director, Konstantin Stanislavsky, spoke of "beats" or "motivational units"—brief moments in a play's action unified by the dominance of a single drive or motivation in the characters. This is the strongest and clearest way of binding action and gaining momentum in a scene. It is also possible for a scene to gain its sense of direction by the dominance of a single force emanating out of the world beyond or out of the past rather than from a character. Whatever the source, a dramatic scene needs to build out of forces. It is then that the scene gains interest. The audience can begin to feel caught up in the action, unsettled in a pleasant sort of way, and intrigued to encounter the next moment, the next "beat."

Here is a poorly constructed scene. There are actions and speeches in it, but it has no "action" in the sense spoken of above. It relies on direct statement to communicate, fails to engage histrionic sensibility, has no sense of direction nor forward momentum, and so falls flat:

DORIS
(At the kitchen door.)

Hi, Milly. Can I come in?

MILLY

Hi, Doris. Sure. Come on in. The door's unlatched.

DORIS

(She enters the kitchen.)

Say, Milly, I was real sorry when you told me that your husband, Harold, left you.

MILLY

Yes. He did that two days ago.

DORIS

I was real sorry.

MILLY

Not half as sorry as I was.

DORIS

I bet you're right.

MILLY

He just packed his bag. Packed his bag and left.

DORIS

Gee. That musta been hard to take.

MILLY

Yeah. I don't know what to do with myself.

DORIS

I can understand that. I'd be the same way. How long you two been married?

MILLY

Ten years.

DORIS

That's a long time. Did he say why he was leaving?

MILLY

Said I was boring.

DORIS

Gee. Tell me more about Harold leaving you.

By this point, short as the scene is, the audience will be about to stand up and scream, "Don't!"—fully convinced that Harold was right: Milly is boring. And so is the scene. It is going nowhere. It has no other purpose than to tell us the news that Harold left. The news has no impact, because it does not affect Milly or Doris in any new way. They have already hashed it over before we meet them. One result is that there is virtually no characterization; Milly and Doris are almost interchangeable. Another result is tedium.

Now it is quite possible for a character to be boring as a person and yet interesting as a character. It requires a context, a circumstance that can throw the character into relief. That, in turn, requires that a character be somehow at odds with the circumstances. In this instance, Milly is not at odds with her circumstance. Admittedly, she does not like Harold's leaving her, but she does not struggle against it. She just talks about it. And Doris, fool that she is, listens. Without changing Milly in any significant degree, we could take her lethargy and her tediousness, make her just a little uncomfortable with her circumstance, and rewrite the scene in a comic tone. We will then begin to make the scene an action:

MILLY
(Seated across the table from DORIS.)
Somehow, I don't feel like doing much today.

DORIS
Oh? Feeling a bit lazy, huh?

MILLY
Well, no, it's not exactly that. It's just that nothing seems to matter much to me, you know what I mean?

DORIS
Well, no, I don't think I do.

MILLY
I mean, what difference does it make if I wash those dishes or not? Who cares? Or clean the house? Or go shopping? Or any of those things I'm supposed to do? What difference does it make?

DORIS
Gee, you seem sorta depressed. Is anything wrong?

MILLY
I'll say. Harold left me two days ago.

DORIS
Really?

(MILLY nods.)
Why'd he do that?

MILLY
Said I was boring. Can you imagine that?

DORIS
He really said that?

MILLY
Yes, he did. It really hurt, him saying that. It was Saturday morning. We usually sleep late Saturday morning you know? But this time he was up early. Showered and shaved, and by the time I woke up, he was packing his bag. I said to him, you know, "What are you doing, Harold?" He said,

"Packing my bag." Well, I didn't know what to say. But finally I said, "Why?" He said, "I'm leaving you." Then I said, "Why?" And that's when he said it, you know, about me being boring.

DORIS

What happened then?

MILLY

He left.

DORIS

Gee.

MILLY

That's why I asked you over. I thought it might do some good to talk to somebody.

DORIS

Well, you just go ahead and talk. What are friends for?

MILLY

Well, see, when Harold and me got married, ten years ago, we were just so excited. We were really in love. But somehow, we just started growing apart from that time on. And now, I don't really know much about what he does. He goes to work down at the warehouse every day, but what he does down there I don't even know. I guess he does good. I mean, he's been getting raises right along and all that. But I don't know much about Harold. Not any more.

DORIS

You suppose there's another woman?

MILLY

Probably so.

DORIS

Let me get you another cup of coffee.

MILLY

No thanks. Coffee makes me depressed.

DORIS

Yeah. I guess you're depressed enough as it is.

MILLY

Like I say, what difference does it all make? Do you think I'm boring?

DORIS

Oh, no, Milly. I think you're real interesting.

The scene is now nearly twice as long, yet it carries interest because Milly is now struggling to put this event into perspective. There is some point in Doris's being here: the action is Milly's reaching out for some reed to hold onto. Of course, Doris won't do, but that is Milly's problem, not ours. And finally, Milly *is* boring. That is her problem, too—her fundamental problem. But for us, it is what makes her vaguely funny, particularly when teamed with her sympathetic friend Doris, who is every bit as boring.

We might rewrite the scene once more, this time enriching the sources of contrast, irony, and tension. The result might not be quite so comic, but it could have a greater immediate impact. In both previous versions, Milly has experienced no discomfort dealing with Doris. She apparently talks with her all the time. Indeed, one reason the second version is humorous is that it implies that all Milly has ever done or will ever do is talk with Doris. If, however, Milly were encountering Doris for the first time, she would no longer be at ease with the immediate situation. She would instead be reluctant to talk about her plight yet torn by the desire to unburden herself to someone. A new polarity, and with it a new dimension, would be added to the scene. The sense of direction would become stronger and more insistent:

DORIS
(Seated across the kitchen table from MILLY.)
It's real nice of you, inviting me over and all, Mrs. Howland, me being new in the neighborhood and not knowing . . .

MILLY
Auckland.

DORIS
Excuse me?

MILLY
Auckland. That's my name. Not Howland. Auckland.

DORIS
Oh. Anyway, like I was saying, it's real nice of you. I don't know any of the neighbors. See, me and Jack (that's my husband's name: Jack) anyway, me and Jack, we just moved in two days ago, and so I haven't . . .

MILLY
Saturday.

DORIS
Huh?

MILLY
I said, Saturday. It was Saturday.

DORIS
Oh, yeah, that's right. Two days ago.

MILLY
That's a day to remember.

DORIS
(Perplexed.)
Oh, sure. It was an important day in my life: moving into our first home, setting up housekeeping, making things nice for my Jack. That means a lot to me. There's such a lot to do, but I'm looking forward to it all.
(Pause.)
Uh, you know that's the fourth spoonful of sugar you're putting in that coffee, Mrs. Howland? Do you always put so much?

MILLY
Is it? I guess I'm a little distracted. I'll have to pour it all out and start over.
(She moves around to the sink behind DORIS.)

DORIS
Anyway, Jack got this real good job at the Good Times Shoe Company warehouse over on Fourteenth Street about a year ago. And now we figured things are going pretty well and maybe we'd look around for a house. Lucky thing we came across this one, right? Gee, ain't married life swell?

MILLY
Swell.

DORIS
Mrs. Howland, you okay?

MILLY
Huh? Oh, sure.
(She crosses back and sits down.)
Let's try that sugar again.

DORIS
Oh, yeah, here you are. Say, what's your husband do?

MILLY
I really don't know.

DORIS
You don't know? What's the matter, he with the Secret Service or something?

MILLY
No.
(Pause.)

DORIS
Uh, look: let's pretend I never asked, okay? We'll just leave it like that. I didn't mean to pry or anything.

MILLY
Harold left me two days ago.

> DORIS

Two days ago?

> MILLY

On Saturday.

> DORIS

Gee, I'm sorry to hear that.
> (Pause.)

> MILLY

Said I was boring.

> DORIS

Look, Mrs. Howland, I'm real sorry. Maybe . . .

> MILLY

Auckland. Mrs. Auckland.

> DORIS

Oh, gee, stupid me. Anyway, like I was saying, maybe it's better if I went home. You don't want me here chattering about my Jack and my new house. I'll just be on my way.

> (DORIS rises to go. Suddenly MILLY catches her arm. After a moment she continues.)

> MILLY

Do you think I'm boring?

> DORIS

Heavens, no. But, listen . . .

> MILLY

Saturday mornings we always slept late. But this time he was up early. Showered and shaved, and by the time I woke up, he was packing his bag. I asked him, "What are you doing, Harold?" He said, "I'm leaving you." Then when I asked him why, he told me I was boring.

> DORIS

> (She is by now seated again, listening intently.)

Harold Auckland?

> MILLY

Yeah. That's his name. Harold Auckland. Good old Harold Auckland.

> DORIS

Oh.

> MILLY

Why do you say it like that?

DORIS

No reason. Like I was saying, maybe it's better if we talked some other time. See, I feel like I'm intruding.

MILLY

No. We'll talk now. I want to know what "oh" means.

Now the scene is an action. In fact, it has moved through two "beats," and is now into its third. The first—up to "Say, what does your husband do?"—develops a tension between Doris and Milly, each occupying (and pre-occupied with) her own world. The second carrying on through Doris's "Oh," concentrates on Milly's internal tension, already evident through such outward signs as the sugar in the coffee and her annoyance at Doris's inability to remember her name. Finally, the third beat returns to a Milly/Doris tension, now redrawn. Something is pending *now*, in the present time. The second version had virtually exhausted itself, but this version wants to carry on.

Ironically, in this last version, Doris does much more of the talking, yet it is Milly who takes focus. Milly even assumes a measure of dignity altogether lacking in the other versions. Neither woman is comfortable with the situation, and they become less so as the scene progresses. Their unease forces them to express their feelings in concrete action rather than expository speeches. Up to this point, the information that Harold worked at the same warehouse as Jack has not appeared, but it is an implicit source of the tension that is developing. Through Jack, it appears, Doris knows about Harold Auckland. At any rate, the scene promises more tension.

The Natural Perverseness of Audiences

Audiences may be open and inquisitive when they encounter a play, but they are simultaneously highly suspicious. They are perverse enough never to believe what they are told directly. They prefer to discover the truth for themselves. When Richard Nixon was busy creating what came to be called "The White House Horrors," he told his watching audience not to believe what his administration might say; instead, "Believe what we do." The American public was perverse enough to do just that. At that moment, Nixon's survival instinct failed him, even if his dramatic instinct was intact.

A dramatist may well engage his audience by deliberately playing up disparities between what is said and what is done. In fact, the third version of the Milly/Doris scene gets some of its interest from such a disparity:

overtly, the two women are having a normal coffee klatch, but simultaneously something else is happening.

You can take this a step further. Action can become "negative reflection"—to borrow a term from Bernard Beckerman's *The Dynamics of the Drama*. When what characters do is at odds with what they say, the disparity can produce a delicious tension. The audience delights in discovering the truth for themselves. This device requires a complete and clear context, for if the actions contradict the words, we need a full background against which to judge it all. For example, suppose two people, George and Sam, meet at a cocktail party. George has just told a compromising story about Sam, little realizing that Sam was in the room the whole time. This is the background. The dialogue itself might be quite simple and seemingly direct, and yet it would imply actions that give every word the lie:

GEORGE

Why, Sam! Imagine meeting you here!

SAM

Yes, just imagine. Here I am.

GEORGE

I trust you just arrived, eh? It's been a lively party. Look, I'd like to introduce you around.

SAM

I believe I have already been introduced around, thanks very much.

GEORGE

Oh. Then you know most of these people?

SAM

I didn't say that.

GEORGE

Well, look, it's really good seeing you again. I hadn't expected the pleasure.

SAM

Nor I. It is always refreshing to have a chance to learn something new about one's friends.

GEORGE

Exactly my feelings.

Even without stage directions, it is clear that this pleasant cocktail chat is a very unpleasant set of actions: clenched teeth, stiff body positions, oblique eye contact. And the background puts it all in perspective.

Negative reflection can work in more subtle ways and Anton Chekhov was a master of this technique. His characters simply cannot come to terms with their lives, and so they end up acting in a manner opposite to what they say. Indeed, the quintessential image of a Chekhovian character is that of a person lounging in an easy chair and proclaiming, "We must work." Perhaps the most famous instance of Chekhov's ironic play of action and words is the so-called "proposal scene" in *The Cherry Orchard.* It is set up to be a proposal scene, yet it contains no mention of marriage. For months, if not years, the family had expected the rich peasant Lopahin to marry their adopted daughter Varya. Now the homestead has been sold in order to pay debts—to Lopahin of all people. He declares himself ready to propose and Mme. Ranevskaya runs off to get her daughter. After some "smothered laughter and whispering" offstage, Varya enters from the room where she had been packing her suitcase to leave home for the last time:

VARYA
(Looking over the luggage in a leisurely fashion.)
Strange. I can't find it . . .

LOPAHIN
What are you looking for?

VARYA
Packed it myself and I don't remember . . .
(Pause.)

LOPAHIN
Where are you going now, Varya?

VARYA
I? To the Ragulins'. I've arranged to take charge there—as a housekeeper, if you like.

LOPAHIN
At Yashnevo? About fifty miles from here.
(Pause.)
Well, life in this house is ended!

VARYA
(Examining the luggage.)
Where is it? Perhaps I put it in the chest. Yes, life in this house is ended. . . . There will be no more of it.

LOPAHIN
And I'm just off to Kharkov—by this next train. I've a lot to do there. I'm leaving Yepihodov here. . . . I've taken him on.

VARYA
Oh!

LOPAHIN
Last year at this time it was snowing, if you remember, but now it's sunny and there's no wind. It's cold, though. . . . It must be three below.

VARYA

I didn't look.

(Pause.)

And besides, our thermometer's broken.

VOICE OFF

Yermolay Alexeyevich!

LOPAHIN
(As if he had been waiting for the call.)

This minute!

> (He exits quickly. VARYA sits on the floor and sobs quietly, her head on a bundle of clothes.)

The scene is very brief, yet it is one of the most memorable moments of the play. It is effective because one can sense the awkward, inward pain of the characters without either of them giving it expression. The overall effect is simultaneously pathetic and amusing.

It is an old truism that one comes to know a character in a play (just as in life) by what the character says about himself, by what others say about him, and above all by what he does. One might extend this statement to say that none of these ways, certainly not the first two, should tell the whole truth. A disparity between them can make the process of discovery fascinating for any audience.

This sense of fascination also grows from the spectacle of characters at odds. They may be at odds with one another, at odds with the audience, at odds with their circumstance, their past, their outside world, or simply each with himself. The tension produced by their being at odds provokes attention, anticipation, and participation. The greater the contrasts, disparities, incongruities, or conflicts thus produced, the more intense the audience's involvement—so long as these grow out of the play's fundamental tension.

The dramatist is obliged to build his play upon some fundamental polarity, using it to give the action unity, but also seeking to give it variety. He must extend the basic tension sufficiently to allow the audience to sense it palpably. For this reason, a dramatic scene may well be longer than the same episode would be in narrative form. The novel reader can pause and savor as he will; the playgoer or moviegoer has not that luxury. He needs ample time to absorb the tension as it occurs.

In this way, the audience also becomes a creative collaborator with the dramatist and the other dramatic artists. The dramatist who will not allow that assures himself of failure. The etymological meaning of the word "entertainment"—"holding between"—reminds us that drama entails creative collaboration between audience and artist.

The Importance of Tone

Tone refers to the author's attitude toward his material which serves to color it and to give distance and perspective. Any writer is concerned with establishing tone. It is a special concern for the dramatist, however, for his material will encounter the audience as a direct, immediate experience. If the audience is to engage with the presentation, it must share the dramatist's tone. This is abundantly clear in comedy, for if it does not inspire laughter, it has broken down. By the same token, a tragedy that does not inspire awe and wonder has not succeeded.

There are occasions when a play-in-the-making will not work simply because the tone is wrong. A dramatist may be struggling to make a scene deadly earnest and he is getting nowhere. If he takes the opposite tack and treats the matter comically, it may suddenly fall into place. Then there are comic scenes that refuse to be funny and yet may work well as serious drama.

Drama works on the basis of combustion in the audience. That can only happen if they share an understanding of the import of the action. Only the dramatist can control this understanding. True, there are occasional anomalies—directors who have saved bad plays or plays that are "so bad they are good again"—but one had better not trust such a crucial matter to chance.

It might be helpful to think of every character as presenting himself to two audiences at once: to the characters with whom he shares the scene and to the real audience. His own personal tone in what he says and does is not necessarily the same as the dramatist's; nor are the reactions of the other characters necessarily the same as the audience's. It bears keeping these levels in mind as you write, seeing to the character's own attitude, the reactions of others (who may vary among themselves), and the effect on the audience all at the same time. Ideally, the meaning of the character's actions will be larger, more all-encompassing for the audience than it ever is for the characters. An audience derives a certain pleasure from a superior vision. This is not to say that they do not relish surprises. Gaining new knowledge is not the same as having wisdom. Tone involves granting audiences a sort of wisdom.

Summary: Stages and Facets of Audience Involvement

The audience's involvement in a play moves through several phases, the dimensions of involvement expanding in the process. A list of these phases can serve as a review:

1. First, the audience approaches a play in a state of open, even naïve, anticipation. The spectacle they are about to see will carry them into another realm, into other levels of reality, while they know full well they also remain in a theatre. In these new realms, new lives will be glimpsed, as well as new ways of seeing life itself. They are alert to every stage or screen suggestion in order to create in their imaginations a full world for the play. In short, they want it to be good, and they are willing to help.

2. As the play begins, the individual audience member assumes a certain anonymity, merging personal identity in the crowd. The gathered audience seeks a kind of communion in the face of an action that raises life to a higher power. Drama depends upon group combustion.

3. Audiences take pleasure in "reading" actions, finding meaning in them through their faculty of histrionic sensibility.

4. They relish the immediacy of the moment, the "illusion of the first time," which gives them the sense of a spontaneous present moment. They give themselves over to the spectacle for the duration, and in recompense demand that it engage them by a sense of continual forward movement.

5. For this reason, they look for ironies, contrasts, conflicts, disparities—any form of tension that may hold them in anticipation. It may range from comic incongruity to tragic irony, but it must suggest an imbalance seeking balance, a driving force working against all resistance.

6. Audiences are perverse, refusing to believe anything told directly to them, and indulging a liking for those truths they discover themselves through various partial truths. No one avenue of expression—not character, not dialogue, not activity, not setting, not atmosphere—singly reveals the truth. It is found in a composite of them all.

7. Finally, they are collaborators with the dramatist in creating the life of the play. It is ultimately in their minds that the play resides. When the tone is right, they gain a pleasant sense of wisdom and shared vision.

Exercises

1. Construct a scene in which the audience is called upon to imagine the world of the play through the suggestions of action and a minimum of scenery, as in the Christopher Columbus play of Dario Fo.

2. Write a sequence of dialogue in which the audience will grasp a meaning different from that intended by the characters, as in the Chekhov scene from *The Three Sisters*.

3. Compose a scene using "negative reflection." It might, for example, be an exchange between two characters who love each other but are afraid to admit it,

or a public scene involving two people who must restrain their detestation of each other, or a sequence in which one person is trying to manipulate the other.

4. Examine again the third version of the Doris/Milly scene. Do one or all of the following:

a. Continue the scene from Milly's line, "I want to know what 'oh' means."

b. Change the locale of the scene and discover how the scene itself changes. Suppose, for example, it took place in a hotel lobby, or in Doris's house, or at a party in someone else's house, or at the Good Times Shoe Factory warehouse.

c. Write a scene that might have occurred between Harold and Jack shortly before this scene between their wives.

d. What might happen if Jack brought Harold home for dinner that evening?

PART II

The Stage Medium

4

Space and Time
on Stage

The dramatic mode, described in Part I, appears in a variety of media: stage, film, television, radio, and others. The conditions of each medium help shape the drama, and these conditions depend on the materials, which vary enormously from one medium to another. Film's strip of celluloid, television's flickering tube, radio's speaker box, and the theatre's stage are scarcely alike. The only element they all share as material is the actor. Even the actor transforms considerably from one medium to another as an image, a sound, or a living presence. Dramatic principles cut across all these media. Any one of them may present a "spectacle of human life conducted through action, based on pretense and bound together by tensions," which is our definition of a play. The spectacle and the pretense, however, depend absolutely on the material of the medium. We shall be examining now the material and consequent conditions of the stage medium, to be followed in Part III by the screen media.

The dramatist, of course, must be as responsive to the conditions of the chosen medium as to the dramatic mode. What tends to vary most from medium to medium are the means of conducting action and the basis for creating pretense. Spectacle and pretense on stage work through the immediate presence of the actor upon the stage, while on screen they work through the interplay of images. As a general rule, most stage plays are less effective as screenplays simply because they were not designed for the screen in the first place. Many stage effects may not find parallel screen effects. Perhaps a good case in point is Peter Barnes' *The Ruling Class*. It has had a brilliant screen version, which nevertheless could not quite duplicate the original stage effects—many of which depend upon the audience's immediate presence before the live spectacle.

Stated most simply and succinctly, the material of the stage medium consists of a human agent caught in space and time. This seems simple enough. Still, the implications are rich; even the most seasoned playwright is still ferreting them out. We can at least set up some signs and pointers in the vast geography of the stage medium.

The Demands of the Stage Medium

For several reasons, the stage deserves our first attention. It is not that the stage is superior to the screen media. True, it has a long and respectable tradition behind it; even now, the playwright commands a respect the screenwriter cannot match. One cannot make a steady living from playwriting as easily as one might from screenwriting, and perhaps we accord this respect to make up the difference. But the real reasons for beginning with the stage medium address much more fundamental conditions.

First of all, the stage allows the playwright much tighter control of material than do the other media. A gap exists in all media between script and performance, but it is considerably narrower in the stage medium. Put another way, the impact a stage director may make on the audience's experience is far less than a screen director may make. In the moment of encounter, the cinema audience experiences the play through the eye of the camera, which the director rather than the screenwriter controls. The playgoer, however, experiences a stage play directly. Because there is no camera to control audience focus, the stage relies on stage action, which the playwright controls somewhat, and on the spoken word, which he controls completely. Moreover, the confines of the stage dictate that the setting—the context of action—be relatively fixed. While the playwright does not design the setting, he does establish the nature and terms of his world as a stage world, and these must be respected for the play to work at all. Finally, although not dictating the appearance of the costumed actors, the playwright at least provides the gross patterns of their behavior and relationships, which no agent, casting director, costume designer, or actor can alter.

Secondly, the stage is a more exacting and demanding medium for the dramatic writer. This results partly from the greater control the playwright exerts, but it also derives from the greater concentration of energies dictated by the confinement of the stage. The stage is a confined space set apart from the audience by one means or another. While that space may represent a wide variety of times and locales, it remains always confined. This forces an economy and discipline on the playwright. What happens in that space over the duration of the play requires concentrated energy, controlled focus, and an inexorable build-up. These no one but the playwright can provide. If things are not going well, we cannot take the camera off to a new location or insert some fancy camerawork in the form of intriguing close-ups or unusual camera angles. A bad scene on stage is simply a bad scene; there is relatively little the directors or actors can do to cover for it.

Thirdly, mastering the rigors of the stage medium is obviously essential for a playwright, but it is also useful for any dramatist regardless of the chosen medium. It demonstrates methods of controlling material one might not otherwise grasp. Some methods, of course, belong only to the stage, but those born of its demand for economy and discipline have value in any dramatic medium. For this reason, playwrights can adapt to screenwriting more readily than screenwriters to playwriting. True, they must adjust to the screen's reliance on visual images and dampen any predilection for the spoken work, but that is less severe an adjustment than accepting the enforced economy of the confined stage.

The Magic of Stage Space and Stage Time

None of this should be taken to mean that the stage presents a set of stifling restrictions. The stage does indeed restrict a play's action, but this is more challenging than stifling. Creativity has a way of being aroused by such challenge. There is a sort of magic about the stage's space and time. That thirty-by-twenty-foot space can become a host of different times and places. The two-hour interval of a full-length play can become a cavalcade of years. Space and time assume an intriguing flexibility. Knowing this gives a visit to an empty theatre and its bare stage a certain eerie feeling. The sensation of the many lives that characters have lived and will yet live on that stage lends a ghostliness to the place. The sensation has inspired numerous stories of ghosts dwelling in theatre buildings. Movies and stage plays have used it as a basis, running the gamut from *The Phantom of the Opera* to Luigi Pirandello's great play *Six Characters in Search of an Author*, which presupposes that the six characters inhabit the continual limbo of the theatre wings, emerging only when that particular play is put into the theatre repertory.

An empty space begging to be filled with life: that is the playwright's challenge. This space is set before an audience and available for a span of time. The task is to fill this space and spend this time in such a way as to engage the audience's imagination, thought, and emotion. The possibilities are endless.

The stage space might become a parlor, a garden, castle ramparts, the bridge of a ship, a battlefield, a cavern, a bar, a hotel lobby, an attic, a factory, a sewer passageway, an insect nest, a cloud, and indeed it has become all those places and many more besides. What makes this variety even more challenging is the many ways in which the stage may become other places.

They range from fully-supported illusion, as in strict Realism, to suggestive theatricalism, as in Dario Fo's platform, masts, and sheets for Christopher Columbus' voyage. Thornton Wilder's "Happy Journey to Trenton and Camden" delighted its initial audiences by the novelty of an automobile trip through New Jersey via four straight-back chairs on a bare stage. Much of the "magic" comes from the fact that the stage remains a stage while simultaneously becoming an illusory place. This double existence of the stage as stage and also somewhere else is the special province of theatre.

Stage time may also be invested with a new dimension. Audiences are quite pleased to accept two different times while watching a play: actual time and stage time. Stage time may be telescoped so that days, months, even years elapse in the world of the play while a scant two hours elapse in the auditorium. This compression can happen on screen as well, but, because the screen delivers a seemingly more literal recording of reality, it generally has to happen between shots. Stage time, however, may run ahead of auditorium time within a scene, as in the twenty-minute night in the first scene of *Hamlet*.

One of the special capabilities and appeals of the stage stems from this double existence: space and time operating on two levels, actual and imagined. The stage is both itself and somewhere else; time is both the running time of the play and the span of the characters' lives represented.

Another peculiarity of the stage as opposed to other dramatic media, and perhaps any other art form, is the fact that it relies equally on space and on time to create its effects. Music, for example, is primarily a temporal art, depending on tempo and rhythm; painting primarily a spatial art, depending on line, mass, and color in space. Even cinema assumes meaning more from time than from space, since its greatest power derives from the juxtaposition of moving images. The stage, however, uses space fully as meaningfully as it does time.

What happens in a play, both between its characters and between itself and its audience, depends as heavily on where it happens as on when it happens. "Where" refers not just to the selection of locale (castle ramparts, battlefield, bar, hotel lobby), but also to the manner in which the locale is defined and suggested to the audience. Definition and suggestion of stage space should imply the forces at work in the play. By the same token, "when" is not just a matter of story, but also of playing up the tensions among the forces. One moment must build on the last to create dramatic momentum. Most plays have a brief notation at the outset (duplicated in the audience's program) indicating the time and place of the play's action. But the definition of these two qualities goes well beyond this.

Thus, a playwright must bear in mind both the temporal and the spatial dimensions of the play, keeping them continually reinforcing one another. A good plot may suffer by an ill-defined space. Equally, a provocative setting may be spoiled if the plot fails to tap its implicit tensions. Two penetrating questions can always be asked about a play to test its dramatic validity: "Why now?" and "Why here?" There should be compelling reasons for the play to occur at *this time* in the characters' lives and equally compelling reasons that it take place in *this locale*. Moreover, there should be good and sufficient reason that this time and this place are defined and suggested to the audience in the way they are. Perhaps the most rewritten part of any play is its opening, with its description of the setting and the opening action. These need to contain the seeds of all that is to happen. The more one discovers about the characters' interaction with each other, with their world and with their audience, the more precise one's idea becomes of how we should first encounter them. And so, a playwright frequently returns to the opening to give it this new precision.

Because it is difficult to discuss space and time simultaneously, we shall begin with space, the stage itself — the theatrical context of dramatic action just as the screen is the cinematic context of dramatic action.

Types of Stages

Through the ages, stages and theatre houses have assumed a host of different configurations. The ancient Greek theatre was an open-air structure with seating surrounding more than half of a dancing circle, itself backed by a narrow stage with three doorways. The medieval stage consisted of a platform backed by a series of "mansions," each representing a different locale to figure in the action. The Elizabethans took that platform into an open courtyard which served as the auditorium; behind the platform they placed a curtained alcove ("discovery space") and two doors and, above them, a balcony alcove ("inner above") and windows. Meanwhile, the Italian Renaissance took the theatre indoors and developed the proscenium arch to frame a perspective vista as backdrop for action and to mask scene-changing machinery. By the mid-seventeenth century that theatre had evolved into the box-pit-and-gallery theatre, with tiers of boxes topped by an open gallery all surrounding a pit seating area. The theatre of the early Realists, at the end of the nineteenth century, put the action into a full environment behind the proscenium arch and placed the audience in rows in a darkened house. All of these are architectural statements of the relationships intended between dramatic action and the gathered audience.

Unlike these earlier theatres, our modern theatre has no single accepted configuration. We live in an eclectic and self-conscious age; one result, among many others, is the enormous variety of theatres. They range from the highly formal and illusionistic proscenium stage to informal "found spaces" of the environmental theatre, with several types falling between. The following descriptions proceed from the informal to the formal.

In recent years, the environmental theatre movement, seeking to merge spectacle and spectator by placing the action in the midst of the audience, has become fond of "found space": airplane hangars, abandoned movie studios, open squares, prisons. Any large but confined gathering space will serve the purpose. For example, Adrienne Mnouchkine staged her elaborate *1789* in an airplane hangar in Paris replaying events of the French Revolution now here, now there in the midst of an ambulatory audience. Dagmar Schauberg staged *Illusions of Freedom* in an abandoned prison in Amsterdam with the audience touring throughout the prison for the duration of the play. *The Passion Play*, an adaptation of the English medieval mystery plays done by the British National Theatre, under the direction of Bill Bryden, was performed in Rome in a mist-filled abandoned movie studio with the audience standing, sitting, walking, and dancing among the actors. The Italian director Luca Ronconi staged his version of *Orlando Furioso* in the midst of a crowd gathered in a public square. All of these asked the audience to walk about in the open space with the spectacle developing in their very midst. Naturally, whenever action began in one spot, the audience made room for it, and the spot became stage for the time. Good environmental theatre requires a constant shifting and redefining of the spectator-spectacle tension, sometimes even assigning roles to audiences. They become, for example, the French revolutionary mob in *1789* and the mob that called for Barabbas in *The Passion Play*. They assume, as it were, two collective identities, an actual theatre audience and an imagined audience in the world of the play. Such a device can work usually only if a collective identity is assigned, since the individual audience member tends to be reluctant and uncomfortable assuming an individual role.

The so-called "black box" theatre is slightly more formal, for it sets a fixed acting area apart from the spectators. It consists quite simply of a room usually painted black to render it neutral. It employs moveable banks of seats capable of assuming a variety of configurations. They may be arranged to surround a central acting area, to stand on two or three sides of the "stage" or to line one side of the room facing the open space. This has the effect of placing the audience in a kind of suspended reality: entering the black box from the outside world seems an entrance into a dreamlike cavern in which actors may conjure images of a totally new world. Jerzsy Grotowski, the famous Polish director, is fond of employing such a changeable, simple room for his so-called "Poor Theatre." It places heavy reliance on the discipline and style of acting rather than elaborate scenic or lighting effects to arouse the imagination of the audience.

A slightly more formal type is the arena stage. Here, the audience sits either in a circle surrounding the acting area or on the four sides of a square or rectangular open space. Unlike the black box, it has a fixed central stage. Like the black box, however, it throws emphasis on the actor, and because of its intimacy, it allows subtle interactions among the actors as characters. All this is done at the expense of elaborate scenic and lighting effects, which, with the open space playing out in all directions, must be held to a minimum. It also gives rather more emphasis to audience interaction,

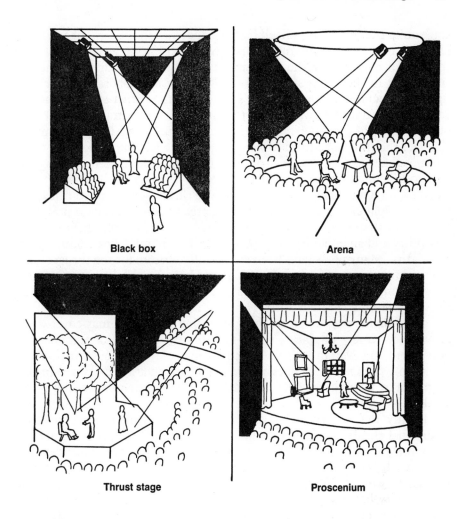

Black box

Arena

Thrust stage

Proscenium

inasmuch as the audience glimpses itself across the stage. A play written for arena staging, or adaptable to it, usually has a small cast of characters, minimal reliance on scenic and lighting effects, quiet or subtle action, and at least a suggestion of audience participation on some level.

Few plays have been expressly written for these relatively informal and new types of theatre: the found space, the black box, and the arena stage. Most of the significant works associated with them come from directorial adaptations. Still, they are viable dramatic stages which provide unique challenges for the playwright. They are appropriate spaces to inspire dramatic imagination and there is no reason for a playwright to put them aside.

A configuration of much greater formality is the thrust stage which, since the early sixties, has become the more favored type of stage. The stage quite literally thrusts itself into the audience in the form of a tapered platform backed by some mechanism provided for scenery. It combines the best of two worlds: the intimacy and reliance on audience imagination found in the arena stage and the capacity for elaborate scenic and lighting effects of the proscenium stage. Still, the thrust stage dictates a certain compromise between these two. It cannot quite attain the intimacy of the arena nor can it sustain the full-scale illusions of the proscenium. The fact that the stage thrusts into the audience leaving three sides open requires that the play rely on suggestion to prompt the audience's imagination to fill in details not provided by scenery, which itself must remain background. Of course, this also grants the thrust stage a greater flexibility. It is a "platea"—a generalized acting area that may become now this locale, now that—relying on the action and lighting to imply changes. This flexibility and an enhanced audience interaction probably account for its popularity. Many plays have been specifically written for the thrust stage: Arthur Miller's *After the Fall*, Lawrence and Lee's *The Night Thoreau Spent in Jail*, Tom Stoppard's *Rosencrantz and Guildenstern Are Dead*, Arthur Kopit's *Indians*, and Milan Stitt's *The Runner Stumbles* are some examples. All these use the stage to create fluid, sweeping action that may cover years and a wide variety of places, while maintaining a degree of audience involvement and even intimacy. The conditions of the modern thrust stage come close to those of the Elizabethan playhouse and they call for a similar dramaturgy, tapping audience imagination to fill in elements of the play's world.

Finally, the proscenium stage is the most formal and by now the most traditional theatrical configuration. In its purest form, the stage area is completely separated from the audience and contained by the proscenium arch which frames the play's world and conceals the stage machinery. It calls for full illusion sustained by scenery, lighting, and properties. The scenery becomes the full environment for the action except on the one side left open for the audience's view. It relies on the "fourth wall" convention, whereby the audience is given the sensation of peering into a room whose fourth wall has been removed without the characters' awareness. Thus, in extreme form, it has been called the "Peeping Tom" theatre. Plays written for the proscenium stage, or adaptable to it, tend to accentuate the interaction of character and environment. They give the feeling of a life being lived in its own reality more or less oblivious to the audience's presence. It is, of course, associated with the Naturalistic experiment and with early Realism, in which a novel appeal was watching life being lived much as it appears in the real world. That appeal is still with us. Plays are still being written in this manner—plays such as Jason Miller's *That Championship Season*, Preston Jones' *Texas Trilogy*, or even Sam Shepard's *Buried Child*.

The proscenium stage also has the versatility to portray elaborate subjective states of mind as called for by Expressionism, Symbolism, and their variants. Such unrealistic plays as Eugene O'Neill's *The Emperor Jones*, Karel Čapek's *Insect Comedy*, and August Strindberg's *A Dream Play*, as well as more recent pieces like Tennessee Williams' *Camino Real* or Sam Shepard's *Geography of a Horse Dreamer*, call for scenic effects that only the proscenium stage can afford.

To overcome the muting effect the old proscenium stage creates by placing all action above the curtain line, many of the newer proscenium houses employ a large forestage area. Certain plays that develop a tension between objective and subjective experience may call for such a configuration. Arthur Miller's *Death of a Salesman*, Tennessee Williams's *The Glass Menagerie*, and Peter Luke's *Hadrian VII* are of this type, alternating sequences in the characters' minds with sequences in objective reality.

These are the essential types of stages available to the contemporary playwright: the found space, the black box, the arena, the thrust, and the proscenium. One might argue that it is not necessary that a playwright know all these configurations. After all, any play is more or less adaptable to any stage, and it is the business of stage directors to find the way. This is true; on the other hand, a vision of the space one's play will occupy sparks the playwright's imagination. Specific effects immediately suggest themselves. To sit down and write Act I, scene 1, and suppose that it will all come of its own accord because one has a good story to tell is wishful thinking. Many great playwrights of the past, Shakespeare and Molière for example, worked for and knew a particular theatre well. This helped conjure an image of the play in performance as they wrote. Moreover, it has not prohibited their plays from being performed on other stages.

Tensions Available in Space

Using these images of the several kinds of stages, let us examine ways in which space might be manipulated. It is not enough to recognize that a play occupies space. As an act of presentation, it also addresses an audience and simultaneously refers to extensions of its fictional world offstage. No matter the type of stage, three realms are always present physically: the stage, the house (or auditorium), and offstage (a neutral ground beyond the stage). With the aid of the audience's imagination, each of these may assume character and the tensions between them become vivid. Moreover, tensions within the stage space may be shaped. On the fictional level, the business of the playwright is to characterize these three realms, multiply them, and create tension between them. Meanwhile, they remain just what they are: physical space.

Anton Chekhov's "On the Harmfulness of Tobacco" provides a beautiful and novel example of characterizing stage space and infusing it with tension. Because it is brief, it is quoted here in its entirety. The economy and precision employed are an inspiration. Notice that the play is ostensibly a lecture. The speaker literally, but unwittingly, makes a spectacle of himself. The audience becomes a second actor in the play, assuming a double existence as both the play's audience and the lecture audience, supposedly gathered to hear a learned lecture on the subject of tobacco. Offstage becomes an extension of this fictive occasion: the wife who waits in the wings toward the end of the piece, the school at Dog Alley, 13, and Nyukhin's imagined realm of a pole on the hillside under the moon. Thus the stage, a simple podium, becomes the meeting ground of lines of tension emanating out of the life Nyukhin lives elsewhere, out of his own subjective mind, and out of the sensibility of the gathered audience. These become complex, but the means employed is simple and direct:

NYUKHIN

(He enters the stage with great dignity, wearing long side whiskers and a worn-out frock coat. He bows majestically to his audience, adjusts his waistcoat, and speaks.)

Ladies and . . . so to speak . . . gentlemen. It was suggested to my wife that I give a public lecture here for charity. Well, if I must, I must. It's all the same to me. I am not a professor and I've never finished the university. And yet, nevertheless, over the past thirty years I have been ruining my health by constant, unceasing examination of matters of a strictly scientific nature. I am a man of intellectual curiosity, and, imagine, at times I write essays on scientific matters—well, not exactly scientific, but, if you will pardon me, approximately scientific. Just the other day I finished a long article entitled: "On the Harmfulness of Certain Insects." My daughters liked it immensely, especially the part about bedbugs. But I just read it over and tore it up. What difference does it make whether such things are written? You still have to have naphtha. We have bedbugs, even in our grand piano. . . . For the subject of my lecture today I have taken, so to speak, the harm done mankind by the use of tobacco. I myself smoke, but my wife told me to lecture on the harmfulness of tobacco, and so what's to be done? Tobacco it is. It's all the same to me; but, ladies and . . . so to speak . . . gentlemen, I urge you to take my lecture with all due seriousness, or something awful may happen. If any of you are afraid of a dry, scientific lecture, cannot stomach that sort of thing, you needn't listen. You may leave.

(He again adjusts his waistcoat.)

Are there any doctors present? If so, I insist that you listen very carefully, for my lecture will contain much useful information, since tobacco, besides being harmful, contains certain medicinal properties. For example, if you take a fly and put him in a snuff box, he will die, probably from nervous exhaustion. Tobacco, strictly speaking, is a plant. . . . Yes, I know, when I lecture I blink my right eye. Take no notice. It's simple nervousness. I am a very nervous man, generally speaking. I started blinking years ago, in 1889, to be precise, on September the thirteenth, the very day my wife gave birth to our, so to speak, fourth daughter, Varvara. All my daughters were born on the thirteenth. But . . .

(He looks at his watch.)

time at our disposal is strictly limited. I see I have digressed from the subject. I must tell you, by the way, that my wife runs a boarding school. Well, not exactly a boarding school, but something in the nature of one. Just between us, my wife likes to complain about hard times, but she has put away a little nest egg . . . some forty or fifty thousand roubles. As for me, I haven't a kopek to my name, not a penny . . . and, well, what's the use of dwelling on that? At the school, it is my lot to look after the housekeeping. I buy supplies, keep an eye on the servants, keep the books, stitch together the exercise books, exterminate bedbugs, take my wife's little dog for walks, catch mice . . . Last night, it fell to me to give the cook flour and butter for today's breakfast. Well, to make a long story short, today, when the pancakes were ready, my wife came to the kitchen and said that three students would not be eating pancakes, as they had swollen glands. So it seems we had a few too many pancakes. What to do with them? First my wife ordered them stored away, but then she thought awhile, and she said, "You eat those pancakes, you scarecrow." When she's out of humor, that's what she calls me: "scarecrow," or "viper," or "devil." What sort of devil am I? She's always out of humor. I didn't eat those pancakes; I wolfed them down. I'm always hungry. Why, yesterday, she gave me no dinner. She says, "What's the use feeding you, you scarecrow . . ." However . . .

(He looks at his watch.)

I have strayed from my subject. Let us continue. But some of you, I'm sure, would rather hear a romance, or a symphony, some aria . . .

(He sings.)

"We shall not shrink
In the heat of battle:
Forward, be strong!"

I forget where that comes from . . . Oh, by the way, I should tell you that at my wife's school, apart from looking after the housekeeping, my duties include teaching mathematics, physics, chemistry, geography, history, solfeggio, literature, and so forth. For dancing, singing and drawing, my wife charges extra, although the singing and dancing master is yours truly. Our school is located at Dog Alley, number 13. I suppose that's why my life has been so unlucky, living in house number thirteen. All my daughters were born on the thirteenth, I think I told you, and our house has thirteen windows, and, in short, what's the use? Appointments with my wife may be made for any hour, and the school's prospectus may be had for thirty kopeks from the porter.

(He takes a few copies out of his pocket.)

Ah, here you see, I've brought a few with me. Thirty kopeks a copy. Would anyone care for one?

(A pause.)

No one? Well, make it twenty kopeks.

(Another pause.)

What a shame! Yes, house number thirteen. I am a failure. I've grown old and stupid. Here I am, lecturing, and to all appearances enjoying myself, but I tell you I have such an urge to scream at the top of my lungs, to run away to the ends of the earth. . . . There is no one to talk to. I want to weep. What about your daughters, you say, eh? Well, what about them? I try to talk to them, and they only laugh. My wife has seven daughters. Seven. No. Sorry, it's only six. Now, wait, it *is* seven. Anna, the eldest, is twenty-seven; the youngest is seventeen. Ladies and gentlemen!

(He looks around surreptitiously.)

I am miserable! I have become a fool, a nonentity. But then, all in all, you see before you the happiest of fathers. Why shouldn't I be, and who am I to say that I am not? Oh, if you only knew! I have lived with my wife for thirty-three years, and, I can say they are the best years of my life . . . well, not the best, but approximately the best. They have passed, as it were, in a thrice, and, well, to hell with them!

(Again, he looks around surreptitiously.)

I don't think my wife has arrived yet. She's not here. So, I can say what I like. I am afraid . . . I am terribly afraid when she looks at me. Well, I was talking about my daughters. They don't get married, probably because they're so shy, and also because men can never get near them. My wife doesn't give parties. She never invites anyone to dinner. She's a stingy, shrewish, ill-tempered old biddy, and that's why no one comes to see us, but . . . I can tell you confidentially . . .

(He comes down to the edge of his platform.)

on holidays, my daughters can be seen at the home of their aunt, Natalia Semionovna, the one who has rheumatism and always wears a yellow dress covered with black spots that look like cockroaches. There you can eat. And if my wife happens not to be looking, then you'll see me . . .

(He makes a drinking gesture.)

Oh, you'll see I can get tipsy on just one glass. Then I feel so happy and at the same time so sad, it's unimaginable. I think of my youth, and then somehow, I long to run away, to clear out. Oh, if you only knew how I long to do it! To run away, to be free of everything, to run without ever looking back. . . . Where? Anywhere, so long as it is away from that vile, mean, cheap life that has made me into a fool, a miserable idiot; to run away from that stupid, petty, hot headed, spiteful, nasty old miser, my wife, who has given me thirty-three years of torment; to run away from the music, the kitchen, my wife's bookkeeping ledgers, all those mundane, trivial affairs. . . . To run away and then stop somewhere far, far away on a hill, and stand there like a tree, a pole, a scarecrow, under the great sky and the still, bright moon, and to forget, simply forget. . . . Oh, how I long to forget! How I long to tear off this frock coat, this coat that I wore thirty-three years ago at my wedding, and that I still wear for lectures for charity!

(He tears off his coat.)

Take that! And that!

(Stamping on the coat.)

I am a poor, shabby, tattered wretch, like the back of this waistcoat.

(He turns his back showing his waistcoat.)

I ask for nothing. I am better than that. I was young once; I went to the university, I had dreams, I thought of myself as a man, but now . . . now, I want nothing. Nothing but peace . . . peace!

(He looks offstage. Quickly he picks up his frock coat and puts it on.)

She is there. My wife is there in the wings waiting for me.

(He looks at his watch.)

I see our time is up. If she asks you, please, I beg of you, tell her that her scarecrow of a husband, I mean, the lecturer, myself, behaved with dignity. Oh, she is looking at me.

(He resumes his dignity and raises his voice.)

Given that tobacco contains a terrible poison, which I have had the pleasure of describing to you, smoking should at all costs be avoided, and permit me to add my hope that these observations on the harmfulness of tobacco will have been of some profit to you. And so I conclude. *Dixi et animam levavi!*

(He bows majestically, and exits with grand dignity.)

This is a play about self-hatred. Typical of Chekhov, it is both a comic and a pathetic spectacle, but it is most assuredly a spectacle. One man, all alone on stage, makes a spectacle of himself. Without the aid of other stage characters, Chekhov turns to the manipulation of space to create dramatic tension. He transforms the audience into a collective character. The space is a lecture podium, which Nyukhin treats as an escape from the "vile, mean, cheap life" of Dog Alley, 13 in the ridiculous hope of some companionship and compassion from his audience. Still, it is an uncomfortable situation. There he stands, blinking his right eye and "to all appearances enjoying" himself. His discomfort becomes also the audience's. Were they witnessing this as an actual lecture, it would be intensely uncomfortable, but aesthetic distance and the double role of play audience and lecture audience mutes this and actually gives pleasure. So the two realms of the podium and the lecture hall set up the first tension. As Nyukhin paints a picture of his life at Dog Alley, 13, a third realm emerges. Granted it is an imagined, offstage realm, but out of it comes the wife waiting in the wings near the end of the play. Pulling Nyukhin in an opposite direction is his vision of a life of peace on a hillside under the moon as a pole or a scarecrow. This constitutes a fourth realm, imagined even

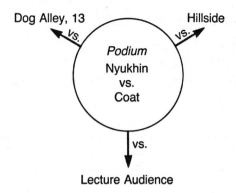

for him, but nevertheless an important realm. Finally, Chekhov contrives at the moment of the play's crux to express Nyukhin's self-loathing in spatial terms. He splits Nyukhin in two by having him take off that frock coat—that coat he wore at his wedding thirty-three years ago and still wears for charity lectures—and trampling on it. All this might be graphically represented as shown above. Repelled by his life at Dog Alley, 13, Nyukhin takes to the podium, from which he seeks the fellowship of the audience. Rebuffed by them, he turns attention beyond them to the hillside under the moon. When that image fades, he directs his energies against himself by way of his frock coat, which stands for everything he hates about his life and himself. Trampling the coat, he kills himself in effigy. And then, tail between his legs, he retreats with ironic dignity to Dog Alley, a defeated man. But his last line, *"Dixi et animam levavi,"* Latin for "I have spoken and relieved my soul," tells us the lecture had been of some therapeutic value.

"On the Harmfulness of Tobacco" provides a clear model of spatial manipulation. Each pole of tension is assigned a realm. As a result, the poles become richer and more vivid. There is ample reason for the play to occur *now*. Nyukhin makes a decision that dooms him to Dog Alley. And there is ample reason for this action to occur *here*, in the lecture hall. We become sensitive to the forces operating on Nyukhin by the awkwardness of the situation and by the polar pulls exerted by the offstage realms.

The play demonstrates not only the use of the three theatrical realms of stage, house, and offstage, but also the three levels on which plays work. These are the actual, the imagined, and the inner life. The first is entirely physical: the actual activity conducted by the actor on stage before the audience. Here, the actor portraying Nyukhin goes through a series of speeches and pantomimes as a performer's presentation. The second level of imagined activity consists of the character, Nyukhin, lecturing us, an imagined audience. Dog Alley and the wife exist on this level with great power, even if they have no actual physical existence. On the third level of inner life, Nyukhin's buffoonery is recognized as a cover for his discomfort and self-loathing. We sense this empathetically as it bubbles under his overt actions and finally erupts in his picture of the hillside under the moon and in his trampling of the coat. These three levels play upon each other, setting up tensions, many of them ironic. Although they are not strictly speaking spatial, requiring as they do time to develop, they nevertheless need a spatial dimension to work. The isolation of realms and the interplay of tensions between them alert us to the interaction of the three levels.

Theatre, taken generally now, operates on three levels (actual, imagined, and inner life) using three realms (stage, house, and offstage). Lines of tension may run between any of these to create drama. This may be graphically illustrated as follows, the circle representing the play and the inverted arrows the potential lines of tension any play might tap:

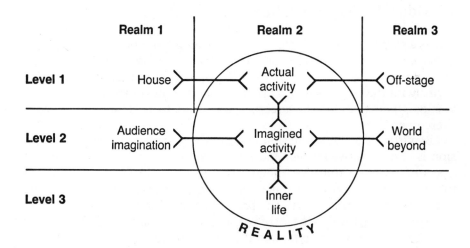

Every play renders these realms as particular places, just as Chekhov had placed Dog Alley in the world beyond and the audience in an imagined lecture hall. Every play must also develop the tensions between the three levels in a specific way. "On the Harmfulness of Tobacco" develops much of it between Nyukhin's overt buffoonery and his inner despair.

A playwright may also divide the stage itself into two or more realms. The Elizabethan playhouse made permanent architectural provision for this by the discovery space, the inner above, the doors and windows. Many modern plays divide the stage to establish different levels of action. Arthur Miller's *Death of a Salesman* uses the upstage area to represent realistic action in the life of Willy Loman, and the downstage area for subjective encounters between Willy and Uncle Ben—encounters that take place in Willy's mind. Tom Stoppard's *Rosencrantz and Guildenstern Are Dead* employs two distinct realms: upstage for Hamlet's Elsinore and downstage for Rosencrantz and Guildenstern's limbo. In a different vein, Eugene O'Neill splits the stage into five realms for *Desire Under the Elms*—four rooms of old Ephraim Cabot's farm house and the yard out front. Some scenes play simultaneously in two of these realms to heighten dramatic tension. Tennessee Williams's *Summer and Smoke* calls for three realms, all distinct places in the same town, all visible on stage at once.

Examples are endless and further insights into the interplay of dramatic levels may be found in Bernard Beckerman's *The Dynamics of Drama*. It would pay to examine the openings of plays you know well to discover how stage realms are defined and isolated to reinforce the coming effects. The point is that you, as a playwright, need to make yourself sensitive to the three-dimensional space of the stage and house and to the implied presence of a world beyond, lurking in the wings of your stage.

Tensions Available in Time

Just as a play is isolated in space, forced to occupy the confines of the stage, so is it isolated in time. What begins must end. A play is a representation of an action; as such it must isolate, focus, and shape that action. A play begins with the emergence of a driving force that moves its action forward. It ends when that force overcomes its ultimate resistance or is itself overcome.

By virtue of a play's isolation in time, the first source of temporal tension is simply between *then* and *now*. We have emphasized before that a peculiarity of the dramatic mode is that it resides in a perpetual present time. The state of affairs we encounter *now* may well contrast sharply and dramatically with *then*—the present set against the past. Moreover, the striving will, the driving force within the play, is always aimed at some future. The sense of entrapment in the present moment set against all time can produce tremendous fascination. It is a tension always available, and some playwrights employ it with great verve. Henrik Ibsen's *Ghosts*, as its title suggests, trades heavily on dramatic interaction of past and present, a present sick and afflicted by the ghosts of the past. Sophocles' *Oedipus Rex* moves forward by discoveries that reach back into the past. Even such an amorphous present as used by Samuel Beckett in *Waiting for Godot* gains dramatic interest by Vladimir and Estragon's entrapment in a present cut off from the past and their desperate reach for a future which Godot will surely change once he arrives. The fact that he never comes produces a perverse tension, leaving their entrapment unrelieved.

Whether or not the polarity of past-versus-present is a major source of tension, it is always a matter of crucial concern for the playwright. The immediacy of dramatic action makes it inevitable. Thus, selecting a point of attack is a decision of such importance for a playwright that it can make or break the play. The point of attack is the moment in the natural story line when the action of the play begins. Story and plot are not the same. Plot is the coherent action of the play, the spectacle of its driving force.

Story is simply a series of events. These events may lead up to, include, and even go beyond the action. Action can only begin when the will emerges. That is the point of attack and the beginning of plot.

Every good story, of course, has its own intrinsic interest just as story. But to dramatize a story is to find a particular set of tensions that matter in an urgent and immediate sense. If that cannot be found, one might as well write the story as a narrative rather than subject an audience to waiting hopelessly for something to matter, now, in the lives of the characters. To dramatize means to give immediate import to events, points of view, and circumstances. Only that will produce action. So the selection of the polar tension that will provide the action with its structure is a playwright's basic decision. The first step in that direction is the point of attack.

In a sense, the point of attack establishes two kinds of "thens" for the play: a "remote then" and an "immediate then." The "remote then" provides a backdrop against which the present operates. It consists of those events that shaped the present circumstance from the very beginning of the natural story. Thirty-three years ago, Nyukhin put on his frock coat and married. His misery began then. Over the years, patterns of behavior established themselves, attitudes solidified, and the misery grew. The "immediate then" propels the action forward. Just before the curtain and our first encounter with the characters, something happened. Events, circumstances, and attitudes have converged to put them in some uncomfortable situation. It needs to be at least vaguely uncomfortable so as to force them to act. This morning, Nyukhin's wife came into the kitchen, ordered her scarecrow of a husband to eat those pancakes, then had him put on his frock coat and sent him out to give another public lecture for charity. Now, freed from his life at Dog Alley, 13, he almost relishes his encounter with the audience: at least they are not his wife. Still, giving another one of these lectures is a nerve-wracking experience, enough to make the right eye twitch. "Now" matters because the lecture is a moment of escape for Nyukhin. It comes to matter even more when it leads to a crucial decision for his life: to return meekly to Dog Alley, 13. Chances are that he will never escape again, certainly not to deliver another public lecture for charity. In those few minutes on the podium, Nyukhin's life is altered almost irretrievably.

This leads us to a third kind of "then" that operates in a play in addition to the "remote then" and the "immediate then." We might call it the "dramatic then." Since a play must move forward in time, every "now" transforms into a "then." Every present moment becomes a past moment. The interaction of these "nows" transformed into "thens" would seem an ever more complex process. It is. But there is a way to make sense of it all. Moments, as the word is used here, are not precise measures of time, such as seconds or minutes, but rather meaningful segments of dramatic action. Ideally, each moment builds on the previous, to create a constant sense of forward movement and anticipation. The stronger the build, the more sensitive we are to the moments contributing to it.

Segmentation of action occurs on two levels: formal and organic. Formal segments are actual breaks in stage action by way of curtains or blackouts. The total action of course is one large formal segment set apart by the opening and closing of the play. Within that sequence, acts and scenes formally break the action into segments. Given the complexity and length of the full-length play, these are usually necessary. They may occur in a short play, but here you run the risk of losing all momentum and so having to reestablish it in the next scene. Formal segmentation seems simple enough, but it does involve that hard decision of what to dramatize: the "why now" test has to be applied to each act and scene. And it involves the equally hard decision of when the action has fulfilled itself and so must end.

Organic segmentation is a subtler matter. These are the "moments": sequences of dramatic action in which one force dominates. When it subsides, replaced by another force, a new segment has begun. This is much the same idea as the "beat" or "motivational unit" as described by Konstantin Stanislavsky in training his actors at the Moscow Art Theatre—the alternation of characters' motivations, first one dominating, then another. Enlarging on this, not only motivations but other forces emanating from the past, the world beyond, or other non-human sources, may alternate. In doing so, they create moments, organic segments.

In *The Elements of Drama*, J. L. Styan presents a chart of a play's movement through time. Liberally adapting the chart to our purposes, it can serve as a counterpart to the previous chart of theatrical space. On Level 1, each activity, each stage suggestion, when coupled with the succeeding one or ones, begins to take on meaning. They come together on Level 2, the audience's imagination, to create the moment. To use an analogy, it works much as we recognize the acts of putting water in a teapot, placing it on the stove, and turning on the heat to constitute the action of boiling water. On stage, the nature of activities 1, 2, and 3 alerts us to a force at work, dominating other forces creating the moment, and ending when that force is supplanted by another.

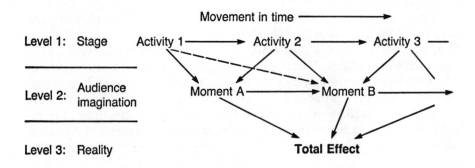

This gives us some idea of the tensions available in time for building dramatic action. How all these tensions may be coordinated with spatial tensions to create a play is a matter of dramatic structure, treated in the next chapter by focusing on the script. We already have a good clue to techniques for coordination in the example of "On the Harmfulness of Tobacco" as Chekhov builds the action out of the tension between Nyukhin's drive to escape his life and his wife and the force of inertia which would have him resign himself to his fate. Behind it all is the power of his self-loathing. And so the action culminates in his trampling his coat, and then his resigning himself to return to Dog Alley, 13. Temporal and spatial tensions are thus effectively integrated.

Exercises

The following little scene, appropriately entitled "The Blah-Blah-Blah Play," is purposefully neutral and meaningless. On this score the lines speak for themselves. The characters are simply A, B, C, and D. The set represents a room, but renders it neutral by calling for only a chair, a window, and a door. It could be anywhere, any time. Even the activity becomes meaningless because the context gives it no framework of meaning. The object of this exercise is to rewrite the play giving it meaning. The place becomes specified, the characters assume identities, the lines become real English, and the activities assume coherence. Here is the scene:

THE BLAH-BLAH-BLAH PLAY

The setting is a room with a chair set just left of center, a window in the stage right wall, and just above it near the right corner, a door.

(AS THE CURTAIN RISES, A is discovered standing and looking out the window. B sits in the chair, with C standing just to his left.)

A

Blah-blah-blah.

(There is a knock at the door. C crosses behind the chair and opens the door. D enters.)

C

Blah-blah-blah.

D

Blah-blah-blah.

(D crosses downstage. C crosses back to his original position, leans down and whispers to B.)

C

Blah-blah-blah.

B

(Looking at D.)

Blah-blah-blah.

D

Blah-blah-blah.

B

(Stands.)

Blah-blah-blah.

(B crosses to the door and exits. D crosses to the vacated chair and sits. A crosses in toward D.)

A

Blah-blah-blah.

Instructions

1. Make the setting a specific locale and give it the additional details such a place would call for. The chair, window, and door remain in their positions, but other items should be added and the whole space characterized.

2. Give the characters names or some identities.

3. Keeping the order of speeches and activities the same, make them mean something. More may be added in the activity, and some speeches may well be longer than others. They need, of course, translation into English.

4. Select a focal point that can serve to produce tension and can allow the emergence of a driving force.

5. Continue the scene beyond its present ending so that it is at least twice as long in terms of number of speeches and activities.

Notice that the selection of a focal point already begins to shape tension and give the action meaning. If, for example, one selects the character D as the focal figure, the scene seems headed for an act of usurpation, since D unseats B, who goes off stage. If one selects C, it tends to become a scene of subterfuge, since C seems to maneuver the other characters. If one selects B, it tends to be a scene of chiding, for then D seems to have failed some mission that B then has to take care of. Finally, if it is to be A, it suggests that A knows things the others do not, and it tends to become a scene of reversal. Other possibilities exist as well. What is out there, in the world beyond, may be the focal point. Then the scene is structured around a tension between the characters in here against a force out there. In any event, this exercise should demonstrate that meaning on stage derives from many sources besides language itself. It derives from action in context, and even the dialogue should consist of actions and reactions.

5

Charting
the Play Script

One way or another, every play must be charted before it is written. Plays, even rather short ones, are complex enough to prohibit being written straight off, from "AS THE CURTAIN RISES," to "THE CURTAIN FALLS." Tall tales are told of course: "I became so inspired by the play that it just wrote itself." Elmer Rice reported that the idea for *The Adding Machine* came to him one afternoon while he sat on his front porch and within a week the play was written. William Saroyan declared that he set aside six days to write *The Time of Your Life,* and decided to make it a five-act play, having finished a day early. Edward Albee claims that he listens to his characters talk for a long while in his head, then quickly writes out the play. There is of course some truth in all these tales. A play may well be written in short order; it may even seem to write itself. Still, none of this happens unless the ideas of the play have been percolating a long while in the playwright's head, if not on paper. This is a form of charting. An audience does not care one way or another *how* the play was charted. They will care, and will surely notice, if the play has not been charted at all.

You must find your own method of working which will be personal, a matter of temperament. This individuality is not an excuse for laziness, but a recognition that working habits need to correspond to your own inclinations. Otherwise, you will grow to dislike the work and shortly give it up. The method must also take into account the conditions of the stage. There are some standard procedures for charting a play script. While one need not always adhere to such formality, the formal process alerts us to what we need to consider while plotting the play's action.

Activity, Action, and Plot

It is useful to remember from time to time that even the finished script is only a chart—a plan of activities to be conducted among a group of actors. Explicitly, a play script is merely a chart of dialogue and stage directions for the use of actors, designers, and directors. Implicitly, the script provides the connections between the activities that render them coherent. The forces that work on and within the characters become clear, making activity also action. Only then do actors become characters. Only then does the play assume the power to engage the audience.

There is a difference between activity and action. A play depends upon activity to develop action, but an abundance of physical activity does not guarantee action. To set actors twirling about the stage like so many dervishes is to give them activity but not action. On the other hand, two characters seated perfectly still may speak knives at one another and create a powerful action without lifting a finger. A well-chosen word may have many times the force of a slap in the face. Both are activity, which is simply words and deeds. Action gives activity meaning, for it is an exchange of forces seeking to alter, avoid, or adapt. In short, it consists of change. The best planned activity implies action which would otherwise not be perceptible to the audience. When activities come together into action, we create a moment in the theatre. It is recognizable and palpable change.

Now we come to plot. Just as action is the structuring of activities, so plot is the structuring of actions. As moment builds upon moment, a play develops a vector, a sense of anticipation and movement, creating an overarching action for the play as a whole. This is plot. Typically, a play begins when its world is somehow thrown off-balance and ends when it finds a new balance. In between, the seeking of balance produces the fundamental action of the play, its plot. This is not to be confused with "story." The plot is the coherent action of the play, the spectacle of a driving force, a will striving against resistance. A story is simply a series of events. It is one way to organize or chart a play's action, but only a way. Indeed, it is thoroughly possible to develop a powerful plot, a compelling action, and yet have no story that is tellable independent of the action. But it is impossible to develop a compelling play without plot, without a central action.

The But/Therefore Principle

Reduced to its simplest terms, a story is a series of events linked together by "ands." We have all heard an excited child rush in after seeing a movie to tell its story: "First there was this king, called King John, and he was real mean, and then he tried to rob the poor by taxing them, and then Robin Hood robbed from the rich and gave to the poor, and King John got mad, and told the Sheriff of Nottingham to go get Robin Hood and his merry men, and then they met in the forest, and then . . . and then . . . and then . . . and so forth." That is a story. Whatever appeal it may have is a basic appeal to sheer curiosity: "What happens next?" E. M. Forster gives this example: "'The king died and then the queen died' is a story. 'The king died and then the queen died of grief' is a plot." Now there is a bridge between the two events, a causal link. Plot appeals to more than basic curiosity: it plays upon our intelligence, our memory, and our emotions. Since drama attains its appeal through the interplay of tensions, the building of actions into plot draws on much more complex links than "and then . . . and then . . . and then." Marian Gallaway's but/therefore principle holds that events in a plot are best linked by "buts" and "therefores." The building of theatrical moments is much stronger if they grow from contrasts, ironies, incongruities, or conflicts. "Buts and therefores" help to ensure that dramatic build.

Applying the rubric to a specific play, one can sense at once how buts and therefores contribute to the development of tension. *Oedipus Rex* by Sophocles is a play carefully built on a storyline. Each succeeding event grows out of or contrasts with the last, setting up a strong driving force for the play's action. The opening action illustrates the linkages.

Word comes from the oracle that the plague in Thebes will be lifted only after the murderer of the former king, Laius, is expelled.

> THEREFORE

Oedipus curses the murderer, vowing to seek him out.

> BUT

No one knows who he is, except possibly the seer Teiresias,

> THEREFORE

Oedipus sends for Teiresias,

> BUT

Teiresias refuses to reveal what he knows,

> THEREFORE

Oedipus flies into a rage, accusing Teiresias of plotting against him,

> BUT

And so forth. Behind all this is the central action of the play: Oedipus's search for the murderer. Enriching the action is the supreme irony, that Oedipus is himself the murderer he seeks. Knowing that from the first, as Sophocles' audience did (and most modern ones do as well) only increases the fascination and anticipation of the play. We want to know, "What will he do when he realizes he is himself that murderer?" Even if we know the story and know that he will put out his eyes and exile himself from Thebes, we want to witness him undergo the agony of realization and proceed to the deed. This is what keeps *Oedipus Rex* from being a mere "who-done-it?" mystery story. And this is what constantly renews it as a stage play. It depends on an action: it has plot, and thus begs to be seen, witnessed, and relished again and again.

Notice, too, that the story of Oedipus is scarcely the same as the plot. The story goes back years before the first event in the play, in fact back to a time before Oedipus's birth. It is the story of efforts to avoid Oedipus' decreed fate to murder his father and marry his mother, a fate he believes he has avoided. The plot, however, is the action of seeking the murderer of King Laius and so realizing the fate had not been avoided at all. Naturally, we learn the full story as the search goes forward—not as a series of "and then . . . and then . . . and then," but as discoveries that have immediate impact on action. There is a very good reason that Sophocles chose not to put the whole story on stage: it would not be relevant to his dramatic purpose. He wished to dramatize the agony of realization which Oedipus undergoes. The whole story is not needed for that—only those events that grow from the decision to seek the murderer. And these are not only events—they are moments that introduce new forces to challenge Oedipus's will.

Every playwright must make similar choices. Because of the restrictions of time—the two hours or so that the play lasts—the playwright needs to calculate what needs to be dramatized (shown in action), as against what may be revealed out of the past or of domains beyond the stage realm (as exposition). If your play is to take place *now* (as all plays do), you must ask yourself why we should encounter the characters at this particular "now." Why does it matter what the characters do at this particular juncture in their lives? This decision depends on where you find the greatest tension in the natural storyline. Dramatize that rather than the whole story. Bear in mind that every "now" rapidly becomes "then," so that the build of dramatic momentum will coalesce around an issue of sufficient depth and interest to sustain action. Seeking "buts" and "therefores" helps to insure that this will happen.

None of this suggests that one must emulate Sophocles. His way of concentrating dramatic energy and unleashing it through the search is excellent, but it is only one way—admirably suited to his purposes, but not to those of every play. There are other ways of building action. Some plays have strong plots but virtually no story: Thornton Wilder's *Our Town*, Samuel Beckett's *Waiting for Godot*, or Lanford Wilson's *Hot L Baltimore*, for example. But what is important is that energy be concentrated, built, and unleashed at a significant snapping point. This requires tension and release, contrast, irony, and disparity. "Buts" and "therefores" are apt to abound even then.

Although he is not dealing specifically with drama, E. M. Forster offers some relevant observations on this score in his *Aspects of the Novel*.

Forster draws a distinction between two kinds of time sense: literal chronological time and time of relative value:

> Daily life is . . . full of the time sense. We think one event occurs after or before another, the thought is often in our minds, and much of our talk and action proceeds on the assumption. Much of our talk and action, but not all: there seems something else in life besides time, something which may conveniently be called "value," something which is measured not by minutes or hours, but by intensity, so that when we look at our past it does not stretch back evenly but piles up into a few notable pinnacles, and when we look at the future it seems sometimes a wall, sometimes a cloud, sometimes a sun, but never a chronological chart. Neither memory nor anticipation is much interested in Father Time, and all dreamers, artists and lovers are partially delivered from his tyranny; he can kill them, but he cannot secure their attention, and at the very moment of doom, when the clock collected in the tower its strength and struck, they may be looking the other way.

This difference between time by the minute and time by value is the difference between time in daily life and time in the theatre. It is the reason that an empty or meaningless minute in the theatre is unendurable while we endure many such minutes in daily life. What is more, the difference between stage characters and the rest of us is that they live lives of concentrated intensity, which we would find unendurable. They are people who might well be looking the other way when the clock struck. Now, playwrights may also choose to look the other way, but not while composing plays, for then they are architects of moments. These moments need value and intensity, but they also need ties to the movement of the clock.

The Dramatic Premise

To decide what to dramatize is to decide that something matters *now*. Something in the figurative lives of the characters matters, both to them and to us. If such-and-such were the case, the characters must decide what to do *now*, and it matters what they decide. Three questions govern the structure of a play: "What if?" "Why now?" and "So what?" If these are presented with clarity and provocative power, you have the makings of a good play. The answers to the questions establish the premise for the play's action—the dramatic premise.

The dramatic premise is the action's "given"—that set of polar opposites that structures the plot. "What if?" is always a good start. Konstantin Stanislavsky was fond of speaking of the "magic if" when he described the context of dramatic action. It suggests that placing a character in a circumstance with which he is at once at odds produces a provocative tension and with it the magic of theatre. Action must ensue. One is reminded of experiments microbiologists conduct by introducing some alien solution into a culture to watch how an amoeba responds. If there is a cardinal rule of playwriting it might be phrased as "Give 'em hell." No matter how fond you are of your characters, you owe it to the play to put them in circumstances that make them squirm, force them to act, and so expose them for what they are. This applies to comedy as well as to serious drama. No character can be fully realized without squirming.

Let's try some examples. What if a gullible, well-to-do gentleman were to take pity on a loudly praying, seemingly devout lecher and take him into his own home to live in close proximity with his beautiful and charming wife? The result is that outrageous spectacle of hypocrisy working on gullibility known as *Tartuffe* by Molière. What if a frightened and insecure young man seeking to avoid the outside world by living in a remote boarding house were visited by two mysterious men from the outside world who insist on giving him a birthday party on a day other than his birthday? The result this time is the chilling yet vaguely comic ritual spectacle called *The Birthday Party* by Harold Pinter. Or yet again, what if an alien Moor, high in the Venetian military and newly married to a beautiful Venetian lady, were brought to suspect her fidelity? Now the result is the awesome tragedy of *Othello*.

A well-framed "What if?" can enrich the potential of a play. It creates a vibrant and dynamic "now" for the play's action. There is at once ample reason for the play to occur *now*, at this moment in the lives of the characters. The "Why now?" question also contributes to the play's premise. It implies that the action is unavoidable; it must happen. Still, you should consider carefully how we will first encounter your characters and their world. Our first image upon the curtain's rise has tremendous power for good or for ill in shaping the play's experience. Generally speaking, the sooner you bring the characters to squirming, the better. Certainly, we do not need long preparatory scenes showing how Orgon encountered Tartuffe the first time, or how Stanley came to live in the boarding house, or how Othello wooed and won Desdemona.

"Why now?" has another, equally important, dimension. Not only does it involve selecting the moment in the characters' lives when we should encounter them, but also *how* we encounter them. Here the specific use of the stage enters into consideration as a means to characterize the "now" of the play. This entails establishing the levels of reality that will operate throughout. A play after all is more than a manipulation of the fictional lives of its characters; it is also a manipulation of the audience's imagination. The artificial place, the stage, taps its physical configuration to create various levels of reality or belief in the audience. Thus, "now" involves not just our encounter with the lives of the characters, but also our encounter with their world as a stage world.

Douglas Turner Ward's play *Day of Absence* provides a clear and provocative example. The premise for this play might be stated as: "What if all the blacks in a sleepy, bucolic, Southern town were to disappear mysteriously one day?" Ward chooses as "now" a moment in the early morning after the disappearance, for he is interested in the town's reaction, not in the disappearance itself. Moreover, to strengthen the tie between the little world of his sleepy town and the larger world of the audience, he employs a blatant theatricalism. The stage is frankly a stage, representing now this part of town, now that. Neither the characters on stage nor we in the auditorium have yet become aware of the blacks' disappearance. To add one last ingredient, Ward calls for the whole play to be a "reverse minstrel show," using black actors in white face. At the outset, seated in chairs on a platform under signs saying "Store" are two Southern "crackers," Clem and Luke, black actors in white face:

CLEM

(Sitting under a sign suspended by invisible wires and bold-printed with the lettering: "STORE.")

'Morning, Luke. . . .

LUKE

(Sitting a few paces away under an identical sign.)

'Morning, Clem. . . .

CLEM

Go'n' be a hot day.

LUKE

Looks that way. . . .

CLEM

Might rain though. . . .

LUKE

Might.

CLEM

Hope it does . . .

LUKE

Me, too . . .

CLEM

Farmers could use a little wet spell for a change. . . . How's the Missis?

                            LUKE
Same.

                            CLEM
'N' the kids?

                            LUKE
Them too. . . . How's yourns?

                            CLEM
Fine, thank you. . . .

            (They both lapse into drowsy silence waving lethargi-
            cally from time to time at imaginary passersby.)

                            CLEM
Hi, Joe. . . .

                            LUKE
Joe. . . .

                            CLEM
. . . How'd it go yesterday, Luke?

                            LUKE
Fair.

                            CLEM
Same wit' me. . . . Business don't seem to git no better or no worse. Guess
we in a rut, Luke, don't it 'pear that way to you?—Morning, ma'am.

                            LUKE
Morning. . . .

                            CLEM
Tried display, sales, advertisement, stamps—everything, yet merchandis-
ing stumbles 'round in the same old groove. . . . But—that's better than
plunging downwards, I reckon.

                            LUKE
Guess it is.

                            CLEM
Morning, Bret. How's the family? . . . That's good.

                            LUKE
Bret—

                            CLEM
Morning, Sue.

                            LUKE
How do, Sue.

                            CLEM
            (Staring after her.)
. . . Fine hunk of woman.

                            LUKE
Sure is.

CLEM

Wonder if it's any good?

LUKE

Bet it is.

CLEM

Sure like to find out!

LUKE

So would I.

CLEM

You ever try?

LUKE

Never did. . . .

CLEM

Morning, Gus. . . .

LUKE

Howdy, Gus.

CLEM

Fine, thank you.

(They lapse into silence again. CLEM rouses himself slowly, begins to look around quizzically.)

CLEM

Luke . . . ?

LUKE

Huh?

CLEM

Do you . . . er, er—feel anything—funny . . . ?

LUKE

Like what?

CLEM

Like . . . er—something—strange?

LUKE

I dunno . . . haven't thought about it.

CLEM

I mean . . . like something's wrong—outta place, unusual?

LUKE

I don't know. . . . What you got in mind?

CLEM

Nothing . . . just that—just that—like somp'ums outa kilter. I got a funny feeling somp'ums not up to snuff. Can't figger out what it is. . . .

LUKE

Maybe it's in your haid?

CLEM

No, not like that. . . . Like somp'ums happened—or happening—gone haywire, loony.

LUKE

Well, don't worry about it, it'll pass.

CLEM

Guess you right.
                    (Attempts return to somnolence but doesn't succeed.)
. . . I'm sorry, Luke, but you sure you don't feel nothing peculiar . . . ?

LUKE
                    (Slightly irked.)
Toss it out of your mind, Clem. We got a long day ahead of us. If something's wrong, you'll know 'bout it in due time. No use worrying about it 'til it comes and if it's coming, it will. Now, relax!

CLEM

All right, you right. . . . Hi, Margie. . . .

LUKE

Marge.

CLEM
                    (Unable to control himself.)
Luke, I don't give a damn what you say. Somp'ums topsy-turvy, I just know it!

LUKE
                    (Increasingly irritated.)
Now look here, Clem—it's a bright day, it looks like it's go'n' git hotter. You say the wife and kids are fine and the business is no better or no worse? Well, what else could be wrong? . . . If somp'ums go'n' happen, it's go'n' happen anyway and there ain't a damn fool thing you kin do to stop it! So you ain't helping me, yourself or nobody else by thinking 'bout it. It's not go'n' be no better or no worse when it gits here. It'll come to you when it gits ready to come and it's go'n' be the same whether you worry about it or not. So stop letting it upset you!

                    (LUKE settles back in his chair. CLEM does likewise. LUKE
                    shuts his eyes. After a few moments, they reopen. He
                    forces them shut again. They reopen in greater curiosi-
                    ty. Finally, he rises slowly to an upright position in the
                    chair, looks around frowningly. Turns slowly to CLEM.)

LUKE

. . . Clem? . . . You know something? . . . Somp'um is peculiar. . . .

CLEM
                    (Vindicated.)
I knew it, Luke! I just knew it! Ever since we been sitting here, I been having that feeling!

Of course, what Clem and Luke sense is the absence of all the blacks, but having grown used to looking right through such people, they cannot put their finger on what is so peculiar this morning. By employing a bare stage, Ward manages to portray a whole town, tapping the audience's imagination to complete the images, including invisible passersby. Moreover, the reverse minstrel show device, turning an old theatrical convention topsy-turvy, has the effect of turning the play back on us as members of a society of racial absurdity. If you were to imagine the play simply as the story of blacks who disappear one day, without these specific characterizations of its "now," you can at once see how diminished its impact would be.

The third question, "So what?" develops out of the premise. It includes both the fictional action that results from the premise and the reflection upon our lives it offers. In other words, "So what?" refers to the result of the premise of action, the natural development out of the initial condition. It also refers to the impact the resulting action has on the audience. The members of the audience have every right to demand "So what?" of the play they witness. A good play ought to matter. It should make a difference not only to the characters, but also to the audience. On some level we need to care. Ultimately, this is a matter of seeing our own lives through the world of the play; we live through the play. The play concentrates our concerns, meanwhile taking us outside ourselves. We identify with a character, or find a parallel with our own lives, or in some way vicariously undergo an experience that doubles back on our own lives. It is on this score that the play must matter. "So what?" is an important test not only for the structure of the play, but also for its impact.

There are two ways of applying the "So what?" test to a play. If you are interested purely in charting your play's action, how it evolves out of its premise on the fictional level, Price's "proposition" may be a valuable way of testing your play's structure. On the other hand, checking your play against the phases of dramatic action may help correct problems on both levels—the action among the characters and the impact on the audience.

Price's Proposition

William T. Price developed the idea of the dramatic proposition in *The Analysis of Play Construction* published in 1908. Subsequently, Bernard Grebanier expanded and refined the idea in his 1961 book *Playwriting*. It is based on the syllogism (for example, "All men are mortal; Socrates is a man; therefore, Socrates is mortal"). In other words, Price saw play construction as a matter of logic with dramatic action based on a major premise and a minor premise leading to a conclusion. If such-and-such were the case and such-another were to happen, what would result? That, in a nutshell, is Price's proposition. He labels the three stages of the dramatic proposition "Condition of Action," "Cause of Action," and "Resulting

Action." These correspond roughly to the three questions: "What if?" (establishing the condition of the action), "Why now?" (referring to the moment action is launched, its cause), and "So what?" (tracing the resulting action).

The proposition is useful in isolating the major tension and giving it focus in the developing action of your play. It is a way of insuring an economy and a coherence in building the action. It does have its shortcomings: it does not take into account the stage medium itself and it tends to treat plot as a matter of storytelling, thus ignoring other patterns of dramatic structure. Still, if you recognize its restrictions, it can prove a valuable tool in playwriting. To be fully useful the proposition must describe only the central action of the play. It should not involve outside events, stories, subplots, or tangents. Only the central action matters. Price and Grebanier notwithstanding, the Condition of the Action states a fundamental cirumstance which may have developed before the action begins: the plague in Thebes for *Oedipus* or the marriage of Othello and Desdemona for *Othello*. Something must happen in the play to alert us to the condition, ideally in a dramatic way—as in Iago's baiting of Brabantio, Desdemona's father, but there is no need for the marriage ceremony to figure in the play's action. The proposition for *Othello* might be phrased as follows:

> *Condition of Action:* The alien Moor Othello marries the Venetian Desdemona.
>
> *Cause of Action:* Iago contrives circumstances to make her appear false.
>
> *Resulting Action:* Othello kills Desdemona.

Baldly stated, the proposition is distinctly uninspiring. It is simply a statement of the structure, the skeleton of a play's action. For the playwright, it helps test the coherence of the structure. Even on this score, the proposition as stated above for *Othello* is lacking an important ingredient. Every play needs some common factor or element that runs through the entire action to bind it together, just as the term "man" binds the Socrates syllogism together. The Condition and the Cause as stated have Desdemona as a common factor, but the play is about Othello. He is the protagonist, the "doer" of this drama. The common factor should relate to him, pointing up the central tension of the play. The common factor is the fact that Othello is a man of an open and trusting nature. Adding this revises the proposition:

> *Condition of Action:* Othello, a man of an open and trusting nature, marries the Venetian Desdemona.
>
> *Cause of Action:* Despite his open and trusting nature, Othello allows his mind to be poisoned against her by Iago's contrivance.
>
> *Resulting Action:* Othello kills Desdemona.

Othello's open and trusting nature is the quality that had endeared him to Desdemona and rendered their relationship so pure and enviable. Iago, for his part, is so rankled by the recognition of anything beautiful in the lives of others (lacking such beauty in his own) that he is driven to destroy it. There is a side to Othello's character upon which Iago can work: his own alien status in Venice and his past experience in the chaotic world of monsters and cannibals all give him cause to doubt the new beauty and love in his life. Thus he is pulled in two directions: towards love, peace, and concord associated with Desdemona and towards alienation, isolation, and chaos associated with Iago.

Shakespeare's use of the stage reflects this two-way pull. The play opens in Venice—portrayed as a city of peace and concord—and then moves directly to Cyprus, Venice's frontier colony on the border of the world of the Turks—a world of chaos and discord. Thus the polar tensions of the play attain even greater relief. Moreover, establishing the stage as a neutral platea, readily becoming now this place, now that, allows the stage to be an outward expression of Othello's inner turmoil. The play's arena—its battlefield—is Othello's mind, but it assumes fuller meaning as the forces of Venice and Desdemona are pitted against those of the Turks and Iago.

Similarly, Nyukhin in "On the Harmfulness of Tobacco" is pulled in opposite directions. He seeks a new dignity—denied him at home at Dog Alley, 13—or, failing that, at least some sense of peace—represented by the pole under the moon. The lecture hall occupies the middle ground. The proposition might read:

> *Condition of Action:* Nyukhin is momentarily freed from the indignity of life at Dog Alley, 13 to give a public lecture.
>
> *Cause of Action:* He fails to find a new dignity with his lecture audience.
>
> *Resulting Action:* He returns to Dog Alley, 13.

Good playwriting makes full use of both the spatial and the temporal dimensions of the stage; one reflects the other. The tensions pulling against each other serve to structure the action as well to characterize the stage space.

Price uses a question to describe the Resulting Action. For *Othello*, given that he has married the loving Desdemona and has allowed his mind to be poisoned against her, "Will he be able to regain his untainted love?" For Nyukhin, the question might be simply, "Will he return to Dog Alley, 13?" There is merit in this device for the audience is engaged in the action by the sense of something pending, a question wanting some answer. Still, if the proposition is a description of action, it ought rightly to end with a direct statement of the final action taken.

While the proposition is relatively uninspiring as a way of describing a play, it is a valuable test for structure. It can remedy a promising but unfulfilling play by pointing up a missing ingredient or indicating where focus may be blurred. It will, of course, tell nothing about the emotional involvement of characters or audience, about intensity, originality of expression, or any of those things that make a play that unique experience it must be. A play may be beautifully structured, producing a proposition that is a marvel of logic and coherence, and for all that, be deadly dull. On the other hand, a play may be fascinating with stunning characters, awesome dialogue, and intriguing actions, and yet, by some structural oversight, not quite fulfill itself. Here is where Price's proposition can be of use to the playwright.

Phases of Dramatic Action

If a play builds through alternating tensions from moment to moment, the total play depends on a single fundamental tension. Each moment offers a variation on it and, as the pattern emerges, we in the audience can begin to recognize these moments as contributing to the total action. The recognition of the build depends on a set of phases through which we are accustomed to follow a play's plot.

Phases of dramatic action have been variously described. The traditional description carries a play through exposition, inciting incident, major dramatic question, complications, crisis, climax, and resolution. These are grouped into "rising action" up to the climax, and "falling action" through to resolution. The one difficulty with this description is its tendency to treat the play as if it were simply a story, sealed inside the world of the play; it neglects the theatrical event itself. It ignores the audience's presence and the fact that they are a source of energy in a play as much as the characters and their "story." To incorporate the theatrical event, we might divide the play into five phases:

1. The precipitating context
2. The emergence of a driving force
3. Resistance
4. Crux
5. Dénouement

Each of these (adapted from Bernard Beckerman's *The Dynamics of Drama*), calls for elaborations.

The precipitating context

Many factors influence the playgoing experience. We may be affected by previous knowledge of the play, the playwright, and the acting company, and by the immediate experience of the theatre auditorium and our companions. Although strong influences on the context of the play, these are beyond the playwright's control. The factors over which the playwright can exert control are:

1. The nature of the relationship between the spectacle and the spectators.
2. The way in which stage is defined.
3. The establishment of a framework of tensions that are to operate throughout the play.
4. The general tone of the piece.

The spectacle/spectator relationship is a matter of how the play opens itself to its audience. A play must invite the audience's imaginative and emotional involvement. The level and nature of that involvement is unique with each play and it must be established at once. Some of this works by convention: the play that begins with an actor on a bare stage addressing the audience calls for a totally different sort of involvement from one that begins with a group in earnest conversation within a fully detailed siting room, and both in turn call for different involvement from a play that opens on a stage bathed in a panoply of lights and projections playing over diaphanous, dancing figures. By convention and association, all these tell the audience a great deal about the world they are about to encounter. In the first few minutes an audience relies heavily on conventions and associations. A play is a form of communication. As such, it needs to provide reassurance that the audience can relate to the play, that its terms are at least recognizable. Still, there is latitude in combining conventions, and there is occasionally advantage in using them in provocative ways, such as the reverse minstrel show of *Day of Absence*. Despite the implication of the word "convention," there is tremendous variety available in combination; a play may be unique because of its particular set of conventions and its style of handling them. More will be said on this score in the chapter on form and style. For the time being, it is valuable to recognize what various conventions imply and how it might be pressed into service for a particular play.

The second area the playwright can control is defining stage space. This is of course the special province of the scene designer, but the playwright lays down the terms within which the designer works. Only the playwright can determine what sort of place the imagined realm of the stage must be and draw the distinction between the world onstage and the world off. Only the playwright can indicate the sources of tension that the spatial configuration should suggest. The playwright may wish to break the stage space into distinct realms or derive advantage from some form of simultaneous setting in which various locales are visible at once on stage.

The play may need a pattern of alternation from one scene and locale to another. Certainly, the definition of stage space should reflect the fundamental tensions operating in the play.

This leads us to the third factor: the establishment of a framework of tensions. Definition of stage space contributes heavily to this; so does the initial impression the actors give us. *Hamlet* begins meaningfully by presenting the Court of Denmark, a crowd of colorfully attired courtiers and ladies, in whose midst we immediately spot the black-garbed, morose, and silent Hamlet. A tension is obviously present. One way or another, when we encounter characters in the process of living their lives, a tension emerges just by our "arrival" on the scene. In his early plays (by his own account), Harold Pinter was fascinated by that sensation of walking into a room occupied by a group of people indulging in activities one knows nothing about. That is the spirit of theatrical encounter. Who are these people? What is going on here? How did things come to this pass? An audience begs to get involved first on this fundamental level of prying curiosity. Beyond that, the initial impression should provide a strong sense of the tensions that are to be tapped throughout the play: tensions between onstage and offstage, between now and then, between one character and another. All this should be evident at once—evident, but not necessarily explicit or explained. One rule of playwriting might be: Never tell the audience everything they want to know until it is urgent that they know it. Even at that, there is no harm in leaving them wondering about something even after the play is over, so long as it is a well-controlled ambiguity.

Finally, the precipitating context establishes tone. It should spark an attitude in the audience. Are the characters like us or distinctly different? Are they exciting and awesome? Laughable and ridiculous? What sorts of things are apt to happen among them and how are they apt to respond? Tone derives from atmosphere, words, qualities of action, and the general appearance of the set and the characters. It also draws on the previous three factors: the spectacle/spectator relationship, the definition of stage space, and the framework of tensions. Probability is also a factor. Altogether, these create a consistency, a feeling with which the audience can identify. Then, and only then, can they begin to react in unison. Playwright and audience begin to work in concert.

The precipitating context *does* precipitate. It precipitates us into the play, catching, characterizing, and focusing our attention where it matters. As a phase, it is over when that focus is complete and that occurs with the emergence of the driving force.

The emergence of the driving force

The emergence of the driving force is a distinct moment in the dramatic action. Indeed, it might be more appropriate to discuss structure as three phases separated by two moments, namely the emergence of the driving force and the crux. The first is a moment separating the precipitating context from the resistance, and the second a moment separating resistance from the dénouement.

The first moment is that event, decision, or act that upsets the balance of the play's world. As such, it incites action, a will to find a new balance. This is the driving force. It may emerge in response to the inciting incident or it may in fact have created the incident. Whichever is the case, the whole of the action of the play from this point forward is tied to this central force. Watching a play, one is not always aware of this moment until after it has passed; it is there nevertheless. Usually, after experiencing a play, one can go back and readily discover that moment. It is what makes sense of the total action, pushing to the surface qualities of character and circumstance that would otherwise be scarcely perceptible. Without it, the play is simply a few activities. With it, the play becomes a compelling action.

Since drama is action, the driving force is best expressed as a will to do something. It is usually embodied in a character, sometimes in a group of characters. Action needs an agent and human action, with which an audience can most readily identify, needs a human agent. A single character serving as agent, a protagonist, has the advantage of lending greater focus and coherence. Nevertheless, there are successful plays which embody the driving force in a group (such as Gerhardt Hauptmann's *The Weavers*), an offstage character (Harold Pinter's *The Dumb Waiter*), or a power beyond the stage, such as time, the past, death, a storm (John Millington Synge's "Riders to the Sea"). However embodied, the force is a will, a drive to do, to accomplish, or to change.

Now, if there is no difficulty about doing, accomplishing, or changing, the play is over at once and it would not have aroused much interest. The appeal of drama—serious, comic, or other—is in the spectacle of striving. And so, resistance follows directly on the heels of the emergence of the driving force. This sets up the play's fundamental tension.

Resistance

Throughout the so-called "rising action" of the play, the driving force works against various forms of resistance. Still, behind all of them is one fundamental opposing force. So, in *Oedipus Rex*, while Oedipus exerts the driving force in his will to find and expel the murderer from Thebes, resistance, derived ultimately from fate, takes on a multitude of forms: the supposed duplicity of Creon and Teiresias, the efforts of Jocasta to divert her husband from his purpose, the reluctance of the shepherd to talk, Oedipus's own gradual realization that he is himself the man he seeks.

Resistance generally takes three forms or some combination of them: antagonistic force, discovery, or reversal. Like the driving force itself, it may be embodied in a character or group of characters, in circumstance, in offstage powers, in the past, or in some combination of all these. It is here that a playwright faces the greatest challenge, for this is the meat of any play. Perhaps for this reason many playwrights are tempted to put off the emergence of the will as long as possible, delighting in explaining the world of the play in the delusion that it is so interesting that the audience will be enthralled. A good play puts its driving force forward early, and gets underway at once. In the words of William Gibson in *Shakespeare's Game:*

> A play begins when a world in some state of equipoise, always uneasy, is broken into by a happening. Since it is not equipoise we have paid to see, but the loosing and binding of an evening's disorder, the sooner the happening the better; these [Shakespeare's] plays open fast.

A second unfortunate temptation for the playwright is to multiply and simplify resistance at the same time. Resistance is multiplied by the sheer number of things that happen to the protagonist, but simplified because they are all unrelated, coincidental, and simple oppositions. A lover wishes to be reunited with his beloved, and so sets out to find her; then he cannot find his car keys, his car breaks down, he loses his address book, he gets there, and she is not in, having left the country an hour before, and so on. Unless this is a snowballing comedy of errors, these complications are likely to become repetitious and boring.

Dramatic momentum depends on an ironic interplay of opposites, a well-bonded sequence of events, twists, counterforces, surprises that work to thwart the striving will. Characters launch activities that counter the will (antagonistic forces), the will produces unanticipated results (reversals), or the will is stymied by the realization that things are not as they seemed at first (discovery). All this requires variety, well-charted interaction, and a modulated, growing tension. Each instance of resistance narrows the options available to the will. Progressively, the driving force comes closer to a confrontation with the basic counterforce. This moment is long-anticipated. When it finally arrives, we encounter the crux of the play.

Crux

The crux, then, is that moment when the driving force encounters the source of all resistance—the major counterforce. In a blatant melodrama, it is the gun duel at high noon at the center of town. But even in subtler and richer plays, there comes a moment of release of the tension built up throughout the play—a snapping point.

Like the emergence of the driving force, the crux is a moment. It separates the resistance phase from the dénouement. Looking at it more closely, however, there is a phase of action that immediately precedes the full crux. This is sometimes called the *obligatory scene* — the scene which the playwright is obliged to give us after all the preparation and anticipation of the rising action. First comes that moment of confrontation, a point of decision, a point of no return. It all has to happen *now*. The driving force is committed to overcome resistance and resistance has risen to its greatest power. Something *has* to happen. This is sometimes called the crisis. Once it is clear that the driving force will dominate or that the force of resistance will thwart the will, the tension is released. This is the real crux or climax of the play.

Dramatic action might be described as the overlapping of ripples and cross-currents deriving from opposing sources and building to a meeting of two great waves, one of which must ride over the other. Once that happens, the waters return to a serene calm. That moment of riding over — the crux — is almost always a very precise moment. It is a sudden release instinctively recognized the moment it happens. Some playwrights, it is true, manage to disguise the crux moment in such a way that only later do we recognize that it had passed by; Anton Chekhov is a master here, for his cruxes are notoriously sneaky and yet always precise. The crux is not necessarily the moment of highest emotional intensity, although it often is. It is the deciding moment in the tension between driving force and resistance. Pirandello's *Henry IV* has its moment of highest intensity at the opening to Act III, when Henry in the dark encounters a portrait that comes to life. That is not yet the crux, which comes when he finds a way to assert his will above his interlopers'.

The crux represents the moment toward which all action has built. It is not, of course, the end of the play. It decides the direction the resolution will take. But there is still turbulence in the waters. Once tension snaps, there remains an emotional need for a gradual subsiding. This accounts for the final phase of dramatic action: the dénouement.

Dénouement

Dénouement is a French word meaning "unraveling." It is an apt metaphor: the play ties its tension into a knot that becomes finally so taut it must snap and then unravel into slackness. The dénouement is longer or shorter depending on how complicated the issues are that build up to the crux. The phase tends to be longer in tragedy, for if the force of resistance washes over the driving force, more time is required for balance to reestablish itself. One should feel, at any rate, that there is no more at stake; there are no more issues to face and the play is genuinely over.

This is not to suggest that a play must be neatly, tidily wrapped up at the moment of curtain. Certain thought-provoking plays, such as Tom Stoppard's *Rosencrantz and Guildenstern Are Dead*, seem to end rather abruptly, leaving a sensation of uncertainty. But this uncertainty has to do with the outward implications of the play for us, who have witnessed it, rather than with the world of Rosencrantz and Guildenstern. Plays that close with finality sometimes fail to concern us and may well remind us of the contrivance of "wrapping it up."

The closing image of a play is a powerful moment that needs to be chosen carefully. One needs to draw the right balance between saying too much and saying too little. The comic strip has as a convention the expectation that fourth square—the last one—will make one pithy statement that throws all the others into relief. The last moments of a play may not be so definitely isolated, but they should provide closure in a similar sense. Many playwrights face an insidious temptation in writing the dénouement: one knows so much about it and feels so nervous about actually ending the play for fear that it has not yet *all* been said, that one goes on and on. Or, the reverse of that, feeling that it *has* been said, one cannot wait to get it over with. With a little relaxation and reflection, one may discover just the right last image and final rhythm. When it is right, the audience will never be able to quite get the play out of their minds. This is true of such plays as *Ghosts, Six Characters in Search of an Author, The Glass Menagerie, The Three Sisters, Long Day's Journey into Night, Death of a Salesman, The Homecoming* and these are worth looking at for just this effect.

These are the typical phases of dramatic action: precipitating context, the emergence of the driving force, resistance, crux, and dénouement. They serve to structure action. They give the play a coherence, a system of relative values, by which the audience knows what has import and what does not. They establish the ebb and flow of forces and counterforces. They provide a rhythm. Still, at best they are only signposts. They tell us nothing about that mercurial, vibrant, individual life a particular play purveys. Only the play itself can do that. The most tightly structured play may for all that be lifeless and dull. We might admire its near perfect shape, but walk away from it entirely unmoved. Other somewhat flawed plays are somehow impossible to ignore. What ultimately matters is that a play attain its power by engaging the audience on all levels—imaginative, emotional, and intellectual—and cause them to stop to reflect on their lives in midstream.

The Use of the Scenario

Price's proposition and the phases of dramatic action are ways of testing the structure of your play. They are, however, abstractions and generalizations; as such they are scarcely inspiring. In the initial phase of creation, they are probably best ignored. At that time, what counts is the vibrancy, the fascination the material itself may have for you. You need to learn as much as you can about that fascination: what dimensions does it have? how can it assume the stage? and how can it be shared with others? If it does truly intrigue you, sooner or later you will find its workable shape. Nevertheless, as you work with the material, you need to pause from time to time and consider the total play, much as a painter must step away from the canvas from time to time. Unlike the painter, however, you cannot see the whole play in one glance. This is the use of a scenario.

A scenario is a brief, concentrated blueprint of the play. Using abbreviated notations, it charts the total action. Thus it exposes the play's structure almost at a glance. It saves you the trouble of rustling through all the pages of a draft to discover where who does what. The structure is apparent at once. In addition, the scenario has the merit of being easily altered. You can try out several possible structures in scenario before committing yourself to one in a draft. As soon as the scenario begins to seem fixed, immutable, and solid, it has lost its purpose. It must always be fluid. You should feel free at any time to alter it, play with it, change scene arrangements, add characters, take them away. To encourage this, it is helpful to keep the scenario always looking at least a little sloppy; do not type it neatly, for that will pursuade you subconsciously that you have the tablet from the mount in hand.

No playwright can do without a scenario in some form. Some experienced playwrights manage on a set of brief notes, holding much of the material in their heads. Others, no matter how experienced, keep elaborate scenarios. How you draft and then use a scenario is in part a personal matter. But, sooner or later, either before or just after the first draft, you need a scenario. There are those who cannot write the first draft without some sort of sketch beforehand. Others find the scenario stifling before the first draft; they find themselves better able to create without an imposed structure. Something can be said on both sides. Certainly you cannot fully anticipate characters, situations, or presentation. It requires a draft to explore the potentials in these areas. On the other hand, one cannot compose a meaningful draft without some sense of the overall action and sooner or later the play has to find its appropriate structure. So, even at the outset, at least some rudimentary scenario is needed and certainly before the second draft can be written, a detailed and thorough one is needed.

At a minimum, a rough scenario consists of notations on the following matters:

1. *Time and place of the action:* notes on where and when the fictional action takes place and on other circumstances that matter to the play as a whole

2. *Mode of presentation:* how the play proposes to use the stage and address itself to its audience

3. *Characters:* descriptive list of the characters and how they contribute to the action

4. *Polarity:* a statement of the basic tension that will propel the action.

5. *Summary of the action:* a synopsis of the phases of dramatic action especially for the opening, the crux, and the closing of the play.

A detailed scenario follows the same pattern, but breaks it down further. It contains a series of notes followed by a complete breakdown of the action. The notes apply to the same items one through four above. Among them, item three is especially detailed, including very thorough accounts of each character, the drives, motivations, background, and relationships with the others. The statement of the play's polarity, item four, may be expressed as a drive to do something versus some form of resistance. It should, at any rate, use infinitive verbs, a drive *to do*. For example, a play might be written based on the polarity: "The drive to control another's fate versus the desire of the other to maintain autonomy." Chekhov's *The Three Sisters* is based on the polarity: "The drive to engage with life and others versus the desire to disperse and so avoid life" and Brecht's *Mother Courage:* "The drive to shape one's own destiny versus the force of the great war machine to enmesh everyone in its enterprise of death." These are statements of the fundamental tensions of the plays. Identifying them is not an exact science, but for any play, including the one you are writing, you should be able to isolate a fundamental line of tension revealed in action, in doing. If you prefer, the statement of polarity might be instead a statement of the proposition, after Price. Or it could address each of the three questions: "What if?" "Why now?" and "So what?"

The meat of the scenario is the action breakdown. This is done in the form of a chart breaking the action into meaningful units or segments. The segments may be created in several ways, the three most useful being the French scene, the motivational unit, and the theatrical moment.

A French scene is a sequence of action involving one group of characters: as soon as one exits or another enters, a new French scene begins. Breaking the action into French scenes has the advantage of telling you at a glance who is onstage when. It demonstrates whether one is making good use of the characters. On occasion, when a play is not doing well in the writing, the reason may be that two characters who need to confront each other never meet. A French scene scenario would expose the problem at once.

A play might have only one French scene, for no one ever enters or leaves the stage. Some perfectly good plays fit this description, most of them relatively short plays. In such a case, the French scene scenario will not work and one of the other two systems will have to substitute. The motivational unit is a sequence of action in which one character motivation dominates; as soon as it subsides, replaced by another, a new unit begins. This is most useful in a play which deals realistically with tensions between characters and may well serve better than any other form of scenario, even if characters do enter and exit.

Some perfectly good plays do not yield to either of these methods of action breakdown. The third system breaks the action into theatrical moments, segments determined by the alternation of tensions: as soon as one tension rounds out and concludes, supplanted by another, a new moment begins. This can be applied to any play, and since the business of playwriting is at base one of manipulating tensions, it is an appropriate way to develop a scenario. The difficulty lies in the fact that the tensions are hard to isolate before the writing and such a scenario may be difficult to compose until after the first draft.

The format of the scenario breakdown of action usually consists of two columns. In the left column, the action of each unit (French scene, motivational unit, or theatrical moment) is listed. The action is described very briefly, concentrating on the essence of each unit. On the right side, for each unit, is a statement of the function the unit serves for the play as a whole. Here is an example of a French scene scenario for the opening to a play:

Scene	*Function*
1. Ned, Alice and Jake discovered. Ned is reading aloud from a story book; Alice is asleep in the armchair; Jake is building a tower with blocks, making irritating noises as he watches Alice out of the corner of his eye. Suddenly, he makes a loud sound and wakes her. Ned is outraged and slams his book shut. Alice bursts into tears. Jake continues as before. Ned comes and stands over his tower threatening to knock it down. Jake stops. Alice stops. Ned knocks down the tower and exits.	1. Established an evening ritual indulged in by the trio. Characterization begun: Ned serious and intent, Alice easily frightened and vulnerable, and Jake a bit of a bully.
2. Alice and Jake. Now Jake bursts into tears. Alice lets him cry a while, then gets out of the armchair and goes to comfort him. He pushes her away repeatedly until she gives up and starts building a	2. Reversal: now Jake is the vulnerable one. Alice shows compassion, but there is a limit to her patience. She succeeds in manipulating him; tension builds as he tries to maneuver her into wanting the book.

tower of her own. Jake soon stops crying. He watches her for a while, then tries to join her. She won't let him. He bursts into tears again. She ignores him. Jake takes up the storybook and starts reading where Alice left off. Enter Ned.

3. Ned, Jake, Alice. Ned goes straight to Jake and takes the book from him. Exit Ned.

3. Another reversal: Jake's scheme backfires.

4. Jake and Alice. Jake cries again. Alice gives up on the tower. She gets another book, goes behind the armchair, and reads silently. Jake thinks he is alone; he goes back to his tower. Alice gets back into the armchair and starts reading aloud surprising Jake. He knocks the book from her hands. She exits in a huff.

4. Leads up to a momentary lull only to return to the same old tension.

The Record Book

While you are planning and writing a play, ideas of use at other points will occur. They may be very valuable: ideas about characters, their mannerisms, a piece of business that could occur, a phrase of full speech, a possible scene, a scenic device—any number of things. These are apt to crop up in one's head at any time at all. To attempt to pursue them all then and there would lead to madness. The solution is to keep a record of them; this is the purpose of the record book.

Most writers maintain a notebook, the commonplace book described in Chapter 2, in which sketches, notations, ideas, and possibilities are kept as they occur, without regard to any intrinsic organization. Once the writer launches a particular project, a separate notebook or a section of the commonplace book is begun expressly for the ideas relevant to the project. This "record book" is maintained while the project is in progress.

The more you know about your characters, about the potentials of the situation, the use you plan of the stage, the more apt you are to find the right details to enrich your play. The record book is a place to explore all the possibilities. It is your private domain in which you can experiment and fail or succeed as you wish. No one else need know a thing about it. Estimating conservatively, for every word that makes its way into the finished script, more than ten others have been written and thrown out. The only way to know the world of your play is to explore it and the best way to explore it is in written form. That is the form in which you must finally express yourself. Moreover, it is one certain way to know the idea well. If it is not written and kept in one place, a new idea will not be tested and may even be forgotten.

Some playwrights write lengthy biographies of their characters; most at least write many notes to themselves about their characters. Certainly the more you know about them the better. If they are to be convincing to an audience, you need a wealth of detail to draw upon. The same is true of the world of the play generally, the offstage realms, and the past. The record book should contain far more information than you will ever use, for only that way will you discover what you most want to know and use. A playwright must always know far more than is ever incorporated in the play.

As the creator of the world of your play, you may feel like a god, but you are not omniscient. The characters may surprise you. If you were truly omniscient about your characters, the magic would probably evaporate and you would give up writing the play. Still, with the help of the record book, you should know as much as humanly possible about your play. Even in the case of a play drawing on historical material, you are in charge of creating the world afresh in stage terms. Here the record book keeps track of research materials as well as your ideas for their re-creation on stage. Whatever the case, it is a private place for you to test ideas, play with your play's potentials and come to know your characters; it is a record, a sort of log, to prevent ideas from getting lost.

Exercises

1. Select a play with an effect that intrigues you. Write the scenario for that play, as if guessing what the playwright's blueprint might have looked like. Doing the scenario for a scene or the whole play should expose the structure, as if you had stripped the flesh away and discovered the skeleton. It may take away some of the mystery of the play, but it will repay you by demonstrating how the play was put together.

2. Examine a group of four or five one-act plays. Isolate the crux moment for each of them. Do the same for a full-length play, finding the crux of each act as well as of the play as a whole.

3. State the premise for each of these plays.

6

Form
and Style

Form and style are abstractions, apparently far removed from the concerns of the playwright. The playwright, after all, must deal with the immediate specifics of the play's characters and locale. Let the scholars who come after decide questions of a play's form or style. The playwright simply writes it. There is some truth to this reaction. Such concepts have a certain stuffiness about them, reminiscent of Polonius telling Hamlet that the actors had arrived:

> The best actors in the world, either for tragedy, comedy, history, pastoral, pastoral-comical, historical-pastoral, tragical-pastoral, tragical-comical-historical-pastoral, scene indivisible, or poem unlimited.

If it is not scholarly stuffiness, then it is artistic, self-conscious posing. It would be ludicrous for a playwright to declare, "I shall now create a Neo-Surrealistic, Quasi-Dadaistic tragical farce" and proceed to the task (although that may be the only way to write such a piece).

Still, the playwright must make decisions about form and style for every play. Sometimes the decisions are unconscious, made in the back of the mind while addressing more immediate matters. At other times, deliberate choices are made in response to problems encountered in writing. Of course, one playwright deals with form and style in a manner very different from the next. Bertolt Brecht was keenly aware of his ideas of Epic Theatre while he wrote. Friedrich Duerrenmatt often commented on the necessity for "grotesque comedy" as he wrote such plays as *The Visit* and *The Physicists*. Arthur Miller similarly spoke of "tragedy and the common man" in connection with his play *Death of a Salesman*. Other playwrights make no issue of their form and style and they are no less successful as a result. The point is that they all do make decisions about form and style.

If every playwright must make such decisions, it would be useful to know something about form and style. Even if form and style are abstractions, they refer to the systematic uses of material in a play. Although playwrights may not need the elaborate concepts of theorists and scholars, they would certainly profit by knowing two things: how decisions about form and style are made and what the options are.

On this level, the terms are no longer quite so abstract and they involve a natural set of conditions. It is perfectly natural that a play will reflect a playwright's attitude and point of view. Natural as this may be, however, there is a sort of two-way pull involved. Paradoxically, form and style are simultaneously private and personal, public and traditional. On one hand, the playwright shapes material in accordance with his personal relationship to it. On the other, a play is always intended for a public audience who bring expectations from previous theatre experience—hence traditions. No audience could relate to an absolutely unique play, even if one could be written. Meanwhile, a play that simply fulfilled audience expectations would be tame, dull, and trite.

Difference Between Form and Style

It is difficult to draw a hard and fast distinction between form and style; they tend to blur into one another. One distinction identifies form as a product of attitude and style as a product of point of view. This is generally true and if the two tend to blur, it is because attitude is heavily influenced by point of view and vice-versa.

Style is a characteristic mode of expression. An artist must handle the materials of a chosen medium, but how he handles them is entirely up to him. Ultimately, this is determined by how he views the world around him. What he considers important and intriguing and why he considers them so, leads him to slant the material one way or another, give emphasis here rather than there, and render language and action in a certain manner. Much of this is second nature, just as Harold Pinter's "weasel under the coffee table" was produced by his second nature. This is so much the case that a well-known playwright is almost always immediately recognizable after only a few lines of dialogue. A play is rooted in what the playwright values, how he sees reality, and the perspective he takes. In short, style has to do with the relationship between the play and reality.

Form has to do with the play's relationship to its audience. The formal elements orient the audience to the play. To the extent that a play is communication, it needs a reasonably recognizable form. Without it, the audience cannot share the experience. The way a play isolates itself in time and space helps establish audience expectations. In addition, suggestions of tone or attitude early in the play alert the audience to expect a particular variety of experience. The first cues are a matter of structural form, the second tonal form.

There is a traditional terminology associated with each of these concepts. Form is described by such terms as comedy or tragedy, one-act or full-length, opera, musical comedy, dance drama, historical drama. Style takes on the guise of various "isms"—Romanticism, Realism, Naturalism, Symbolism, Expressionism, Absurdism are all styles. They each handle the materials of the stage in characteristic ways determined by a vision of reality. Any of these styles could be applied to any form. One might have a Realistic comedy, a Romantic tragedy, or even, perhaps, an Absurdist opera, incongruous as that seems.

The terms are simply signposts that refer us to historical patterns in form and style. To some extent, every play has its own form and style born of the unique personality of its playwright and of the culture in which its theatre operated. It is virtually impossible to separate form and style from content. For the playwright, this means that much of the struggle of creation has to do with discovering his own way of relating to his material and to his theatre.

Structural Form vs. Tonal Form

Form may be described in two ways. First, it may be described in terms of tone. Tone refers to the author's (and implicitly the audience's) attitude toward the play's experience, its characters and the overall world of the play. It may assume a tragic or a comic pattern, and accordingly the play would become a tragedy or comedy. Form is also a matter of structure. How the play defines its stage space and divides its stage time are formal matters governing structure. The fact that a play exists isolated in time and space means that the playwright must structure both these dimensions. Structural form, then, includes the way a play opens and closes, breaks its action into acts or scenes, and focuses its crucial moments. Both are ultimately determined by attitude. As a result, our view of the material of a play-in-the-making always indicates something of its most appropriate form, both structural and tonal. It is impossible to conceive of a play without some sense of its form nor of a form without some feel for its probable content. Bearing in mind that there is nothing fixed in all this, it would be useful to examine the two sides of form, beginning with the structural side.

Historically, structural form has moved between two extremes: concentrated and comprehensive form. Comprehensive form draws into the play's structure all the pertinent action of the natural story. It uses an early point of attack, thereby showing in action all the significant moments. To do so, it uses the stage as a neutral ground becoming easily now one place, now another, or now one time, now another. Much medieval drama, Shakespearean and Elizabethan drama, and modern Epic Drama are of this type. At the extreme opposite end of the spectrum is the concentrated form. The concentrated form focuses all attention on the final crucial moments of the natural story, accordingly employing a late point of attack and relying heavily on exposition to fill in earlier moments pertinent to the present. The stage in this case usually represents a particular locale more fully and retains the same scene throughout an act if not the entire play. Classical, Neo-classical, and Realistic dramas tend to use this form.

Both forms have value. The comprehensive form tends to engage the audience's imagination in order to fill out the theatrical illusion. The audience thus has a greater sense of collaborating in the play's creation. The concentrated form tends to involve the audience's emotions more fully, since it compacts the dramatic tension more tightly.

Structural form may also apply to the way a play divides its time into segments. By definition, a play is itself a segment of time. It begins and therefore must end. The initial impression and the "parting shot" are both structural matters of great importance. So too are any curtains or blackouts that may occur during the course of the play. Each act or scene thus created is a formal unit of the overall structure. There are formal considerations deriving from the one-act play structure in contrast to a multi-act or full-length structure. For several centuries, the five-act structure was regarded as essential. For much of the present century, the three-act play has been the norm, recently replaced by the two-act structure. The overall length has been determined over the years by various extrinsic factors as well. The ancient Greeks had a stamina unknown to us and indulged in a whole day of tragedies presented in the form of a trilogy—three plays usually unified by theme or storyline. Broadway prefers plays that can be over before the trains to the suburbs stop running. American television is the most rigorous form of all, calling for half-hour shows that are actually twenty-four minutes long, with exact intervals allowed for commercials. Generally, television drama is the shortest form, cinema next, and finally stage drama. Still, audiences nowadays are not accustomed to enduring a play over three hours long. Occasionally, enduring a marathon session is a fashionable thing to do, as in the case of Eugene O'Neill's nine-act *Strange Interlude* or the recent *Nicholas Nickleby* based on Charles Dickens's work and presented by the Royal Shakespeare Company. These are exceptions made possible by the enormity of the prestige of those behind them.

Tonal form is closely tied to tradition and audience expectation. The attitude of the playwright, which he of course hopes to inspire in the audience as well, leads to patterns of shaping the play. Traditional forms take the dominant tones to a logical structural conclusion, creating tragedy, tragicomedy, comedy, farce, melodrama. These traditional forms demonstrate the relationship between attitude and form and they provide options always worth considering.

Historically, tonal form, much like structural form, has moved between two extremes: fixed and organic. The doctrine of fixed form holds that a play must maintain a definite pattern partly because it renders the play accessible to audiences and partly because there is an innate beauty and challenge in adhering to form. There is an appeal to purity in it. The doctrine of organic form holds that a play must assume the form uniquely suited to it and that there should be no definite or fixed forms. The truth probably lies somewhere between. Inasmuch as no play can avoid coming to terms with its audience, it must adhere in some measure to audience expectations and hence traditional form. On the other hand, every play is its own experience, free to lay down its own terms, and audiences tend to grant that license to the playwright, at least up to the point where they can continue to enter into the world of the play.

Currently, there is little allegiance to the doctrine of fixed form. It had its day during the seventeenth century when only two forms of drama were regarded as legitimate: comedy and tragedy—each having fixed and pure features. Nowadays the world has begun to strike us as so baffling that no form can adequately express our responses. Contemporary plays often employ a provocative and ironic mixture of tones, leaving audiences both amused and horrified, delighted and mystified, or charmed and awed. Still, the implications behind the standard forms passed down through the ages are worth exploring. They tell us a great deal about how attitude, empathy, and emotional response create patterns in drama. A play, we need to remind ourselves, is an artifice contrived to affect people. Form is a deliberate means to that end.

Traditional Forms

Putting aside the many special forms of theatre such as opera, ballad opera, operetta, musical comedy, dance drama, musical review, there are three basic tonal forms: tragedy, comedy, and tragicomedy. These are related directly to mood, attitude, or tone and can indeed cut across the special theatre forms, applying as well to musical or dance forms as they do to the so-called legitimate theatre. All three have sub-forms and variations, all have assumed new patterns with each succeeding age, but they remain identifiable by tone. The tone is evident by the emotional response the piece seeks to create. Tragedy tends to arouse a sense of awe and wonder in the face of the seriousness and universality of the suffering at the center of the spectacle. It is what Aristotle called pity and fear. Melodrama is a variation on the tragic mood, creating an alternation of fear, indignation, and relief. Comedy arouses amusement at the absurdities and human vagaries that make up its spectacle. It relies on incongruities, the sense that things are somewhat out of joint, and it usually resolves in a spirit of camaraderie. Farce is a variation, emphasizing physical buffoonery and outrageous exaggeration. Tragicomedy is a mixed form, calling for a controlled ambiguity of tone. It is the most common form in the modern theatre perhaps because of the ambiguity of modern life itself.

Each of these traditional forms is described in greater detail below. These are descriptions of traditional patterns, not prescriptions for how such plays should be written.

Of the various tonal forms, tragedy is the most fixed, the most traditional, the most highly esteemed. The dramatic counterpart to the challenge of writing the "great American Novel" is that of composing a "Modern Tragedy." Somehow, by definition a tragedy is expected to be great. So few are written in the contemporary theatre that to write one at all would be remarkable. Actually, the problem here is that tragedy has become as much a value judgment as it is a distinct form. Putting aside the values connoted by the term tragedy, the form is not so unusual after all.

Tragedy seeks to excite empathetic awe at the spectacle of a human being (or beings) face-to-face with the most threatening and challenging circumstances life can entail. The human condition does entail threats and challenges we normally shy away from; they are too dire for us to wish to face. Nevertheless, they intrigue us and pique our curiosity. In the relative safety of the theatre, we can indulge that curiosity at no expense to our personal security. The spectacle itself and our response to it can enlarge our awareness of the conditions of the life we lead. This purpose implies a series of characteristics.

Tragedy is usually structured around a single protagonist, a person strong enough to meet the challenges implied, but weak enough for us to identify with as a fellow human being. The challenge is both urgent and dire. If not surmounted, it poses grave dangers not only to the individual, but frequently to associates, if not society at large. The source of the challenge is not trivial. It might derive from fate, an error in judgment, another character, and usually from all three. In some ironic way, the protagonist himself frequently collaborates in bringing on this threat or challenge. In any event, the play's progress takes it from relative calm and contentment to catastrophe. Whether or not the protagonist survives, the test has been dire. Often at the end there is a sense of an emerging new order. It is the spectacle of man confronting the worst life can offer and, in the act of confronting it, assuming a dignity that is not lost even if the protagonist must succumb.

The audience of a tragedy undergoes an emotional release which Aristotle labeled "catharsis": an unleashing of our deep-seated, suppressed fears through the vicarious experience of the play. He defined tragedy's focus to be pity and fear, the emotions aroused and expended on "a worthy subject"—the protagonist being someone better than average, yet fully human.

These are the traditional characteristics of tragedy. The great tragedies of the past, especially those of the Greeks and of Shakespeare in the Elizabethan age, have, rightly or wrongly, become the models. They are tragedies that pit the protagonist against the gods or against the forces of the cosmos; they assume grandeur through the magnitude of the confrontation and the loftiness of their style. While *Oedipus Rex* and *Hamlet* may be quintessential tragedies, many others, even from the contemporary theatre, are certainly also tragedies—plays such as Bertolt Brecht's *Mother Courage*, Luigi Pirandello's *Henry IV*, Arthur Miller's *The Crucible*, and Friedrich Duerrenmatt's *The Visit* (even if he preferred to call it "grotesque comedy").

Although a variation on tragedy, melodrama carries a negative connotation. It is a term sometimes applied to those plays that might be tragedies if only they were better plays. If tragedy is made trivial and if it ends happily with virtue triumphant, the result is "mere melodrama." We tend to think of the melodramatic as synonymous with the sensational. There may be good reasons for this, but again the term is only a category, not a value.

The essence of melodrama lies in its spectacle of disaster. Like tragedy, it deals with dire threats and challenges, but they are produced now by forces outside the protagonist. They result from some hidden offstage force or from the machinations of an evil antagonist. There is no ironic collaboration between fate and the protagonist. These things tend to happen of their own accord, without the protagonist having decided to take a step toward disaster. For this reason, villains tend to abound in melodramas.

All this suggests that melodrama generally contains less substance than tragedy. That is true. On the other hand, melodrama is well-suited to certain sorts of human experiences. All of us face the chance of sudden disaster or victimization. There are always circumstances which, though completely beyond our control, drastically alter our lives. If the emphasis is placed on the human response to disaster, a melodrama can be meaningful. Moreover, melodrama is inherently theatrical, producing strong tension and spectacular effects. Some excellent plays fit this description: Harold Pinter's *The Birthday Party*, Charles Gordone's *No Place to Be Somebody*, or Friedrich Duerrenmatt's *The Physicists* (which he again would call a grotesque comedy). If emphasis is placed instead on the disaster itself, as in many nineteenth-century melodramas such as Dion Boucicault's *The Octoroon* or in present-day disaster films such as *Airport* or *Jaws*, the drama suffers a loss of substance even while gaining high spectacle. These are pieces that give melodrama its bad name.

Comedy depends on the creation of the ludicrous, in the largest sense of the word. It develops spectacles of incongruity, deliberate inconsistency, and absurdity. One way or another, characters are again caught up in circumstances beyond their control, but the emphasis this time is on the laughable. This means that the circumstances be more disconcerting than dire. Laughing is both a mysterious and a peculiarly human activity. Why we do it, nobody quite knows. We can point to the sorts of things which provoke laughter, even if we cannot explain it. As Henri Bergson indicates in his essay "On Laughter," we tend to laugh at the spectacle of mechanical or inelastic behavior. Any sort of behavior that cannot adjust to a new circumstance because of its own rigidity can be laughable. Adaptability is one of humanity's better traits. Society seeks to maintain that by ridiculing those who refuse to adapt or cannot. Another way to see it is to recognize that human beings, each and every one of them, have their weaknesses in which we like to indulge, but in our wisdom do not. We derive amusement in the theatre from witnessing others indulge them and letting them take the consequences. There are of course varieties of laughter. The amount of laughter produced, as measured on a laugh-meter, is no gauge of the quality of a comedy. Laughter may be an inward amusement or an outward guffaw. Similarly the source may range from gentle humor to bitter satire. All of them tend to portray individuals caught up in absurd or incongruous situations that defy rational analysis.

There are a great many sub-forms of comedy: situation comedy, comedy of character, comedy of ideas, comedy of manners (high comedy), and just plain farce (low comedy). Farce is the most extreme form of comedy. It relies on physical spectacle. The contrast between the exalted notions we have of our human glory and the mundane necessities to which we must submit provides the grist for the farcical mill. For all our dignity, farce reminds us, we still occupy physical bodies. For example, the man of great purpose and dignity who steps on a banana peel or the woman of amiable good-nature who gets a pie in the face are old surefire farcical pieces of business.

Other forms of comedy may rely on the sight of human beings caught in suddenly disconcerting circumstances, but they do so on different levels and with greater subtlety. Situation comedy pits relatively normal human beings against absurd situations. Comedy of character pits absurd characters against situations that would ordinarily seem normal. Comedy of ideas tends to construct whole worlds out of topsy-turvy ideas and values, which prove as valid as the counterparts we so thoroughly believe in our world. Finally, comedy of manners pits pretentious characters against more knowledgeable ones who usually do the disconcerting.

Whatever the form, comedy concentrates on the incongruous, producing pain for the characters, but pain that is not strong enough or permanent enough to interfere with our recognition of the ridiculous. It has the effect of making us feel for the moment just a little superior. In order to do so, comedy virtually demands characters who take themselves and their circumstances very seriously indeed. The character who thinks he is funny and his playwright who knows he is are both doomed to failure.

Because it is a mixed form, tragicomedy does not allow as precise a description as comedy and tragedy. Its form is correspondingly more organic, altering more radically from one play to another. What perhaps most clearly marks it is a controlled ambiguity of tone. In the case of any bad playwright, there is first and foremost an ambiguity of tone. One simply does not know what to make of the play. Should we take it seriously? What is this all about, anyway? But in the case of tragicomedy, this ambiguity is carefully controlled; indeed, it is a source of dramatic tension. A single event may strike a provocative balance between the humorous and the pathetic or between the whimsical and the tragic. We feel both reactions and hesitate to give full vent to either one. These plays may give enormous comic pleasure from time to time, and yet bring us up short— recognizing that what we had laughed about is after all very serious and threatening. It is perhaps the most favored form in the present age because we perceive our own world with a similar ambiguity: things are simultaneously absurd and out of joint while they threaten our very existence. Some fine examples of the tragicomic form might include Anton Chekhov's *The Three Sisters,* Luigi Pirandello's *Six Characters in Search of an Author,* Tom Stoppard's *Rosencrantz and Guildenstern Are Dead,* Samuel Beckett's *Waiting for Godot,* and David Storey's *Home.*

Tragedy, melodrama, comedy, farce, and tragicomedy are the major traditional forms, but they are by no means fixed, especially today. Classification has become progressively difficult as playwrights shape forms to suit their particular plays. Chekhov was fond of calling his plays comedies, while his director Konstantin Stanislavsky called them tragedies, and we here have called at least one of them (*The Three Sisters*) tragicomedy. Duerrenmatt called his plays "grotesque comedies," while we have called one (*The Visit*) a tragedy, and another (*The Physicists*) a melodrama. Even a modern tragedy is apt to produce a healthy dose of laughter and amusement, and a modern comedy, moments of sudden horror or amazement. Still, the traditional forms can tell us something about how tone influences form.

Establishing a Feel for the Material

It is clear now that you must discover tone before you can find the right form for the material. In other words, as you examine material that, for one reason or another, intrigues you, your first step is to find out why it intrigues you. What is it that matters to you? That, in turn, leads to the attitude you take toward the material in recognition of its importance. You may rest assured that material that means nothing to you will mean exactly that to an audience. If you are attracted to a certain story, a character, a set of circumstances, or a setting, it stands to reason that it has meaning for you. You would not be interested in transforming it into a play unless you found meaning in it that seemed worth communicating to someone else. But what is that meaning?

The word "meaning" is used here not to refer to the theme that the play might eventually convey, although there is certainly a relationship. If you were to discover the theme early, it would probably stop the development of the play dead in its tracks. To be able to say at the outset that your play will demonstrate "the necessity for patience and forebearance in times of social unrest" would suggest that this material never "wanted" to be a play in the first place. It would be perfectly happy as a declarative sentence. "Meaning" refers to the sense of urgency and importance the material carries. Why do you care and why should an audience care? Caring can happen on all levels and need not be taken to demand that all plays need a weighty, earth-shattering significance. One can care about little things. "There is a special providence in the fall of a sparrow," said Shakespeare. Somehow, something in that material matters to you. As soon as you know what it is, you can begin to explore the form that might best contain it.

An intriguing two-way struggle goes on between playwright and the material that matters. As you play with it, writing notes about the characters, trying out sample bits of dialogue, and imagining different settings, the material begins to talk back. The more you know about it, the more clearly it tells you the form it "wants to assume." This requires a kind of humility before your own material, so as to let it talk. Of course, it is not true that it talks or wants anything, but it appears to in the same sense that characters sometimes seem to take on a life of their own in the process of writing them. What is really happening is that you are inventing and discovering new and more promising connections between the details of the characters and their circumstance. Each one tells you something more about what you yourself care about.

Samson Raphaelson, in *The Human Nature of Playwriting*, remarks on this dialogue that a playwright might have with his material:

> You plan a piece of work—you can almost weigh it. Can I hold it in my hand? Does it have body, weight? It shouldn't weigh like lead and it shouldn't weigh like tissue paper. It should weigh like a bird and should have a pulse like a bird. I find certain ideas actually feel that way in your hand, and other ideas, as you imagine them written, are just words. You know they're no good. Good work must have body of some kind and pulse and, let us add, wings. Also, you may start with a tragedy—you begin to weigh it and it wants to be a comedy. Try it as a comedy in writing or in your mind. If it is too powerful, too moving, too terrible to be a comedy, then you know it demands to be a tragedy, but don't force it. If it is little and you can write it with ease and with pleasure, then be little, be Max Beerbohm instead of William Shakespeare. He's little and he will probably live for a long time. Be what you are and let your material be what it basically is.

The process is much the same as what must transpire in the subconscious mind when we dream. We seem to have a little playwright in our heads who constructs these brief nocturnal experiences and decides what to emphasize and what form to use in light of what matters to you, the audience member.

What we have been calling material always exists in some form already. Even if part of your material is a prior experience, it has already assumed form as memory. Memory blocks out certain things, makes other things rather bigger than they were, and so gives them shape in accordance with the meaning the experience has for you. Other material might be in the form of an anecdote, a short story, a joke, a dream, an action, or any number of other things. Composing a play, you are trying to develop the form that comfortably contains them all. You are in charge. You can tell your characters what they must be, where they are, when they must do what. But in doing so, any lack of respect for the genuine feelings the characters create will result in mismatched, awkward combinations. The form will be wrong.

Both structural and tonal form are involved in this search for meaning; both result from the meaning found in the material. Structural form entails decisions about the dimensions of the material, the nature of the dramatic tension, the pinpointing of the crux moment, and the appropriate ending. All these decisions turn on the importance the material has. Tonal form has to do with the feeling, the attitude the material strives to create, and it begins with your own attitude.

For illustration, it is useful to take material from one form to a completely different one. The process of having to make adjustments to the new form is much like the process of dramatizing material. Suppose we were to begin with material in the form of an anecdote and then transpose it into a comic strip. The anecdote is a narrative form, the comic strip a graphic form, but both entail action. The comic strip is further removed from the medium of theatre, but it is closer to the dramatic mode, since characters exist visually in a seemingly present time for each frame of the strip. Like drama, the comic strip does not have the luxury of narrative sequences or the comparative open-endedness of a written story. All action must take place within the confines of three or four frames, just as a drama must concentrate on a restricted number of scenes. Here is the anecdote:

> Bert and Jack came upon a leather-bound case sitting in the middle of the sidewalk. They were very intrigued by it, but they surmised that it must be some sort of trick. They peered into the corners and alleyways nearby, but saw nobody. It seemed that they were alone with this leather-bound case. They edged closer to it. It had a lid held shut by an elegant gold clasp. Neither wanted to be the first to pick it up, wincing against the chance that it might blow up. Finally, Bert did pick it up. Nothing happened. Jack then took courage. He took the case from Bert and opened it. The case went off with the sound of a clanging alarm. They dropped it and ran. A little man stepped out of a door nearby, picked up the case, turned off the alarm, and ran after them. The

closer he got, the faster they ran. They ran around a corner, stopped suddenly, leaned against the wall, and tried to catch their breath. Suddenly, the little man stepped in front of them, smiled, and said, "Excuse me, but you dropped this."

The anecdote form, with its brevity and sudden sharp effects, naturally imposes a degree of "meaning" on the material. It tends to be objective and detached in tone, encapsulating in a few quick strokes a very small segment of human experience.

To render this material in the form of a comic strip, we need to recognize the nature and limitations of the new form. The comic strip is one of the most restrictive and structured forms of art, rivaling the sonnet—even if it lacks its prestige. The form consists of three to four frames within which two-dimensional drawn figures as characters act and speak via balloons over their heads. Each frame can contain only limited material. Economy is enforced and with it the need to clearly isolate the segments of the material for each frame. The last frame might be called the "clincher frame," for it must make the statement the others have led up to. Depending on how these questions are resolved, the story could change considerably. The following version provides an example.

These four frames contain the essence of the anecdote's story. The economy imposed by the four-frame structure required deletion of some material and a new emphasis on what remained. Other choices could be made. The frames might accentuate some other aspects of the story, as this second version does.

In this case, the four frames accentuate a different phase of the story. The little man appears in both versions, but he makes a very different contribution. In the first version, he appears to be an innocent bystander who good-naturedly restores the dropped item to its "owners." In the second he is important as the perpetrator of the trick: he creates the whole action and appears in all but the third frame. And yet, in the first version, he assumes an importance of a different kind, for the cartoonist uses him for the final effect.

A play is not a comic strip, but it does pose similar demands. Dramatic structure may not be as rigorous but it does demand economy. Audiences will not sit endlessly. Stage action must convey the storyline. As a result, the play concentrates on an act, which is a unified set of activities. They may be broken into formal segments of acts and scenes or they may constitute a single act, as in a one-act play.

There are one-act plays that are split into two or more scenes by blackouts or curtains: Noel Coward's "Fumed Oak," Douglas Turner Ward's "Day of Absence," and Leonard Melfi's "Birdbath," for example. This apparent contradiction may be resolved by recognizing a difference between an act and a scene. These are not absolute terms. The difference between them is relative, but one may say safely that an act involves a more complex development. It pulls together a number of intricate strands. A scene tends to be a briefer, more incisive sequence of action, intended as a quick insight rather than a development. Some full-length plays, however, are composed of scenes rather than acts — plays such as Tennessee Williams's *The Glass Menagerie* or *Camino Real*. Arthur Schnitzler's *La Ronde*, or Bertolt Brecht's *The Good Woman of Setzuan*.

One-act plays are rarely split into scenes because they are generally so short that any break in the action can seriously mar the unity of the play. Normally then a one-act play presents its action in one sequence, one formal segment — an act. It is usually a brief play, completed within an hour. These features have implications. If the play is to complete its effect within the span of one act, it generally relies on a single incident. It seeks to create a quick sensation, a glimpse into a life being lived, and it derives more of its dramatic development from our discoveries of new factors than would a full-length play. Accordingly, the characters rarely undergo any fundamental change in the course of the action. The cast is correspondingly smaller — usually three to five characters. As a result of all these factors, the one-act also tends to place its crux moment near the end of the play. It occurs as a vivid revelation rather than a culmination of long developments.

Some material lends itself more readily to the one-act form, generally material that attains its greatest effect in vivid revelations and discovery. Material calling out for development, change, and more complex characterization will probably not work as a one-act. Conversely, one can fool oneself on this score, working very hard at a full-length play only to discover that the rich development was not there; it was a fine one-act all the while.

Formal Economy

Even in the case of a full-length play, form imposes an economy that demands your respect. If you have ever been strongly affected by a play and then study it closely for its structure, it is surprising how small the means can be to create a great effect. The curtain that goes up must also come down; the audience rightfully expects the interval between to condense in action what is most pertinent and telling about the life of the play.

A great temptation on first mapping out a play is to show everything. It is a wonderful story and an interesting group of characters, after all. Audiences ought to love everything about them. It is a dangerous temptation. First, a wonderful story about interesting characters loses its appeal rapidly if there is nothing for us to guess at or wonder about. It insults our intelligence and dulls our imagination. A play requires a certain density in order to engage an audience. Showing everything robs it of density, leaving the play thin indeed. Second, showing everything will mean splitting the play into several scenes to show several different times and places. This can be done; the stage is a marvelously flexible device. But you need to consider that great effort is required to build dramatic momentum and, if it is to be broken by a blackout or curtain to esablish a new time or place, all momentum will be lost. A hefty portion of the new scene will have to be devoted to rebuilding that lost momentum. Third, there is a kind of beauty or wonder in a neatly self-contained object of any sort. A play is no exception. Through allusion and implication, you can convey a great deal about the characters and their circumstance. It need not all be told directly. The more compact the play, the more likely it is to emphasize what matters. An audience appreciates the feeling that they are being spared all the middling details in the interests of something that has genuine import or interest.

If you find yourself wanting to ring down the curtain and pick up the action at another point in time, perhaps that is where it should have begun in the first place. It is easy to write scenes that serve to set up and explain your characters; it is more difficult to write scenes in which something happens. The former are not worth writing, unfortunately. If a scene arouses interest by portraying an action that affects the characters or creates a meaningful change, the audience will be at once alert to anything they can learn about the situation. That is when exposition should be delivered. Exposition, the information we need to know about the characters' world, works best when it makes a dramatic impact itself.

Formal economy in drama ultimately resides in the capacity of its act of presentation to contain a complex of factors. A human action can refer beyond itself. We can read in what another person is doing a great deal of information and feeling that is not explicitly there. The encounter, that basic motif of drama, is exciting and promising exactly because it engages us on so many levels.

Below is a story describing a day in the life of a certain middle-aged gentleman. It gives us a portrait of his whole way of life, but it is not rendered in action. It is a narrative composed of description of people, places, and activities. On stage, we might be tempted to make two scenes out of it, one in the kitchen and one on the hillside. At any rate, here is the story:

He had already passed his thirtieth anniversary. It had been a miserable marriage. His wife ran a boarding school in which he had been a slave from the first day. He ordered supplies, kept the accounts, stitched together the exercise books, taught this, that, and the other thing, and took his wife's dog for walks. He also gave public lectures for charity and promoted the school. His whole life was tied up in the school, morning, noon and night. His seven daughters drove him crazy, especially now that they all ought to be married anyway. He was expected to see to everything, provide for everyone, and account for anything that went wrong. It was, for example, somehow his fault that none of those girls had managed to find a husband.

One morning, several of the boarding students had trouble with their glands and could not eat breakfast. Too many pancakes had been made. His wife cursed him for allowing the extra ones to be made and ordered him to eat them all. He did, for he was very hungry. As he sat digesting them and expecting his wife to interrupt that peaceful moment without warning, the thought struck him to slip out of the school for a while.

He did. As he emerged from the school gate, he noticed a pole set into the ground on the hill across the street. He studied it awhile, then walked up to the top of the hill and stood there by the pole. He stood there all day, while the operation of the school went haywire. By nightfall, his wife's nerves were frayed. She stormed out of the school and stopped short when she saw her husband standing on the hill next to the pole under the moonlight.

"What are you doing up there? You pipsqueak devil, get down here! Have you any idea the number of things that have gone wrong because you disappeared? What's the matter with you, anyway?" and on and on.

He returned to the school and took care of a toilet that had overflowed and a fuse that had blown. Thereafter, he often thought of that peaceful day he had spent on the hillside and was as often tempted to repeat the experience.

This fellow is our friend Nyukhin from Anton Chekhov's "On the Harmfulness of Tobacco," the play dealt with in Chapter 4. All the information about Nyukhin's life is contained in the play, but there it is part of the act of lecturing. Nyukhin might have indulged in a variety of different actions. But one which certainly comprehends virtually all the others and conveys his plight and his will to escape is an encounter with a lecture audience. Certainly, it is far more efficient and effective than any number of scenes showing us Nyukhin's life at Dog Alley, 13. Instead, momentarily freed from his life at the school and face to face with other human beings, he is inspired to unburden himself. As a natural result of that motivation, we learn about his life, and the exposition has urgency for he is trying to come to terms with his life. When he fails, naturally he must return to Dog Alley, 13. It is an act, a decision and a result. That is concise and effective theatre.

While wrestling with the material for a play, you should overcome any compunction to be faithful to the details. It is the basic appeal and interest the material has which demands your loyalty. The particulars are alterable to the demands of the form and style you choose. Chekhov did not write "On the Harmfulness of Tobacco" from the story told above, but if he had, it would have been a perfectly reasonable decision to transpose it all into a lecture hall. By the same token, the one-act form, or the tragic form, or your own sense of style may lead you to consider drastically altering some part of your original idea. So long as you do not lose its appeal in the process, and find new ways of enhancing effect, you are only gaining by it. If you lose that appeal, however, you lose the play. When that happens, you will know it at once. You will have two options: go back and recover the appeal or abandon the project for something new.

Formal economy bears most heavily on structural form. But for the sake of both that and tonal form, all your decisions come back to the question of the feel and meaning the material of your play has for you. Structurally, you want to encapsulate the material in an action, provide the most apt framework, focus the tension, and fix the crux moment. Tonally, you need to find the quality of language and action that would most enhance the feeling or attitude the play is to inspire. There is a danger here, too. One may try to second-guess an audience. It leads to pushing too hard for a particular response. Remember that audiences tend to be just a little perverse, refusing to believe anything they are told too directly or with too much emphasis. Relax and let the feeling you yourself have for the material dictate how you want to approach it. If the feeling is genuine, the tone and structure will emerge. Of course, it takes hard work: you need to explore the material thoroughly before the feel and attitude can emerge.

Style and the World of the Play

Gaining a feel for the material entails not only the attitude you take toward it, but also the perspective. One has to do with form, the other with style. It is difficult to make absolute distinctions between the two. One's style tends to merge with one's form; in fact, a proclivity for a certain form is part of one's style. Of all terms, style is probably the most difficult to define with any precision. Basically, it is a characteristic mode of expression rooted in the way one views reality. Since any art form is a deliberate alteration of reality, occupying as they all do a new ground, its manipulation derives from a personal vision. Since a play, as a particular art form, occupies a stage, and fills its space with living, breathing human beings, it is a world to itself. For that reason, there is a strong tie between style and the world of the play.

The real world does not make decisions about style; nothing is necessarily more important than anything else so far as nature is concerned. But for us, some things matter very much. Style is a reflection of that concern. We care very much about deaths, for example, indifferent as nature may be. Since it is human nature to care, a play (which really is an expression of care) naturally takes on a certain coloration reflecting that care. Form, too, is the product of care, but in the case of style the care appears chiefly in the treatment—the quality and color of the action which provides a continual reminder that there is a consciousness and a sensibility behind what we witness on the stage. A playwright maintains a presence through the style and coherence of the play's world. Even an Absurdist, believing the world empty and devoid of meaning and value, writes plays out of care—a concern for the agony that that emptiness produces in us human beings who so need meaning.

Theatre is an act of communication. A play restructures the world using living beings encountering each other in three-dimensional space. And as they encounter us, the theatre experience produces a shared vision. Our view of the world merges momentarily with that of the play. Dissimilar as our individual views of reality may be, we agree on enough points to make theatre possible. We disagree enough that it is virtually impossible for any two people to write the same play, even if they agree beforehand on the plot, characters, and setting. This is the source of style.

In any form of expression, the same principle operates. Again the comic strip provides some good illustrations. The Sunday comics are a potpourri of styles. Pogo's world is sharply different from Dr. Morgan's, whose world would never be confused with Blondie's, nor could hers with that of Dennis the Menace. Each artist uses the same elements in creating the comic strip, but the viewpoints, sensibilities, and manners of expression vary enormously. Each artist has worked long enough with the world of their strips that all the elements have taken a very comfortable place in the world of the strip and we cannot help but share a little of that world. In the theatre, the encounter is so much deeper that the absorption in the world of the play can be very strong indeed.

A playwright is constantly designing new worlds, one for each play. Although many stylistic qualities carry over, they still have to be reestablished at the outset of each new play. In keeping with Aristotle's probability (discussed in Chapter 1), when we as an audience encounter a play, we look at once for any insights into the nature of this new world. What sorts of things are apt to happen here? How are they apt to happen? Style is a code giving some of this insight. The world of the play becomes more or less coherent and believable in direct ratio to how authoritative its style is. The stage must become its own world. We must believe not only that it has every right to be there, but also that it could be no other way, at least for the time being. When that happens, style is present.

Personal vs. Established Style

Style reflects the social dimension of theatre. It develops as a means of sharing a vision of reality. Such visions vary not only from one individual to another, but also from one culture to another. Individual perspectives are the source of personal style, cultural perspectives the source of established style. They are not mutually exclusive; a personal style operates within an established style. Shakespeare shared many stylistic qualities with other Elizabethan playwrights, and yet there are distinguishing elements to his personal style.

Established style has usually held sway throughout an entire age, receding only as a new view of reality comes to supplant it and thereby call for a new style. An ancient Greek, an eighteenth-century Japanese, and a modern American obviously would not see reality the same way. *Oedipus Rex*, the Kabuki play *Chushingura*, and *The Glass Menagerie* give testimony to that. Doubtless, *The Glass Menagerie* would strike Takedo Izumo as strange, fully as strange as his play would strike Sophocles. The reason is that the plays are based on views of reality that are alien to one another. For all the reality we read into the stage worlds of our own plays, the more alien the play the more apparent the stage's contrivance. It reminds us again that at base the stage is all pretense. Being so, its ability to reflect reality depends on whether the audience can read a reality in the complex of pretenses. For most of us in the West, Kabuki's illusions do not work because, not sharing the view of reality, we cannot understand the stage conventions it had produced.

Through the ages, reality has been seen in constantly changing ways. In response, theatre has constantly developed new styles. Until recently such styles generally endured for more than a century. Neo-classicism, for example, emerged out of the Italian Renaissance and became a fixed style in France after the 1630s. It continued as an accepted style through most of the eighteenth century. For that long period, the style corresponded to accepted ideas of the nature of the world and the sort of theatre that could best reflect them. Since the late nineteenth century there has been no such unanimity about the nature of the world. Truth has become more and more relative and a proliferation of styles has accompanied this development. The twentieth century has been aptly called the age of "isms." The period has indeed witnessed a cavalcade of styles: Realism, Naturalism, Symbolism, Expressionism, Futurism, Dadaism, Surrealism, Epic Theatre, Absurdism, Theatre of Cruelty, the Happening, Environmental Theatre, Total Theatre. These are established styles; they might also seem a Tower of Babel. More will be said concerning these styles at the end of the chapter.

Within established styles, individual dramatists have their personal styles. Henrik Ibsen, Anton Chekhov, and George Bernard Shaw are three early Realists, yet there is no mistaking the personal style of one for either of the others. They are all Realists in the sense that they all employ every means to render the appearance and sound of the stage as much like appearance and sound of the objective real world. To our eyes and ears, their plays have the sense of everyday life. Of course, to achieve this they must resort to pretenses, such as a fourth wall that pretends to cut us off from the action, as if the characters were in one room and we in another. Beyond that, each of the dramatists uses language, action, environment, and antecedent action in his own way. Following are three scenes, one from each playwright. Each one is a scene between a man and a woman who have already developed expectations of one another. The scenes are parallel in this respect and they share their Realism. If you know the playwrights at all, you will guess at once which scene is whose:

HILDA

All these ten years I have believed in you so utterly — so utterly.

SOLNESS

You must go on believing in me!

HILDA

Then let me see you stand free and high up!

SOLNESS

(Sadly.) Oh, Hilda — it is not every day that I can do that.

HILDA

(Passionately.) I will have you do it! I will have it! (Imploringly.) Just once more, Solness! Do the impossible once again!

SOLNESS

(Stands and looks deep into her eyes.)

If I try it, Hilda, I will stand up there and talk to him as I did that time before.

HILDA

(In rising excitement.) What will you say to him?

SOLNESS

I will say to him: Hear me, Mighty Lord — thou may'st judge me as seems best to thee. But hereafter I will build nothing but the loveliest thing in the world. . . .

HILDA

(Carried away.) Yes . . . yes . . . yes!

SOLNESS

. . . build it together with a princess, whom I love . . .

HILDA

Yes, tell him that! Tell him that!

SOLNESS

Yes. And then I will say to him: Now I shall go down and throw my arms round her and kiss her . . .

HILDA

. . . many times! Say that!

SOLNESS

. . . many, many times, I will say.

HILDA

And then?

SOLNESS

Then I will wave my hat . . . and come down to earth . . . and do as I said to him.

HILDA

(With outstretched arms.) Now I see you again as I did when there was song in the air.

This is not the end of the scene, but it is a sequence long enough to impress its style. Here is the second short scene:

RAINA

You look ever so much nicer than when we last met.

(He looks up, surprised.)

What have you done to yourself?

BLUNTSCHLI

Washed; brushed; good night's sleep and breakfast. That's all.

RAINA

Did you get back safely that morning?

BLUNTSCHLI

Quite, thanks.

RAINA

Were they angry with you for running away from Sergius's charge?

BLUNTSCHLI

(Grinning.) No: they were glad; because they'd just run away themselves.

RAINA

(Going to the table, and leaning over it towards him.)

It must have made a lovely story for them: all that about me and my room.

BLUNTSCHLI

Capital story. But I only told it to one of them: a particular friend.

RAINA

On whose discretion you could absolutely rely?

BLUNTSCHLI

Absolutely.

RAINA

Hm! He told it all to my father and Sergius the day you exchanged the prisoners.

(She turns away and strolls carelessly across to the other side of the room.)

BLUNTSCHLI

(Deeply concerned and half incredulous.) No! You don't mean that, do you?

RAINA

(Turning, with sudden eagerness.)

I do indeed. But they don't know that it was in this house you took refuge. If Sergius knew, he would challenge you and kill you in a duel.

BLUNTSCHLI

Bless me! Then don't tell him.

RAINA

Please be serious, Captain Bluntschli.

Again, this scene cuts off in midstream, but there is enough there to catch its style and flavor. Finally, here is the last short scene:

DUNYASHA

I'm so nervous, I'm worried. I went into service when I was quite a little girl, and now I'm not used to common life, and my hands are white, white as a lady's. I'm so tender and so delicate now, respectable and afraid of everything. . . . I'm so frightened. And I don't know what will happen to my nerves if you deceive me, Yasha.

YASHA

(Kisses her.)

Little cucumber! Of course, every girl must respect herself; there's nothing I dislike more than a badly behaved girl.

DUNYASHA

I'm awfully in love with you; you're educated, you can talk about everything. (Pause.)

YASHA

(Yawns.)

Yes. I think this: if a girl loves anybody, then it means she's immoral. (Pause.) It's nice to smoke a cigar out in the open air . . .

(Listens.)

Somebody's coming. It's the mistress, and people with her.

(DUNYASHA embraces him suddenly.)

Go to the house, as if you'd been bathing in the river: go by this path, or they'll meet you and will think I've been meeting you. I can't stand that sort of thing.

DUNYASHA
(Coughs quietly.)
My head's aching because of your cigar.

The first scene is from Henrik Ibsen's *The Master Builder*, the second from George Bernard Shaw's *Arms and the Man*, and the last from Anton Chekhov's *The Cherry Orchard*. All three plays are now classics of the modern repertory. The characters behave in fully Realistic manner, as if the audience were not there and they occupied only the represented space: the large verandah of Solness' house, the library of Raina's father's house, or the garden of Mme. Ranevskaya's house. The three scenes portray life as we might witness it had we been there. Still, there is considerable difference in the styles.

What is sometimes most telling about a playwright's style is the dividing line between what is literally contained in the dialogue and action and what is implied. For example, the Hilda-Solness scene stresses an exultant striving pushed forward by Hilda's passionate encouragement. Implicit is a sense of overreaching and of impending doom. The Raina-Bluntschli scene is word banter in which what at first seems important gives way to something else. Implicit is the conviction that there is indeed something important underneath it all. Typically, Shaw works his scenes on the premise that what we may think is significant is insignificant and vice-versa. Finally, in Chekhov's case, the Dunyasha-Yasha scene is literally a love scene gone sour. Dunyasha gives direct expression of her feelings and witnesses her hopes curdle there before her eyes. Implicitly, we feel both Yasha's outrageous disdain and Dunyasha's private agony.

The decision to emphasize this and imply that contributes more than anything else to developing style. The stage cannot show us all and no one would want it to, because it would rob it of its excitement. What the stage may imply about the characters' lives is sometimes more fascinating than what it tells us directly. Implying something powerfully yet subtly can be one of a playwright's greatest gifts.

Current Styles

In the contemporary theatre several styles can be isolated and described as dominant styles. Although there are certainly others, they are in constant flux and danger of disappearing. Here is a brief catalogue of five major styles.

Realism

Full Realism consists of portraying human life through close duplication of the details we observe around us. It plays upon the objective experience of seeing and hearing, trying faithfully to reproduce the way we see and hear real life. Accordingly, it tends to place the action within the proscenium, having the characters behave as if the audience were not there. It nevertheless presents itself to the audience in such a way as to lend emphasis where it is needed; it is not as closed as old Naturalism. As a result of these features, Realism tends to employ concentrated action, an act portraying a time span roughly equivalent to its playing time. Examples include Jason Miller's *That Championship Season* and Preston Jones's *The Last Meeting of the Knights of the White Magnolia*.

Modified Realism

Modified or Psychological Realism continues to rely on the presentation of life through detail and to play on our senses of sight and sound, but it places a different emphasis on the psychological drives that motivate us and thus introduces a subjective level. This subjectivity frequently appears in the form of dreams, daydreams, reminiscences, or inner dialogue. Time is more fluid; flashbacks, jumps forward in time, or telescoping of time are not uncommon. More than one locale might be represented on stage simultaneously; in extreme cases the stage is virtually bare, easily representing a variety of places in either objective or subjective reality. Nevertheless, Realistic details still serve to give a binding effect of a real world. Examples include Arthur Miller's *Death of a Salesman*, Tennessee Williams's *The Glass Menagerie*, Lawrence and Lee's *The Night Thoreau Spent in Jail*, and Milan Stitt's *The Runner Stumbles*.

Allusive Realism

This is closely allied to "Modified Realism," but it replaces an emphasis on psychological motivation with allusions to forces beyond the characters—sometimes social, sometimes metaphysical. Typically, the play seems simple and straightforward, but then proves to be driven forward by strange or at least unseen forces. The characters and their world are, one way or another, suggestive of other things in our own world. Plays run the gamut from the almost cartoon-like allusions of Slawomir Mrozek's *Tango*, John Guare's *House of Blue Leaves*, or Kurt Vonnegut's *Happy Birthday, Wanda June*, to the more chilling allusive quality of plays like David Rabe's *Sticks and Bones*, Harold Pinter's *The Birthday Party*, or Sam Shepard's *Buried Child*.

Absurdism

This style is based on the conviction that the world is inherently meaningless and out of harmony with itself and with us. It attempts accordingly to characterize the stage in a deliberately chaotic manner, assuming
a kind of coherence only by building a deliberate climactic rhythm reflecting the characters' and our own response to the vision of the abyss the
play opens up. Frequently, it works by encasing the play on a stage that
seems stranded or cut off from what must really matter—something out
there. It tends to rely on vivid physical images to create a searing effect,
such as people turning into rhinoceroses, people consigned to living out
their last days in ashcans, or the spectacle of characters being gradually
buried in sand or furniture. Examples include Eugene Ionesco's *Exit the
King*, Samuel Beckett's *Waiting for Godot*, and Tom Stoppard's *Rosencrantz
and Guildenstern Are Dead*.

Epic Theatre

This style developed out of the early theatricalism of directors such as
Vsevolod Meyerhold and Erwin Piscator and the theories and plays of Bertolt Brecht. It is based on the conviction that society-at-large is the shaper
of our destinies, working in collaboration with the mean small-minded
side of human nature. As a type of theatre of social awareness, it attempts to
alert us to the social forces around us, sometimes activating us to do battle
against them. It portrays the world with extreme economy, resorting to
theatrical suggestion and avoiding any thorough illusion. The devices of
illusion are blatant and apparent. Stage space is neutral, becoming easily
now this locale, now that. Time represented may consist of decades, even
centuries. It is sometimes based on actual history, sometimes on invented
history, but always on a parallel between the play's strange world and our
own world, which should begin to seem strange in the process. Examples
include Bertolt Brecht's *Mother Courage*, Edward Bond's *Lear*, Max
Frisch's *The Firebugs*, John Arden's *Serjeant Musgrave's Dance*, and Arthur Kopit's *Indians*.

These current dominant styles are not fixed phenomena and different
people may well draw different lists. Descriptions may also vary, but this
catalogue contains most of the salient characteristics discernible in the
present-day theatre.

The business of the playwright is not to study these styles and strive
to be up-to-date. Certainly, you should know about the work going forward; but to ape it in order to seem *au currant* is professional suicide. Your
style should derive from the approach to the dramatic mode and theatrical
medium that suits you and your chosen material best. You need to be fully
comfortable with it. Style is not something developed overnight; it takes
long and close experience working with the material and your chosen

medium (stage or screen) and witnessing over and over the way material transforms in the process of dramatizing. Style is the natural result of working long and intimately with your material. To attempt suddenly to develop a new style will only draw attention to contrivance. Style may be a patterned contrivance, but it only works to the extent that it conceals itself and appears natural.

Exercises

1. It makes a considerable difference what a dramatist chooses to show in action onstage or to have reported from offstage. Study a scene in which something is indeed happening offstage, whether acknowledged or not by the characters. Then, write that offstage scene as if it were on stage, emulating the playwright's own style. (This is the structural premise of Alan Aykbourne's trilogy *The Norman Conquests,* in which each of the three plays dramatizes the same events, but as they occur in a different room.)

2. Using the same scene, or if necessary choosing another, rewrite it by giving it a completely different tone. If it is a comic scene, make it tragic. If it is lyrical and sentimental, make it satirical and sardonic, and so forth.

3. Select any dramatist whose work you know and whose style is distinctive. Then attempt the following:
   a. Study the style; then write a scene of your own invention using that style.
   b. Rewrite a scene from the work in your own way, avoiding the original style.

4. Adapt a short story or a scene from a story or novel to the stage. How does the new medium change the way the events must happen? What new material must be added to make it work? What original material must be deleted?

5. Write a short piece for radio or for mime. The first form depends entirely on sound to convey action, while the other depends on silent physical activity. Notice how the form both limits you and encourages imagination.

7

The Dramatic Script

Chapter 5 examined the charting of a playscript; now the dramatic script itself is the subject. The play script stands in relation to the play as the scenario does to the script, so writing the script is still a matter of charting. The play script, as a set of directions for the play, can only hint at its final stage experience. A good script hints with such vigor, insistence, and consistency that it is hard to imagine the wrong staging. Still, the writer and the reader must both imagine the staging: the script is not the play.

For these reasons, the play script demands detail. New potentials constantly emerge that had not been reckoned with while charting the script. Ideas for a play are one thing, the script quite another. Ideas that seemed perfectly appropriate, even exciting, when initially contemplated, may turn sour when you try to make actual characters carry them out. Other ideas that had initially seemed merely satisfactory may assume unexpected life. Ideas are slippery; they quickly metamorphose into surprising shapes once they hit the page. A play (especially a good one) contains so many variables that it is impossible to predict what form an idea will take until you write the script—and sometimes not until you see it in rehearsal. While you write, new possibilities are always pressing for your attention. Some may lead to a high road of excitement, while others lead down a primrose path to frustration. At every turn you are also apt to encounter a weakness in the script you had not anticipated. Each new potential and each exposed weakness will occasion some reconsideration of the original idea. One new potential may preclude another; one solution to an exposed weakness may alter later plans. At times, you will want to chuck the whole mess. At others, you will become so enthralled with new turns of events, you cannot wait to write the next page.

Scripting a play is full of so many pinnacles of excitement and quagmires of frustration that it is a wonder anyone does it at all. Although one is tempted to think of script writers as masochists who like hitting themselves over the head with a hammer because it feels so good when they stop, this does not have to be the case. Drafting a play script can and should be an exciting but relaxed undertaking—a matter of exploring the material, testing it, finding its most appropriate form and tone. The first draft lays down the groundwork and opens up the weaknesses and possibilities to full view. Each successive draft brings you closer to the play's potential. More will be said about the process of drafting in a later chapter; for now the important thing is to recognize that the script is the product of one's best guess at the intended play. It is as though the play had a will the playwright seeks to discover. This involves looking for the common ground on which the most promising possibilities can all operate and anticipating a stage existence which is a step removed from the words being written on the page.

Making a good guess at the intended play is the best any playwright can hope to do. Even the most seasoned playwright encounters surprises in the process of scripting and even in rehearsal. When a play arrives on the boards and becomes now a play rather than a play script, it assumes many new dimensions. Among all those facets of the play directly experienced by the audience (setting, lights, costumes, properties, activities, sounds, and dialogue), only dialogue is directly controlled by the playwright. All the others are provided by co-workers in the theatre: directors, actors, and designers. Nevertheless, the playwright may exert an indirect control over all these other facets. In contriving a particular set of tensions for the play, characterizing the world in a particular way, and setting in motion a clear action, the playwright implies all facets of the play's experience. The dialogue itself is an overt symptom of the forces at work in a play, forces that produce other effects as well. Since dialogue is the one effect the playwright controls directly, a discussion of scripting appropriately begins with dialogue.

Dialogue as Action

We have already seen how action is the essence of the dramatic mode. This principle has far-reaching implications. In the case of dialogue, it means that a speech must first and foremost be an action. This is the telling difference between dramatic dialogue and dialogue in a narrative. Dramatic action calls for characters to do things, in the widest sense of the word "do." They exert their wills, have impact on their situations, create new situations, and affect each other. A speech is every bit as capable of carrying an action as a physical act; in some respects speech has greater capabilities because words can carry subtleties and shadings no overt physical act can. Some plays, such as those of Racine or Chekhov, contain relatively little physical activity, yet they are full of action. When characters speak they are acting upon or reacting to their situation. One character's remark may be a response to a prior speech or to something in the circumstances. These actions and reactions are the stuff of drama.

Physical activity and dialogue serve to reinforce each other. The movement of an actor about a stage tells a great deal about the character's state of mind, emotion, and intent. The audience is affected on a first—even primal—level. In much the same way as two kittens at play read each other's minds, we can sense physical activities on stage. Each movement can (and should) vivify the inner world of the characters. Physical activity, however, is restricted to conveying the emotion and tone of the characters. It can provoke strong reactions from us on a visceral level, but it cannot convey either the subtleties or the wider significance that dialogue can. In cinema some of these subtleties may be caught in close-ups unavailable in the theatre, but it still requires words to catch meanings that can carry us beyond the immediate. There has been a movement afoot to annihilate "the theatre of language" on the grounds that pantomime is the pure stuff of theatre. This view, orginating with the Futurists and the Theatricalists of the early twentieth century and championed later by Antonin Artaud, appears today in the work of such directors as Jerzsy Grotowski and Richard Schechner. What seems to be emerging now, however, as reflected in the plays of Edward Bond and Peter Handke, is a renewed interest in the way words enrich dramatic action precisely because they can be actions themselves. The era of stage writhing and moaning seems to be over.

Because all stage action is intended to affect an audience, the place to start with dialogue is to see it in relation to audience. In the theatre no interaction is more important than that between the actors occupying the characters' world and the audience occupying their own. Dialogue is the richest, fullest bridge between the two worlds, so anything that strengthens that bridge enhances the play as a whole. A list of the functions of dialogue may help to clarify its contributions:

1. *Dialogue is a purveyor of action:* In any play, the audience is made aware of action in the forms of physical activity, body language, gesture, facial expression, vocal tone, and dialogue. At best, all of these are action. Certainly, no speech justifies itself without being an action.

2. *Dialogue enhances meaning.* A mute play, a pantomime, has remarkable capacity to convey meaning. Nevertheless, physical activity and bodily expression are limited, capable of communicating only certain kinds of information and emotional tone. Behind these sensations may be rich or complex ideas and subtleties of feeling only words can express. Ideally, dialogue builds from the overt expressions of mime, enlarging and lending variety to the dramatic experience.

3. *Dialogue establishes rhythm and tempo.* Rhythm, the play's pattern of forward movement through time, and tempo, the speed of the movement, derive from both overall tone and the release of emotional energy. In performance, they are controlled by the actors' actual movement and vocal patterns. For the playwright, dialogue is the one dependable tool available to control the play in performance on these scores. If the dialogue captures a strong sense of rhythm, it will be difficult to run counter to it and all movement is apt to reflect it.

4. *Dialogue is a means of characterization.* Dialogue is one of the primary ways an audience grasps the differences between one character and another—which is what characterization is all about. It is true that what is most telling are the decisions and actions undertaken by the character; but the most vivid and immediate clue we have is dialogue. The frequency and timing of speeches, the manner of speaking, the uses of imagery, how speeches relate to other actions, how they relate to the speeches and actions of others—these are all telling signs of the inner workings of a character.

5. *Finally, dialogue is a way of characterizing the world of the play.* Through style (patterns of sentences, uses of imagery, selection of words), dialogue gives us a vivid sense of the nature of the world the characters occupy. To some extent these emanate from the "local color" employed to convey the sense of an actual place (as in Synge's Ireland or Williams's American South) and to some extent they are the product of the particular perspective of the playwright (as in Shakespeare's soliloquies or Pinter's pauses).

More than one of these functions should be in operation at any one moment in the course of a play. One speech cannot be dedicated to characterization, the next to the world of the play, the next to rhythm, the next to meaning, and the next to action. Ideally, all functions are in operation all the time.

As a bridge to the audience, dialogue must first of all be comprehensible. This is not a matter of playing down to an audience, of making sure that even the slowest among them understands what is going on. The ideas involved might be very complex, but the audience needs to sense at once how any one speech is an action. Consider for a moment how a gathered audience differs from a solitary reader. They have not the freedom to skip forward, to take things faster or slower, or to look back at something they did not quite grasp the first time. They must engage with the play *as it happens.* They need to sense the import of every means of expression (body stances, activities, gestures, facial expressions, vocal intonations, and the lines themselves) the moment they occur. This does not prevent dialogue from having meanings beyond those immediately apparent; it only means that without this, the audience will not grasp any other meaning. If they are not engaged on the level of action, they are not engaged.

The surest way to present comprehensible dialogue is to be sure that each speech is indeed an action—something said in order to affect another character, the situation, or the character himself. The speech should be, as well, a *single* action because if it is made to carry the burden of multiple actions, it quickly becomes incomprehensible. Respecting this principle, one can even write quite long speeches. A good Shakespearean soliloquy illustrates a long speech which is still a single action. In contrast, here is a sequence of incomprehensible dialogue. The lines are not actions. As a result notice how difficult they are to follow, especially if you were only to hear them:

HIERONYMUS

In other matters, all facets being equal of course, as we should have to say, the need for attentive care is demonstrably apparent, as you well know, having dealt with this over some weeks to the detriment of your health, as it were.

HILDEGARDE

Yes, but you recall, I am sure, how it was that Father's idea for the amelioration of the family's economic status became distorted in the hands of Uncle Humbert, who had always been contrary.

HIERONYMUS

Yes, indeed I do remember that Humbert was never to be relied upon in matters of finance. As a matter of fact, it has been often observed that the beneficence of your forebears had been more than a little dissipated by that side of the family.

HILDEGARDE

That most certainly is a verity. To which I might add that cousin Hazel was ever imprudent, and presently her whereabouts are totally unknown, no doubt due to her having always been altogether too casual in her dealings with men.

HIERONYMUS

I had always thought that my own cousin Hesther was the most blithely inattentive young lady in the world, but I have had to reverse my thinking once you narrated the stories you know about your cousin Hazel.

There are several reasons why this dialogue is incomprehensible. First, it is about nothing that matters now; it is empty and vacuous talk. Second, as the speeches and sentences are all approximately the same length, they become deadly after a while. Trying to listen to them, we gradually become anesthetized to any meaning they might have. Third, the choice of words prevents any richness or extension of meaning. The words are esoteric and simply unexciting. Words such as "facets," "demonstrably," "amelioration," "beneficence," and "verity" are not particularly engaging words. They are flat, pretentious, and abstract. Fourth, the speakers resort to the passive voice ("it has often been observed," "became distorted in the hands of") and this also deadens the effect. Finally, the sentence structure is awkward and self-conscious. So many clauses and sub-clauses interfere with the main idea that we begin to wonder if there is one. Behind all these failings is the simple fact that none of these speeches attempts to change anything or affect anyone. They are not actions.

These are probably the most common failings in bad dialogue; fortunately, no playwright is likely to exhibit all of them at once. Still, if there is any single root cause of these failings, it is the failure to make lines actions. An audience will not comprehend dialogue unless it matters, and it will not matter unless it is leading somewhere, and it will not lead anywhere unless it is action.

Suppose we remedy the dialogue between Hieronymous and Hildegarde by dealing with the superficial failings: that is, by varying the length of speeches and sentences, by making the wording concrete, and by rendering the structure less awkward and self-conscious. This might be the result:

HIERONYMOUS
What you have been through these past few weeks must make you realize how careful you should be about money.

HILDEGARDE
Yes, but this was not all my fault. Father tried to get the family out of this scrape, but Uncle Humbert squandered what little we had on some flim-flam scheme.

HIERONYMOUS
Like everyone on that side of the family, Humbert was always a sucker.

HILDEGARDE
Exactly. Remember how his daughter Hazel disappeared one day, probably taken in by one of her sugar-daddy friends?

HIERONYMOUS
She was every bit as bad as my cousin Hesther—no, worse. Much worse!

This is a vast improvement. For one thing, we can understand what they are saying. There is some variety now so that some things seem more important than others. Although Hieronymus and Hildegarde are saying essentially the same things as in the prior version, we now have the idea that these might be real people whose lives involve other people. We are much more willing to attend to what they are saying. Still, the scene is going nowhere. The discussion is academic and does not seem to have any immediacy for the characters or for us. So while we may comprehend the dialogue in the narrow sense of the word "comprehend," in a larger sense, we still do not. "Comprehend" means to take in, to embrace, to make something a part of oneself. If dialogue is written in such a way that we do not care to take it in, it ends up not fully comprehensible.

The second requirement of dialogue is that it be strongly rooted in character. Our Hieronymus-Hildegarde scene failed on this score, even in the revision. In neither version do the lines seem to express a personality. No clear motivation prompts these lines. Hieronymus talks just like Hildegarde and vice versa; they are virtually indistinguishable one from the other. The fact that all the names, relatives included, start with an "H" does not help. Characters need to be comprehensible, too. The first way this can happen is to take every opportunity to distinguish one from the other and dialogue is a prime opportunity. Manner of speech vividly reveals character. It tells us something specific and concrete about the nature of the character's inner life as well as about social background. If dialogue is action, it will also reveal motivation.

Stage Directions

Important as dialogue may be, it is ultimately only a facet of a stage play. The full play entails setting, lights, costuming, sound, properties, and actors moving, miming, gesturing, and accomplishing stage business. Among them all, the primary theatrical mode is in the encounter of actor and audience. The word is ancillary to this; it enhances, enlarges, and enriches action. But words are not the only actions. The Theatricalists of this century are fond of pointing out that pantomime is the pure stuff of theatre. They are right—but the theatre has never bothered itself much about being "pure." Words have a way of so augmenting the meaning of a play and its outward relevance that dispensing with language inevitably weakens the theatrical experience.

It is also true that, above all else, an audience believes what it sees— "seeing is believing." A character speaking one thought and conveying another in action is taken as a liar. While the word "audience" comes from the Latin *audire* ("to hear"), the word "theatre" comes from the Greek *theatron* (or "seeing place"). The etymology suggests that theatre is first and foremost a seeing experience.

All this might indicate that a playwright would be wise to pay greatest attention to the stage directions. If theatre is a "seeing place," then what the audience is to see would seem the playwright's main concern. It is true that the playwright must write with the whole stage in mind, but this does not mean that stage directions should consume the playwright's attention. Stage directions have a value, but it is very limited. They are, after all, only descriptions—they are not the actual event. Notice how few of them appear in the works of Shakespeare or Molière, whose plays nevertheless play vividly upon visual effect. The rich theatrical worlds of their plays were implicit in the overall context and in the dialogue; little else is needed.

Stage directions do not in fact control anything. A playwright may reasonably expect the dialogue to be spoken on stage as written; he cannot expect stage directions to be so honored. Indeed, some directors conscientiously cross out all stage directions before they start their work. This is not a comment on the perversity of stage directors. It is a comment on a fundamental condition of the stage: the stage existence of a play is tied each time to its particular theatre, stage, actors, and audience. That is the province of the director. The playwright has no business invading it, if for no other reason than the fact that he can know nothing about those particular theatres, stages, actors, and audiences. The playwright needs to attend to charting the course of the play, laying down the essential context and set of tensions for its action. The director may then adapt this to the actual space of a theatre and its stage, to the actors who are to embody the characters and to the expected audience. "Stage directions" is perhaps a misnomer, since the real directions are those issued by the director.

So what use are stage directions? They serve to visualize whatever is not evident in the dialogue; they help to establish rhythm and tempo. Beyond that, they are useless. In the early drafts of a play, stage directions may help the playwright maintain a mental picture of the stage. If many remain in later drafts, however, they sound a warning that dialogue is not doing its job—a fundamental weakness. There is a simple test for this: any stage direction which clarifies a crucial use of stage space, establishes a rhythm, or describes essential gestures or business belongs in the script. All others do not and these include most of the single adverbs many unsure dramatists are fond of using: "tenderly," "violently," "pensively," "passionately." These usually appear because the lines themselves are insufficient; only rarely should there be such ambiguity that an adverb is needed to clarify the effect sought. In general, remember that the audience does not hear your stage directions.

There are two kinds of stage directions. The first is the stage direction which describes a technical effect, belonging to scenery, lights, sound, properties, or costumes. The second is the direction which details an action to be accomplished by the actors. The first is useful at the outset of the play in describing the setting of the play and the way it relates outward to the audience. After that, this type is used sparingly to describe only essential effects. The second type appears only when there is a possible ambiguity of meaning in the dialogue or when physical action takes precedence.

Below is a sequence of dialogue from Arthur Miller's *Death of a Salesman* which illustrates both the restrained use of stage directions and the rich yet economical use of dialogue. At the outset of the whole play, the stage directions establish the crucial need for several realms of action: the simultaneous presence on stage of the Lomans' kitchen, master bedroom, and upstairs bedroom, with the implied presence of a parlor behind the kitchen. The house is set against a panoramic view of apartment houses. In addition, the yard surrounding the house provides yet another realm of action. In this scene, two realms are in use: the upstairs bedroom in which the brothers Happy and Biff are about to retire for the night, and the kitchen, in which their father Willy moves about reliving the past in his imagination. As a result, there is a third realm implied, the world Willy Loman once knew. Notice how the dialogue and the described uses of the stage enact the scene's basic tensions:

BIFF

Remember Bill Oliver?

HAPPY

Sure, Oliver is very big now. You want to work for him again?

BIFF

No, but when I quit he said something to me. He put his arm on my shoulder, and he said, "Biff, if you ever need anything, come to me."

HAPPY

I remember that. That sounds good.

BIFF

I think I'll go see him. If I could get ten thousand or even seven or eight thousand dollars I could buy a beautiful ranch.

HAPPY

I bet he'd back you. 'Cause he thought highly of you, Biff. I mean, they all do. You're well-liked, Biff. That's why I say to come back here, and we both have the apartment. And I'm tellin' you, Biff, any babe you want . . .

BIFF

No, with a ranch I could do the work I like and still be something. I just wonder if Oliver still thinks I stole that carton of basketballs.

HAPPY

Oh, he probably forgot that long ago. It's almost ten years. You're too sensitive. Anyway, he didn't really fire you.

BIFF

Well, I think he was going to. I think that's why I quit. I was never sure whether he knew or not. I know he thought the world of me, though. I was the only one he'd let lock up the place.

WILLY

(Below.) You gonna wash the engine, Biff?

HAPPY

Shh!

(BIFF looks at HAPPY, who is gazing down, listening. WILLY is mumbling in the parlor.)

HAPPY

You hear that?

(They listen. WILLY laughs warmly.)

BIFF

(Growing angry.) Doesn't he know Mom can hear that?

WILLY

Don't get your sweater dirty, Biff!

(A look of pain crosses BIFF's face.)

HAPPY

Isn't that terrible? Don't leave again, will you? You'll find a job here. You gotta stick around. I don't know what to do about him. It's getting embarrassing.

WILLY

What a simonizing job!

BIFF

Mom's hearing that!

WILLY

No kiddin', Biff, you got a date? Wonderful!

HAPPY

Go to sleep. But talk to him in the morning, will you?

BIFF

(Reluctantly getting into bed.)

With her in the house. Brother!

HAPPY

(Getting into bed.)

I wish you'd have a good talk with him.

(The light on their room begins to fade.)

BIFF

(To himself in bed.)

That selfish, stupid . . .

HAPPY

Sh . . . Sleep, Biff.

(Their light is out. Well before they have finished speaking, WILLY's form is dimly seen below in the darkened kitchen. He opens the refrigerator, searches in there, and takes out a bottle of milk. The apartment houses are fading out, and the entire house and surrounding become covered with leaves. Music insinuates itself as the leaves appear.)

WILLY

Just wanna be careful with those girls, Biff, that's all. Don't make any promises. No promises of any kind. Because a girl, y'know, they always believe what you tell 'em, and you're very young, Biff, you're too young to be talking seriously to girls.

(Light rises on the kitchen. WILLY, talking, shuts the refrigerator door and comes downstage to the kitchen table. He pours milk into a glass. He is totally immersed in himself, smiling faintly.)

WILLY

Too young entirely, Biff. You want to watch your schooling first. Then when you're all set, there'll be plenty of girls for a boy like you.

(He smiles broadly at a kitchen chair.)

That so? The girls pay for you?

(He laughs.)

Boy, you must really be makin' a hit.

(WILLY is gradually addressing—physically—a point offstage, speaking through the wall of the kitchen, and his voice has been rising in volume to that of normal conversation.)

I been wondering why you polish the car so careful. Ha! Don't leave the hubcaps, boys. Get the chamois to the hubcaps. Happy, use newspaper on the windows, it's the easiest thing. Show him how to do it, Biff! You see, Happy? Pad it up, use it like a pad. That's it, that's it, good work. You're doin' all right, Hap.

(He pauses, then nods in approbation for a few seconds.)

In this sequence, several things are worth pointing out. The scene builds on a set of tensions:

1. Between Biff and Happy on plans for Biff's future.
2. Between them and Willy on his embarrasing loss of touch with reality.
3. Between the present and the past.

The action begins on the first tension and moves through the next two. There is just enough dialogue and stage direction to clarify the tensions, but not so much as to work them to death. A certain amount of implied tension is left to suggest a greater depth. This is good playwriting. It takes into account the stage, uses the dialogue to suggest a fuller existence, yet leaves a margin of latitude for the actors, designers, and director to exercise their talents. It might be noted that some of these ideas concerning the staging of this particular play derived from consultation with the designer Jo Mielziner and from the rehearsal process. Those that appear as stage directions are only those necessary to clarify the uses of the stage and the rhythm necessary to the play's effect.

The Second Dialogue and the Third Factor

The term "second dialogue," as coined by Maurice Maeterlinck, refers to an unspoken interaction between characters taking place simultaneously with the overt dialogue. It is as if the characters were speaking two dialogues at once, the second implied by the first. It is substantially the same as the "subtext" spoken of by Konstantin Stanislavsky. Whatever term one might use, the presence of an implied dialogue to accompany the overt one enhances and deepens dramatic action. The action assumes new dimensions when action is conducted on levels other than the spoken word, and implication and allusion are useful dramatic devices. People in real life do not always say what they mean, yet the implied meaning is perfectly clear—even when it contradicts what the person is actually saying. When you are asked "How are you?" you know this is rarely a request for information on health. Moreover, you can distinguish readily between a perfunctory courtesy and a genuine interest. Whenever in life you encounter someone clearly meaning something other than what is said, you are brought up short and you listen more closely. In the theatre, that is just what we want, so characters often communicate this way.

There is another reason for implied dialogue: although the theatre depends upon the objective experience of seeing and hearing, it also seeks to give us a glimmer of the inner lives of the characters, letting us in far enough that we may join their experience vicariously on one occasion or shudder in the recognition of a wicked impulse on another. For us to glimpse the inner lives of the characters, the playwright and fellow theatre artists must resort to a complex of expressions. No single avenue of expression will do. Audiences grasp the truth through a combination of context, exposition, stage effects, physical activity, and dialogue. From them, the audience fashions a "second dialogue" in their minds. Of course, they can do this only if details are carefully calculated to dovetail on a significance or meaning.

This dovetailing calls for an outside reference point to pull the concerns of the characters to the surface. Two characters talking at each other, airing their conflict directly, will produce thin and flat drama. Drama depends on a polarity to produce tension. But the tension drawn between two poles alone has no dimension or depth. We learn all we need to know about the characters so quickly that we feel we know more than we want to know and we tire of it all. The "third factor" is the most useful way to gain dimension and depth, and with them, interest.

The third factor is that outside reference point that puts the dramatic tension into relief. The third factor may be a third character—and most often is. For this reason it is much easier to write a three-character scene than a two-character scene. Three characters provide the opportunity for constantly shifting polarities. You may at first draw tension between characters A and B, using C as a third factor. The next moment, character C may find himself at the opposite pole from A, while B serves as third factor. In terms of the overall dynamics of a play, the action frequently requires an outside force, a third character for example, to provide the catalyst to push the play to its crisis.

When scenes and whole plays involve only two characters, an absent character or some object may serve as third factor. There may be any number of third factors in a play, but only one is in use at a time. For awhile, the Negro in the basement is that third factor in Harold Pinter's play "The Room"; similarly, at different moments throughout the play, Godot functions as a third factor in Samuel Beckett's *Waiting for Godot*. Objects may carry out this function too. The park bench—and later the knife—are third factors in Edward Albee's "The Zoo Story." The third factor can even be imaginary (the knife in Eugene Ionesco's "The Lesson") or it may be a simple device suggesting other people (the telephone in William Gibson's *Two for the Seesaw*). A curious case in point might be the tape recorder in Samuel Beckett's "Krapp's Last Tape." While only one character is physically present on stage, a second character representing his former selves is present through tape recordings. For the third factor, Beckett at times turns to the tape recorder, then tape spools, and bananas. There is only one character in Chekhov's "On the Harmfulness of Tobacco," quoted in Chapter 4. His audience serves as the second character; the offstage wife, the pole under the moon, and his frock coat are third factors.

Here is a simple, straightforward example of the third factor serving to produce a second dialogue:

ALICE

Are you out of your mind? Those socks don't match. Can't you see that? Look! One's brown, the other's blue.

GEORGE

Umh.

ALICE

Well? Take them off. Find the right ones and put them on.

GEORGE

I don't have time.

ALICE

Well, you take time. What kind of impression do you want to make out there? They'll snigger.

GEORGE

I suppose it does your soul good to find my socks don't match. Gives you a chance to feel superior.

ALICE

You know why they don't match, don't you? Because you never pay any attention to what you're doing. That's why!

GEORGE

Is that so?

ALICE

Yes, it's so. Now you're going to tell me your mind is on higher things. Oh, sure, it's always on higher things. They're so high your life right here on earth is a mess.

GEORGE
(Putting on a sport jacket.)
Well, my mind is now on a higher thing than my socks. I'm thinking about my jacket.

ALICE

Oh, fine.
(She sees the jacket.)
Wait a minute. You can't wear a plaid jacket with striped trousers.

GEORGE

I can, too. Look. And I'll take this polka dot tie to go with it.

ALICE

You look like a clown.

GEORGE

Off I go.
(He starts for the door.)

ALICE

You can't go out looking like that!

GEORGE

Sure I can. Just watch me.

ALICE

All right. See if I care. You're the one that looks like Bozo, not me.

GEORGE

Right. When I enter the boardroom, people will mutter, "What's the matter with that guy's wife that she doesn't tell him he's all mismatched?" That's what they'll say.
(He leaves.)

ALICE

George! Stop! Come back here and make yourself look decent. George!

(There is no answer. She sits on the bed in frustrated exhaustion. After a few moments, the door opens slowly. GEORGE enters quietly, taking off his jacket. ALICE does not notice him until he speaks.)

GEORGE

Oh, hell, I can't do it. I look ludicrous.

(She looks up. He smiles sheepishly.)

ALICE

You sure do.

(They laugh and embrace.)

George's clothes constitute the third factor here. They are not the real subject of conversation, but they provide a point of reference to pull to the surface the feelings of the two characters. The second dialogue is clear and concise. It might be phrased this way:

ALICE

I get so tired of the way you ignore the little things that count. Your life is a mess just because of that.

GEORGE

And I get tired of the way you're always pointing out my petty failings.

ALICE

You're ridiculous.

GEORGE

Yes, I guess I am.

ALICE

I love you, anyway.

GEORGE

I love you, too.

This is nice and short; it is also rather thin and uninteresting. The dispute over the socks and sports jacket helps to sustain the scene, give it variety and interest, and provide a reference point that crystalizes the relationship.

The third factor may also be a ritual, an outward activity that gives focus to the scene. While one thing is transpiring between characters, altering their relationship, they are ostensibly doing something else. Kaufman and Hart used this to grand advantage in their comedy *You Can't Take It With You* in which every character had a favorite activity. Sometimes that activity may take on strange, mysterious, or sinister qualities and so enhance dramatic interest. Playwrights such as Sam Shepard, Tom Stoppard, Harold Pinter, and Samuel Beckett are fond of this device. We think at once of the haircut in *Buried Child*, the coin flipping in *Rosencrantz and Guildenstern Are Dead*, the shredding of a newspaper in *The Birthday Party*, or the meticulous placement of Hamm's chair in *Endgame. The Birthday Party* has a bizarre scene with an interrogation of poor Stanley Webber conducted by the strange duo of Goldberg and McCann. Notice how something else seems to be happening while the interrogation goes forward. The sequence below is preceded by a line of questioning about Stanley's wife—whom he may or may not have killed and who, for that matter, may never have existed. Suddenly, the questions take off in a new direction:

GOLDBERG

Is the number 846 possible or necessary?

STANLEY

Neither.

GOLDBERG

Wrong! Is the number 846 possible or necessary?

STANLEY

Both.

GOLDBERG

Wrong! It's necessary but not possible.

STANLEY

Both.

GOLDBERG

Wrong! Why do you think the number 846 is necessarily possible?

STANLEY

Must be.

GOLDBERG

Wrong! It's only necessarily necessary! We admit possibility only after we grant necessity. It is possible because necessary but by no means necessary through possibility. The possibility can only be assumed after the proof of necessity.

McCANN

Right!

GOLDBERG

Right? Of course right! We're right and you're wrong, Webber, all along the line.

McCANN

All along the line!

GOLDBERG
Where is your lechery leading you?

McCANN
You'll pay for this.

GOLDBERG
You stuff yourself with dry toast.

McCANN
You contaminate womankind.

GOLDBERG
Why don't you pay the rent?

McCANN
Mother defiler!

GOLDBERG
Why do you pick your nose?

McCANN
I demand justice!

GOLDBERG
What's your trade?

McCANN
What about Ireland?

GOLDBERG
What's your trade?

STANLEY
I play the piano.

GOLDBERG
How many fingers do you use?

STANLEY
No hands!

GOLDBERG
No society would touch you. Not even a building society.

McCANN
You're a traitor to the cloth.

GOLDBERG
What do you use for pajamas?

STANLEY
Nothing.

GOLDBERG
You verminate the sheet of your birth.

McCANN
What about the Albigensenist heresy?

GOLDBERG
Who watered the wicket in Melbourne?

McCANN

What about the blessed Oliver Plunkett?

GOLDBERG

Speak up, Webber. Why did the chicken cross the road?

STANLEY

He wanted to—he wanted to—he wanted to . . .

McCANN

He doesn't know!

GOLDBERG

Why did the chicken cross the road?

STANLEY

He wanted . . .

McCANN

He doesn't know. He doesn't know which came first!

GOLDBERG

Which came first?

McCANN

Chicken? Egg? Which came first?

GOLDBERG and McCANN

Which came first? Which came first? Which came first?

(STANLEY screams.)

By virtue of relentless yet incoherent force, the line of questioning Goldberg and McCann inflict on Stanley becomes menacing. Stanley is expected to account on the spot for the Albigensian heresy and picking his nose and the Irish question and his sleeping habits. By pounding away at him in this manner, Goldberg and McCann manage to demolish the last vestiges of Stanley's ego. The hammering of meaningless questions becomes a ritual and a third factor in the tension between Stanley and the two strange men. The ritual virtually becomes an outside force that propels the scene forward.

The third factor, whether in the form of an object or an activity, is a valuable way to augment dramatic tension and interest. Indeed, the greater the disparity between the third factor and the second dialogue, the more powerful the scene. In the "proposal scene" in *The Cherry Orchard*, quoted in Chapter 3, the third factor comes in the form of the galoshes Varya pretends to be looking for, while the second dialogue is about a longing to marry. In the scene in Anton Schill's grocery store in Friedrich Duerrenmatt's *The Visit*, the yellow shoes constitute a third factor, while the second dialogue has to do with greed and murder. In the preceding scene from *The Birthday Party*, the third factor is absurd questioning and the second dialogue is one of menace and threat.

Ironies: Who Knows What When?

If dramatic momentum is intensified by disparity between the third factor and the second dialogue, it is also strengthened by the use of ironies deriving from a disparity between what one person knows and what another knows. The forward movement of a play derives from curiosity. One character strives to know something which another already knows, while we in the audience know only that the other does know it. We are curious in our way and the characters in theirs. A play is a voyage of discovery for characters and audience alike.

So it is for the playwright as well, especially while composing the first draft. For all the charting you may do beforehand, the actual script is another matter. You discover things about your characters you had not known were there. They sometimes seem to take on a will of their own and insist on moving in directions the scenario does not provide. The immediate circumstances of your play, moment by moment, cannot be entirely foreseen—nor can the full potential of any of the characters. So writing the first draft produces fascinating new possibilities with each new speech, action, and reaction. In successive drafts these can be smoothed out to take advantage of those that count and squelch the others.

In some ways, the final dramatic script reflects this process in a compact and controlled way. Over the weeks and months of composing the play, the playwright has undergone an elaborate series of discoveries, not altogether coherent but often exciting. Over a two-hour period the audience, encountering the play, its world, and characters, undergoes an exciting, but hopefully coherent series of discoveries. Furthermore, the characters have no knowledge of what will happen next and they should find themselves continually surprised, having to adapt, adjust, make new decisions, abandon old ones.

With such unfoldings, ironies become immensely useful. Part of the thrill of *Oedipus Rex* derives from the audience knowing what Oedipus does not know: that he is searching for himself when he launches the effort to rid Thebes of the murderer of Laius. Humor or tragic pathos in a play depend upon irony. A speech from the conclusion of Tom Stoppard's play *Jumpers* provides a striking example. The humor derives from the appearance of a man who seems to know what he is talking about, the words themselves seeming to make sense for a moment, until suddenly we recognize that it is outrageous gibberish:

CROUCH

I think we might proceed with our opening statements—"Man—good, bad or indifferent?"—Sir Archibald.

USHER

Call Sir Archibald Jumper!

ECHO

Call Sir Archibald Jumper!

> (ARCHIE swings in, hanging on a rope. GEORGE remains prone. Enormous applause, unrealistically cut off, for ARCHIE.)

ARCHIE

Mr. Crouch, ladies and gentlemen. "Man—good, bad or indifferent?" Indeed, if moon mad herd instinct, is God dad the inference?—to take another point: If goons in mood, by Gad is sin different or banned good f'r'instance?—thirdly: out of the ether, random nucleic acid testes or neither universa vice, to name but one—fourthly: If the necessary being isn't, surely mother of invention as Voltaire said, not to mention Darwin different from the origin of the specious—to sum up: Super, both natural and stitious, sexual ergo cogito er go-go sometimes, as Descartes said, and who are we? Thank you.

> (Shattering applause. The USHERS hold up score cards: "9.7"—"9.9"—"9.8".)

This, of course, is sheer playfulness. It is funny because the irony works on so elaborate a scale. First, the man seems to be making sense, with phrases that strike familiar resonance, but the harder we listen, the less sense we can find, until we give up in a spasm of laughter. The irony is even richer for an audience who knows something about the history of philosophy, because then the disparities between the original phrases of Voltaire, Descartes, Darwin and the phrases Sir Archibald has concocted, add still more absurdity. Tragic effects depend as much on irony as comic ones, as we shall see shortly. For tragedy or comedy, irony is a strong and effective way of catching up the audience's interest.

The characters too experience disparities in knowledge; some in fact suffer for it. None of them should ever know all he wants or needs to know. We the audience know some things that one of the characters—but not the others—might know. We may be aware that another character knows something we would dearly like to know. One character might know something another character's life depended upon, and it will make all the difference when and how he finds out. Sometimes, a scene which is not working well in the writing may suddenly open up by the simple remedy of robbing a character or the audience of a piece of knowledge.

At the outset of a play, we the audience know next to nothing, while the characters, who supposedly have been living their lives all along, are well-versed in what is happening. It is like stumbling into a room unannounced and are trying to get the wavelength of what is happening. Gradually we catch on. Then we may surpass the characters in understanding, learn things they do not know, and perceive things in ways that are distinctly our own. All of these are ironies and all of them contribute both depth and momentum. When, for example, the Chorus in *Oedipus Rex* rejoices at the news of the death of Polybus, Oedipus's supposed father, we know better. We are wiser and know that there is no cause for joy, but quite the reverse. Here is a more recent example—the opening to *A Soldier's Play* by Charles Fuller:

> (AS THE PLAY OPENS, the stage is black. In the background, rising in volume, we hear the song "Don't Sit under the Apple Tree," sung by the Andrews Sisters. Quite suddenly, in a sharp though narrow beam of light, in limbo, TECH/SERGEANT VERNON C. WATERS, a well-built, light-brown-skinned man in a World War II, winter army uniform, is seen down on all fours. He is stinking drunk, trying to stand and mumbling to himself.)

WATERS

(Repeating.) They'll still hate you! They still hate you. . . . They still hate you!

> (WATERS is laughing as suddenly someone steps into the light. (We never see this person.) He is holding a .45 calibre pistol. He lifts it swiftly and ominously toward WATERS' head and fires. WATERS is knocked over backward. He is dead. The music has stopped and there is a strong silence on stage.)

VOICE

Le's go!

> (The man with the gun takes a step, then stops. He points the gun at WATERS again and fires a second time. There is another silence as limbo is plunged into darkness and the barracks is just as quickly lit. We are in the barracks of Company B, 221st Chemical Smoke Generating Company, at Fort Neal. Five black enlisted men stand at "parade rest" with their hands above their heads and submit to a search . . .

Almost all of this opening is visual, accompanied by sparse dialogue. Yet it gives us a privileged piece of knowledge. We have seen Waters shot. We are not able to see the man who did it. He seems to have a companion who shouts "Le's go!" Chances are that we are going to meet the murderer in the course of the play. Perhaps we are looking at him now as the barracks scene begins. We and two characters know some things about this murder that the others do not know. Part of the momentum of the play derives from this disparity.

Comedy also calls for such a disparity, although it is often more complex. Misunderstandings and mistaken identities are the stuff of extreme comedy and farce and the orchestration of who knows what when can make all the difference. What one character knows rarely corresponds with what another knows and, while we in the audience generally know more than anybody, there are still gaps that make us curious. The action moves forward through all manner of misunderstandings and mistaken identities until all the pieces of information fall into place. We are carried along knowing that they have to fall into place sooner or later. In Oscar Wilde's *The Importance of Being Earnest*, we know for a long time that Jack Worthing was a foundling left as a baby in a handbag at the cloakroom of Victoria Station, the Brighton Line. We know that ever since Jack has lovingly kept that handbag as the only mother he ever had. We do not know that Miss Prism, governess to Jack's ward Cecily, had once lost such a handbag with a baby in it. The minute Jack learns this news, he rushes off to get the handbag and show it to Miss Prism:

JACK

Is this the handbag, Miss Prism? Examine it carefully before you speak. The happiness of more than one life depends on your answer.

MISS PRISM

(Calmly.) It seems to be mine . . . The bag is undoubtedly mine. I am delighted to have it so unexpectedly restored to me. It has been a great inconvenience being without it all these years.

JACK

(In a pathetic voice.) Miss Prism, more is restored to you than this handbag. I was the baby you placed in it.

And now Jack rushes to embrace his new-found mother, only to discover that Miss Prism is intensely embarrassed, never having been anybody's mother. "Then, who am I?" Jack would like to know. These shifting ironies are the stuff out of which Wilde built the whole comedy.

As a general rule, whether comedy or tragedy, disparities of knowledge (ironies) lend depth, interest, and momentum to the action. The audience should always be aware of things they would like to know. No character should know all he needs or wants to know. This prompts a desire to know, a motivation for action, and a sense of anticipation. If everyone knows everything, the play is guaranteed to be dull.

Timing—*when* someone discovers a new bit of knowledge—is also important. It should happen when it makes a difference. The audience should not learn anything too soon or too late: too soon and it is gratuitous, a moot point, a matter of no importance; too late and the audience feels cheated. For the characters, however, it *can* be too late—learning something when it no longer can help, when the desperate need has passed and the decision made, can produce a poignant effect. But characters must not learn too soon. It is probably no accident that Aristotle's idea of *peripeteia* links discovery with reversal. The powerful reversal, a sudden change in circumstance, is much more powerful when linked with discovery. The crisis moment of most plays hinges on some kind of discovery, ranging from simply finding out a piece of news to realizing a significant truth. The latter is more common in serious drama and it usually occurs some time before the end of the play because realization entails a severe adjustment. Comedy, as in *The Importance of Being Earnest,* more commonly depends on a piece of news, so the crisis tends to occur much nearer to the end. Once we learn that Jack's name really is Ernest, and has been from birth, the play can end—and it does.

For you, the playwright, composing the play is initially a process of discovery. If a scene is not working well, it may be dull for the plain reason that people know too much. You may discover new possibilities simply by altering what one or another of the characters (including the audience) happens to know.

Exercises

1. Use one or more of the following objects as a "third factor" in a dramatic sketch:
   A hat
   A letter opener
   A book
   A rope
   A pair of binoculars

2. Select five photographs at random. Study them to find some common denominator, something that could link them as parts of the same story, much as movie stills seem separate until you see the movie. Write a scene based on the photographs.

3. Compose a dialogue in which two characters attempt to keep a third from knowing something. Compose another in which one character knows something the other two need to know. In this case, the two may or may not know that the other has this crucial information.

PART III

The Screen Media

8

Flashing Images:
Writing for Films

The title "flashing images" applies to both television and cinema, for both rely on images flashed across a screen. These flashing images substitute for the live presence of actors to convey dramatic action. Because such images can present a spectacle of human action in fictional worlds, the screen serves the dramatic mode well. The dramatic mode is no purer, no truer to itself, on stage than it is on screen—it simply has a longer tradition behind it. The screen comes from relatively recent technological developments: film has been with us barely a century and television only a few decades. Neither one looks at all like a theatre and both plainly use different material. Still, the great silver screen and the little screen both have the capacity to use time and space to present human action in imagined lives. Whenever the screen serves this purpose, the principles of drama apply as they do for the stage. Conflict, irony, incongruity, contrast, tension are fully as relevant here as for the stage. Those who manipulate the medium—screenwriter, director, actors, editor, and others—aim to affect an audience just as their counterparts in the theatre do. On these basic points, regardless of medium, the dramatic mode operates in much the same way.

Still, dealing with moving images instead of living actors has to make a difference—and it does. To make those images convey action calls for a different sort of manipulation than the stage requires. This alters matters considerably for everyone, dramatist included. The screen reduces the space to two dimensions, while the moveable camera enlarges it imaginatively into any place the camera can turn its eye. Time is cut up into the small units made by single runs of the camera — the shots. Actors and objects can be seen from all variety of angles and distances. The play of light and dark and of various colors can contribute to dramatic effect. All of these things render filmmaking a very different enterprise from play production.

Because of these differences the screenwriter is further removed from his medium than the playwright. Conversely, the screen director has more control over the dramatic experience prepared for an audience than the stage director. Another figure with no counterpart in the theatre, the film editor, also has a decisive voice in filmmaking. Thus, many factors feeding into the making of a film are outside the screenwriter's purview. Discouraging as this may sound, the fact remains that the basic premise of a film and the line of action it pursues are laid down in the screenplay, the work of the dramatist.

Any dramatist must bear in mind the distinctive features of a chosen medium. Screen media differ from the stage in five ways:

1. Images on a two-dimensional screen replace living actors in the three-dimensional space of the confined stage. The movement and interaction of these images, rather than the actual activity of living actors set immediately before us, convey the dramatic action.

2. The screen media depend heavily on technology. They require machinery and equipment both to produce a play and to witness it. The stage on the other hand requires only the proverbial two boards and a passion.

3. Screen time is much more flexible than stage time. Time is broken into the very short intervals of shots, the duration of single runs of the camera. Sustained blocks of time, whole scenes and acts, are required in stage plays.

4. Although the screen is reduced to two dimensions, the space it represents is remarkably variable. The camera can ignore the limitations of space and time. It can show now this, now that, pan, tilt, and dolly about. The camera can look at any corner of the fictional world the filmmakers choose. The stage, however, is a confined space and must remain so.

5. The screen media provide the possibility for constantly altering the relationship between the spectacle and the spectator. Audience members at a playhouse will see the play from fixed positions determined by the location of their seats. Moviegoers will seem to see things from a variety of viewpoints. The camera can take them in close, raise them above, drop them below, move them out, at will. The camera can even move into the subjective minds of characters if it chooses.

The implications of these five characteristics are far-reaching. The screen is an exciting arena for dramatic action and one that has exerted a far greater impact on the public than the little "cottage industry" of the stage could ever hope to do. Some of these implications strongly affect the work of the screenwriter; others are beyond a dramatist's control.

The silver screen reflecting projected images also differs in some ways from the little screen creating images from electronic impulses. Indeed, television tends to share more features with the stage than does film. To identify key differences in media, we will begin with a discussion of film.

The Interplay of Images

Cinema is essentially a visual art. In fact, until the invention of the "talkies" in 1927, it was solely a visual art. Many filmmakers were initially chagrined with the introduction of sound, unable or unwilling to adapt to this apparent fad. Others latched onto it with such fervor that they reproduced stage plays directly onto film and hired playwrights and stage actors to help create the new films. The intervening years have taught us that sound can provide depth and variety, but it serves chiefly to reinforce the visual experience—and not always through talk. Sounds of all sorts—music, noise, sound effects, as well as dialogue—can enhance visual images. But sound serves the image and it is the image that dominates. This is worth remembering, for the screenwriter must think visually and the screenplay ultimately is a description of visible action.

All the work of the screenwriter, the director, the technicians, the actors, the editor and others emerges in the form of a long, narrow band of celluloid. As a physical thing, it is quite unprepossessing, but the individual transparent photographs on that band can be run through a projector to create the illusion of movement, and can even create the further illusion of a life being lived among the characters. So, this flimsy band is at the heart of the magic of cinema. The cries of frustration and the foot-stamping of an angry movie audience when the mechanism breaks down are testimony to the power of this magic.

The physical film itself pulled off its reel, trivial as it seems, can tell us something about the material manipulated in making a movie. The film contains many individual transparent photographs which will pass through the projector at the rate of twenty-four a second. It requires 129,600 photographs to fill an hour and a half, the usual length of a feature film. That will make the narrow celluloid band about a mile and a half long. Looking at the band, we might notice that after a certain number of frames, often lasting only a few seconds when projected, the image changes completely, either seen from a new angle or replaced with another. These are shots created when the camera was turned off and restarted pointing somewhere else.

To someone unfamiliar with the language of film, these breaks might be puzzling, but the convention of alternating shots has become a familiar device readily accepted as a way of creating an imagined world in our minds. The juxtaposition of shots is the basic syntax of film. It tells us a world of things about the characters, their environment, what is important, what is at issue, and, in short, where the drama lies. Selecting shots is also none of the screenwriter's business. The director calls the shots and the editor organizes them. Still, the story, its atmosphere, the characters, and the overall tone help define them and these the screenwriter provides.

The cinema experience, once this band of celluloid starts its journey through the projector, gives us the sensation of riding about inside an all-seeing, dark box with a rectangular eye looking about another world, now closely, now at a distance, now from high up, now at eye-level. We trust it to turn its eye on things that matter. Since we must look at what it looks at, we naturally feel cheated if it shows us irrelevant, meaningless details.

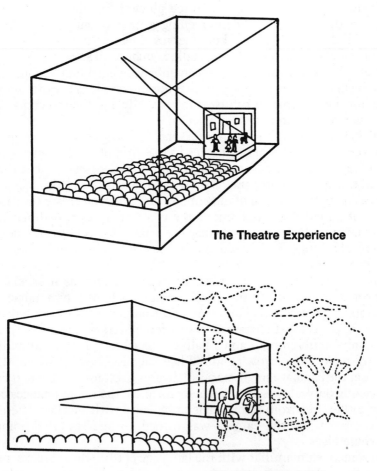

The Theatre Experience

The Film Experience

Traveling about in that box makes us identify somewhat less with our fellow audience members than we do in the playhouse. The journey is a little more personal and private. Notice how quiet and self-absorbed a movie audience is emerging from the movie theatre as compared with an audience leaving a playhouse.

This darkened box we ride in is, in effect, the camera. We see the play's world as the camera sees it. Thus the camera has a presence in the drama that must be reckoned with. The stage play has no such intermediary; we see the action directly. But at the movies, the camera is the storyteller. While the screenwriter never puts a finger on the camera, its presence as storyteller should remind him that what he composes in the form of a screenplay is a story, a narrative made visible. Indeed, a screenplay is fundamentally a narrative of what we are seeing on screen by way of the camera.

Film Production

How this camera does its work is the concern of other people: the director, the cinematographer, the cameraman, and the editor. The ins and outs of technology are complex and most of them have nothing to do with the screenwriter who, nevertheless, should be aware of the process by which a film is put together. This includes the dramatic uses of the camera, the way the film builds its effects, and the production process.

For the screenwriter, these factors boil down to one simple statement: we see what the camera sees. We might also add that we see *as* the camera sees. Most of the variables that influence how we view a movie are contained in the shot. These include the framing or composition of the shot, the camera's angle and distance from the subject, any movement of the subject or the camera or both, the qualities of location, lighting, effects of lenses and lens filters, and the way one shot relates to the next. Since the director designs the shots and the editor puts them together, the screenwriter has no direct control over any of these factors. Those that bear on *how* the camera sees things (framing, angle, distance, lighting, lenses, and filters) are wholly outside the screenwriter's control. He can influence them only by requiring certain emphases, atmospheric qualities, and tones. For example, a screenplay that describes "a locomotive bearing down on us," will surely influence the director to shoot the locomotive at a low angle. Those other factors that bear on *what* the camera sees are closer to the screenwriter's concern. The script describes essentially what we see as a running narrative, so naturally it exerts considerable influence over such factors as the movement of the camera, the movement of the subject, the succession of shots, and especially the locations. Other people will make the actual decisions on all these, but the storyline will determine the limits for them.

One of the most telling differences between a stage play and a film lies in the units of time they use. The stage play uses large formal units: scenes and acts. Every time the curtain falls or the lights black out, we come to the end of one of these formal units. Within that time, the action is continuous and fully scripted by the playwright. The smaller units are organic ones, determined by the shifting of tensions or motivations. The reverse is true of the film. Now the formal units are small and the organic ones large. The shot lasts about eight to ten seconds, and within that time the action is controlled by the director. The scene, created by a shift in time or place, is not nearly as formal or complete a break as a curtain in the theatre, for it occurs between one shot and another and so is of the same order as the shots themselves. The screenplay, true enough, sets forth the succession of scenes. The largest unit in films, the sequence, is a collection of successive scenes that complete an action, analogous to the chapter in a novel or to the act in a play. The audience is only vaguely aware of these shifts, and they serve mostly as a device to keep the dramatic action clear for the screenwriter, director, and editor.

The various kinds of shots are determined by angle and by distance as illustrated on page 175. For the most part these are of no particular concern to the screenwriter, but from time to time they are worth bearing in mind. For example, at the outset of a scene, standard practice calls for an extreme long shot which serves to create the context of the scene's ensuing action. On occasion, the drama may require a close-up or extreme close-up in order to lend emphasis to a telling detail such as facial expression or an object that may somehow push the action forward. Similarly, you may have a low angle shot in mind in a moment when someone or something seems to loom over us. There are other special shots such as the "point of view" shot representing a character's view of his world, a "reverse angle" shot showing us what was behind us, and an "over the shoulder" shot, using the shoulder of one character to partially frame another. While you will rarely have occasion to use these terms or call for a specific shot, it is well to bear them in mind while you visualize the film your screenplay describes.

What we see on screen is the movement of images and because they can move, they must. Planned by the director and executed by the actors, the cameraman and others, the movements include shifts of the camera (panning, tilting, dollying), of the actors within the frame or in and out of it, and of objects as well. Frequently, this motion serves as comment of the action rather than as action itself. Insofar as they carry import for the story, movements are of major concern to the screenwriter. The screenplay describes movement on the screen.

The contexts in which these movements occur, the fictional places of the scenes, also matter. Each scene has its location and time of day, and these factors can strongly affect the action. Whether a scene is indoors or outdoors, the specific locale, and the time of day are matters of concern

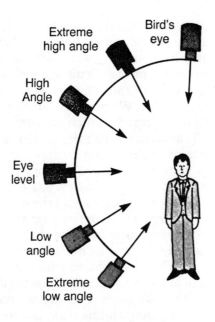

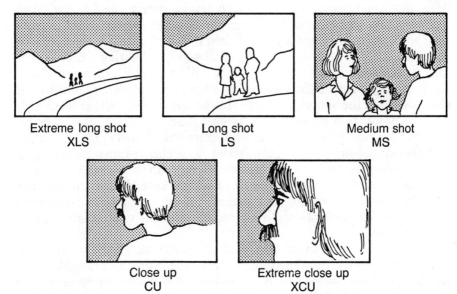

both for the story and for the filming of it. The director and staff use the information in planning the production. The story itself can take on added dimension and power with the right choices for the action's context. Whether a scene takes place in the dead of night or in broad daylight, in a house, a bar, a church, a bus, or a hotel lobby, can make a big difference. A scene may be flat for no other reason than its setting. An intimate love scene, for instance, can take on interesting values if set in a busy subway station where the frantic lovers are oblivious of the crowds. Changing the setting or the time of day can enliven an otherwise dull scene.

For a playwright probably one of the most difficult adjustments in moving to screenwriting is the loss of authority and control over the medium. One would like, after all, to call the shots. Whether playwright or not, you need to have an understanding of the way in which the film artists collaborate in the process of film production. This information clearly sets the responsibilities and limitations of the screenwriter.

The process of creating a film entails three distinct phases: pre-production, production, and post-production. The first phase involves all the planning for the shooting of the film. It begins with the scripting. The screenwriter or screenwriters first write a four- or five-page outline of the film's action. It is shared with other members of the production staff and then given a fuller version as a "treatment"—the narrative of the film as a sort of novella of about 40 pages. This too is shared with the production staff and, with their suggestions in mind, the screenplay is finally drafted—a present-tense novel of some 120 to 140 pages. The director meanwhile works at selecting locations, arranging crews, hiring actors and technicians. After the screenplay has gone through several drafts, the director takes it in hand and writes a shooting script, breaking the action into the shots he plans to take. It is usually transferred into a storyboard, consisting of quick sketches of each shot. He then makes out a shooting schedule calling for the day and hour when each shot will be done. The order in which the shooting is done is determined by efficiency, not the order in which shots occur in the shooting script. This brings pre-production to an end.

The production phase is the "shoot." Rarely is the screenwriter involved. There are occasions when the director will discover problems or potentials that call for a change in the script. Such changes are usually simply made—unless they make a substantial difference in the dialogue, in which case the screenwriter may be brought back in. Several takes are made of each shot, as well as various "cover shots" (cut-away shots or reaction shots of secondary characters)—all to provide the editor with alternate ways of bridging shots.

At the end of the shoot, post-production begins. The editor receives all shots and cover shots in all their takes, and begins to assemble them into a "rough cut"—a first draft of the final film. Again the screenwriter is rarely involved unless a major change is contemplated, which is indeed possible even at this stage. When the editor completes the final cut, the film is done.

The Structure of the Screenplay

What should now be clear is that the screenwriter's work is one of telling a story in a series of scenes. These are relatively short, compared to those of a stage play. In fact a screenplay reads rather like a novel, except that it describes a movie we are watching in the present rather than an experience others underwent in the past.

This in turn means that the scene is the basic building block for the screenwriter. Location and the action to take place there, not individual shots, occupy the screenwriter's attention. Scenes are of various lengths. They are rarely long, and often they may be a simple impression created by a few shots or even a single shot. They are composed generally of descriptions of activity, punctuated with dialogue. The scenes merge easily and readily into one another since they are linked in the same manner as the shots themselves, cutting directly from the last shot of one scene to the first shot of the next. Screenwriters may from time to time stipulate various special ways of making transitions from scene to scene, such as fades (the image fading into blackness or one emerging out of blackness) or dissolves (one image fading as another emerges). Because such decisions will be made by others much later during production or post-production it is probably useless to make these stipulations. Screenwriters continue to do so anyway since the script is intended to make the reader visualize a movie.

Ease of movement from scene to scene is one of the charms of films, but it is also insidiously tempting. Because it is so easy to change scenes, the moment a scene loses interest one is tempted to jump to a new time or place and start a new scene. One way to exert restraint is to chart a progression for the scenes so that they build toward a climax—the completion of a line of action—and then start afresh. The shift marks the end of a sequence and the beginning of another. So, shots unified by location and a passage of time become a scene, and scenes bound together by the pursuit of a line of action become a sequence. Sequences that follow the play's driving force to its conclusion make up the entire film. In this sense, the play of tensions renders the film a dramatic form akin to a stage play. On the other hand, the presence of the camera as the intermediary storyteller gives the film narrative qualities akin to those of a novel.

Concentrating on the line of action ensures that the scenes are not aimless. One avoids the temptation to jump to a new scene should the last one lose interest. There are films whose screenplays jump about in a frantic frenzy and audiences forgive them only because the star actor is so fine or the director and editor found ways to cover the fault. There is nothing inherently wrong in a welter of jumps from scene to scene, so long as they illuminate the action and propel the story forward. But to create new scenes constantly just for the sake of change is plainly bad screenwriting. We might, for example, have a series of quick scenes that put us first outside viewing a speeding train, then in one of its compartments, then in a living room, then in the garden, then back to the train roaring down the tracks. Such bouncing about is apt to annoy an audience, who has barely time to get oriented before being hustled off somewhere else. Still, if the action provides a connecting link between all these scenes, they can work. It may be in this case that those who are riding the train are rushing to their friends in the living room before a madman, already lurking in the garden, can get to them. We need only provide enough information for the audience to make these connections.

Connections are the source of cinematic structure; images on screen take on significance by their connections. The screenplay should therefore provide the thread in the form of forward action. More often than not, a well-calculated visual effect will establish the action without resort to a word of dialogue.

Novel, Play Script, and Screenplay: An Example

One way of seeing clearly the effect of a medium is to treat the same material in several different media: in this case, in a novel (narrative), a play script (theatre), and a screenplay (film). Here is a sample scene as the novelist might render it.

When the five boys were ushered into the Principal's office, they stood in the middle of the room, looking at the floor, all of them except Sam, that is. While shame filled the others with chagrin, Sam could not contain his curiosity. He let his eye rove all over the office, for he knew it had to contain somewhere that dreaded instrument of torture, Old Paddington.

"Sit down here and wait," they were told, and the door closed. Sam watched the level handle return to its level position to know that they were alone. Meanwhile his friends shuffled about finding places to sit on the couch and on a few straightback chairs they pulled out. Still, Sam could not catch sight of Old Paddington. Craning his neck, he backed into a spot on the couch next to Jack and nudged him.

"Hey, Jack . . ." he hissed.

"Hmm?" replied Jack, who clearly wanted to be left alone.

"Where do you suppose it is?" Sam insisted.

"What?"

"You know. Old Paddington."

"Shh. Don't say it." The conversation irritated the other boys, who were squirming in their seats hoping Sam would stop this. Jack looked at them, and on their behalf whispered, "Be quiet. The less you say, the better off we'll all be."

Sam looked at Jack and his other friends. "Bunch of cowards!" he thought. But he kept still. The room's presence began to weigh on them. The clock seemed to tick louder and louder and each boy could hear the others breathing. They tried to breathe more slowly, but it only made things worse.

Through all this, Sam's irritation grew, until he jumped up and faced them all: "Look, you guys. You know for what we done, Mr. Marsh's gonna bring out Old Paddington. We're in for it. The only way around it is if we can find Old Paddington ourselves before Mr. Marsh gets here. Then we can hide it, and maybe while he's looking . . . "

Just then, footsteps sounded in the hallway. Sam's eyes shot to the door. The door handle began to turn. Sam looked this way and that. There had to be some escape, some window or door, but there was none, and now the door was opening. That's the escape! Sam lunged for the door, yanked it full open, and shot through between Mr. Marsh's knees. He felt a hand grab at his arm, but he twisted and jerked himself free and shot off down the hall.

"Stop that boy! Stop him!" cried Mr. Marsh. Sam whirled around at the corner of the hall and looked back. No one was coming after him, but there silhouetted in the door frame was the figure of Mr. Marsh holding in his hand an enormous paddle, Old Paddington! Sam turned the corner and ran outside into the sunshine.

The scene is dramatic in that it works on a palpable tension. Still, the novelist can do things with the material that the playwright cannot quite do. He can move into and out of the heads of his characters whenever it suits his purposes. He can develop as full a description of any object, feeling, or thought as he pleases. On the other hand, the scene is restricted to what can be conveyed in words on the printed page. It is an event over and done with, now being told with words that have no quality of inflection or intonation. There is no sense of immediacy, no feeling that the scene is happening now before our eyes.

The playwright can catch some of these qualities, but, unable to enter the head of his characters, he will have to resort to some other means to alert us to the private agonies of a character such as Sam. The stage version of this scene might then read something like this:

> (The door opens, and the five boys, FRED, JACK, SAM, DICK and HAL, all enter very slowly and quietly. They stand in the middle of the room shuffling their feet and looking at the floor. They are followed by MISS CAROTHERS, looking very stern and angry.)

MISS CAROTHERS

You boys wait right here. We don't want to hear a peep out of you. Mr. Marsh will be here in a minute, and then you'll start thinking twice about what you did. This is a day he'll make you remember for the rest of your life. Sit down and be quiet.

> (She exits and closes the door behind her, and as she does so, SAM shoots a look in that direction. When he is sure she is gone, he starts looking around the office, moving to every corner of it. Slowly, the other boys find themselves places to sit on the sofa and a few straightback chairs they pull out. Finally SAM comes and sits next to JACK.)

SAM

Hey, Jack . . .

JACK

Hmm?

SAM

Where do you suppose it is?

JACK

What?

SAM

You know. Old Paddington.

HAL

Hey, you guys, shut up. You wanna get us in worse trouble? Just keep your yaps shut, okay?

JACK

It's not my fault. It's Sam here wants to talk all the time.

HAL

Shh. Be quiet. The less you say the better.

> (The room is silent. The boys sit kicking their legs back and forth, twiddling thumbs, and squirming. Finally SAM stands up and begins to explore the room. After looking in several places, he looks under FRED's chair.)

FRED

What are ya doin', anyway, Sam?

SAM

Looking for Old Paddington, whaddya think?

DICK

Come on you guys. Keep it down, willya?

SAM

> (He stands and marches around to face his fellow conspirators.)

Look, you guys . . .

DICK

Hey, cool it, Sam. We're in enough trouble as it is. Now just shut the heck up.

SAM

No, I won't. Are you guys gonna just sit there and let Mr. Marsh pull out Old Paddington without so much as a squeak of protest? You know we're in for it. Look: the only way out is if we can find Paddington ourselves before Mr. Marsh gets here. Then we can hide it, and maybe, while he's looking . . .

HAL

Here he comes!

(The door begins to open. SAM looks at it, then quickly around the room, then he bolts for the door, yanks it open, pulling MR. MARSH into the room. MR. MARSH grabs for SAM, but he is gone.)

MR. MARSH

Stop that boy! Stop him!
(He watches for a while, then in irritation he turns to the boys in the room, carrying a large paddle in his hand.)

JACK

(With quiet fear.)
There it is. There's Old Paddington.

MR. MARSH

Yes. Here is Old Paddington. You think your friend did you a favor running out like that? You have another think coming. All right, let's get started. You, there.
(He motions to FRED.)
Come here. Lean across that desk.

There are some interesting contrasts between the novelist's and the playwright's versions of this scene. The playwright's version is somewhat longer because the tension must fill out a span of time in order for the audience to sense it fully. Deprived of the novelist's capacity to describe and to enter into the thoughts of the characters, the playwright must resort to dialogue and action to make their feelings evident. This also calls for the characters to lend their presence to the scene. In the narrative version, it did not matter much who the other four boys were, but in the stage version, they are present, right there on the stage, and each must make his own contribution. So now we have all of them speaking, along with a certain Miss Carothers, who was only a vague presence in the original version. In short, the stage has to take action and the physical surroundings and play upon them to communicate the feeling the novelist was able to accomplish with a few descriptive phrases.

Now, let's have the screenwriter undertake the same scene. This time, the effects have to be tailored to a succession of images, and so the script might read something like this:

1. INT., SCHOOL PRINCIPAL'S OFFICE—DAY

While in the background a clock is ticking somewhat louder than normally, five boys sit uncomfortably in a couch and a couple of straightback chairs set up beyond the Principal's desk. They are FRED, JACK, SAM, DICK, and HAL. All except SAM have their eyes fixed on the floor, looking altogether ashamed. SAM, however, looks all over the office. It is apparent that the Principal is not there. SAM is not idly looking over the premises; he seems to be looking *for* something. A rapid series of shots of SAM's face and POV (point of view) shots of objects here and there give us this impression. Finally, he nudges JACK sitting next to him.

> SAM
> Hey, Jack . . .

> JACK
> Hmm?

> SAM
> Where do you suppose it is?

> JACK
> What?

> SAM
> You know. Old Paddington.

> HAL
> Shh. Don't talk. Be quiet. The less you
> say the better off we'll all be.

The group falls silent. The ticking of the clock grows louder. SAM's eyes dart all over the room. He looks at each of his school chums, one after another, as we see them in POV shots alternating with momentum, until SAM jumps up and faces the group. He hisses this speech at them:

> SAM
> Look, you guys. You know for what
> we've done, Mr. Marsh is going to
> bring out Old Paddington. We're in for
> it. The only way around it is if we can
> find Old Paddington ourselves before
> Mr. Marsh gets here. Then we can
> hide it, and maybe while he's looking
> for it . . .

The sound of approaching footsteps stops SAM dead. All eyes turn toward the door, which looms out over them. The door lever turns down. The eyes dilate. The door begins to move. Suddenly, SAM lunges for the door and yanks it open. In a rapid series of shots, we see MR. MARSH try to grab SAM, who twists and turns and finally jerks himself free and runs.

> MR. MARSH
> Stop that boy! Stop him!

2. INT., HALLWAY—DAY

We follow SAM as he tears down the deserted hallway away from the office. When he reaches the corner of the hall, he stops and turns around to look back. In a reverse angle shot, we see MR. MARSH's silhouette in the doorway, the outline of the huge paddle, "Old Paddington," clearly visible in his hand. Again, we see SAM take off down the hallway at right angles to the one down which he had fled.

3. EXT., SCHOOLYARD—DAY

SAM emerges from the school building into the sunshine. He looks right and left, and then runs off frame.

A word is needed about screenplay format as illustrated here. It breaks the action into scenes, each labeled as an interior scene (INT) or exterior one (EXT), as a particular location (PRINCIPAL'S OFFICE, HALLWAY), and according to time of day (DAY or NIGHT). Names of characters are capitalized except in the text of the dialogue. Since images are so important, descriptions of what we are to see occupy the full width of the format, while the dialogue is kept to closer margins, usually ten spaces inside the action descriptions, left and right. Generally the format is an aid in concentrating on the line of action and clarifying the uses of locations for the various scenes.

Some interesting things have happened to the Paddington story in the hands of the screenwriter. Like the playwright, the screenwriter does not have the novelist's luxury of full description and so he must resort to what an audience may see and hear. For all that, the screenplay is closer to the novel than the stage script because the camera functions as a narrator of sorts. Where the playwright had to involve all the characters as agents of the drama with a greater amount of dialogue and action, the screenwriter could allow the camera to see things objectively, from any character's point of view, or even subjectively as the character's emotions influence his perspective. So, although the screenwriter may not describe directly, he can let the camera tell much of his story. The film and the stage play must both *show* the story, but the film can assume a narrative voice via the camera, and this capacity brings it close to the novel in many respects.

Since time is broken into the tiny components of shots, each one lasting not much more than ten to fifteen seconds, the film is more fluid in structure than the stage play. The action within a shot lasts about the same amount of time it would take in ordinary life, which is roughly true of a theatrical scene as well. Between any two shots the screenwriter can jump over a span of time, move to a new location, and create a new scene. The playwright has to await the end of a much longer scene for this liberty of movement, and frequently will prefer to retain the scene in its concentrated action. So the playwright's version works with the interactions of the gathered characters in the Principal's office, while the screenplay moves out of the office into the hallway and out into the schoolyard.

The screenwriter's freedom of movement, however, requires good motivation in the drama for any change in scene. Although jumps in time and space may be easily accomplished and even expected in a film, they must still illuminate and forward the action. One must not change scenes just to change scenes.

Because the screen reduces space to two dimensions, the film reduces actors, objects, and setting to a single plane. Curiously enough, this provides the screenwriter and the director with a new source of interest. It means that objects and settings can forward the action with almost the same power as actors. The stage play relies heavily on actors, while scenery and properties remain in the background for the audience. The film, on the other hand, brings these to the same plane, and by close-ups or a moving camera, it can imbue them with expressive power. Objects can reveal a great deal about the human life revolving around them. The camera can translate them into provocative images of drama. Some films are ostensibly about objects or animals: Walt Disney's *Herbie*, about a Volkswagen car; *Jaws*, about a shark; or Hitchcock's *The Birds*. No one who has ever seen *Citizen Kane* can forget the bottle of poison, nor can anyone who has seen *The Pawnbroker* forget the spindle on his countertop. Many of these effects related to objects or setting derive from the choices made by the director, but the screenwriter must bear in mind that the image is the most powerful instrument of cinematic storytelling. If anything can be told in images instead of dialogue, it should be.

All this suggests different frames of mind for cinema and playhouse audiences. In the playhouse the audience occupies essentially the same place with the actors: the world of the stage play is a three-dimensional extension of our world, occupied by flesh-and-blood human beings like ourselves. We naturally interact with them and part of the excitement of a stage play comes of that interaction. The movie house, on the other hand, creates its excitement by seeming to carry us magically throughout the fictional world of the play, the camera often bestowing life on otherwise lifeless things. The movie gives us a sense of being all-seeing, especially privileged beings.

By way of summary, the following chart (adapted from a list in Eugene Vale's *The Technique of Screenplay Writing*) gives some indication of the salient differences between three forms of storytelling, three ways of portraying human living: the novel, the stage play, and the film.

	Novel	*Stage*	*Screen*
Length	Indefinite	1–3 sittings; 90–200 min.	One sitting; 90–150 min.
Time units	Narrated	Presented	Represented

	Novel	*Stage*	*Screen*
Treatment of time	Open, comprehensive	Closed, concentrated	Open, comprehensive
"Language"	Words	Actions	Images
Use of Space	Open	Closed	Open
Selection of locales	Full freedom	Restricted	Slightly restricted
Access to characters' minds	Direct	Only through action	Only through images
Point of view	Variable	Objective	Variable

Charting the Screenplay

More obviously than a play script, a screenplay is a blueprint for a play yet to be completed. It sharply underscores the fact that composing a script is an act preparatory to the work of others. People do not publish or read screenplays as often as they do play scripts. The screenplay is more removed from the final work because the screen requires a greater variety of planning before the completion of the play than does the stage. Fortunately or unfortunately, depending on how you look at it, not all the planning belongs to the screenwriter. The shooting script, laying out precisely the activity of the camera, is the work of the director. Once shot, putting the film together is the work of the editor. All these activities overlap with what seems the playwright's prerogatives, for they all bear on the charting of the play. The screenwriter, in short, works at a further remove from the medium and exerts less control over the final play than the playwright. This also means that we need to be very clear on the prerogatives and responsibilities of the screenwriter.

With the director charting the camera's activity and the editor arranging the shots produced, the screenwriter's charge is to plan the action. That is a simple way to say it. The screenwriter is no more and no less than a teller of visible stories. Ironically, the distance from the medium makes the screenwriter's job somewhat easier than that of the playwright, for it frees him to concentrate on the action alone. He may simply focus on the story and leave almost all the details of its realization on screen to others. Nevertheless, even if he is relieved of the obligations to chart the camera's activity and arrange the shots, he needs to recognize the camera's presence and the impact of the editing process. He must compose with the screen in mind.

Three factors heavily influence the screenwriter's work: the play of images, the presence of the camera, and the lack of full, formal breaks in action beyond the individual shot. We have dealt with the first of these already. Suffice it to say now that images have the importance on screen that words do on stage. They constitute the film's basic language. The kinds of images and the way we see them are at the base of a film's experience. This means that the screenwriter must think of his story in images, "see" the story as he writes. He may have no say in the selection of images themselves, but if he does not render the story visible, capable of being told in moving pictures, his screenplay will be useless.

As for the second factor, the presence of the camera makes it virtually a character itself. The audience engages with the drama through the camera. We in the audience tend to identify with the camera, for we see the play's world through its eye. The camera can take attitudes toward the characters; in fact, it cannot help doing so. This poses a special challenge to the screenwriter who, like a novelist, must make a decision about viewpoint. Here he differs from the playwright who reaches an audience directly, without an intermediary. But the screenwriter differs from the novelist, too, in that the film permits the camera to alter viewpoints readily, while the novelist must plan and prepare carefully for such change and usually prefers to maintain the same viewpoint throughout. The choices for novelist and screenwriter, however, are substantially the same: the omniscient, the objective, the third-person, or the first-person (subjective) voice. These will be treated in a later discussion of "camera consciousness."

The third factor—the absence of large formal units of action in film and the screenwriter's lack of control over the shots—means that the screenwriter needs to exert special discipline over the charting of the play's action. He receives no reinforcement in the way of acts and scenes, as the playwright does. He cannot fix clearly the arrangement of shots. As a result, it can be difficult to sense the rhythm and flow of the play, and it requires a special effort to give the play a firm structure. To keep control, the play is usually broken into scenes (continuous action taking place in one location) and into sequences (spans of action that build to the release of tension). Scenes are almost formal units in that they clearly take place in different locales or at different times. Sequences are totally organic, defined by a strong sense of the evolving action. They do not represent full breaks: the end of one sequence and the beginning of another is not signalled by anything except the awareness of a shift in issues, the recognition that something new is at stake in the action. Usually not even the script signals a new sequence; the unit chiefly serves the purpose of organizing action as the screenwriter composes.

For all these reasons, the whole process of composing drama, the relationship of writer to fellow artists in the enterprise, and the format of the script differ considerably from the playwright's practices. The second two of these three factors—that is, the camera's presence and the units of action—deserve some special scrutiny under the rubrics of "the idea of continuity" and "camera consciousness."

The Idea of Continuity

On the surface, a film is simply incoherent—nothing but a series of photographs. They relate easily enough one to another within a shot, but between shots they would have no meaning at all to someone unfamiliar with the conventions of film montage. If someone from an alien culture were made to watch a film, he could make little sense out of the jumping from vision to vision, even if he could adapt to two-dimensional representations of reality. "Continuity" refers to the full, rounded physical relationships of the images on screen as parts of a coherent world. One might say that the world itself has its own natural continuity which the camera destroys. Filmmaking requires creating a new artificial continuity to take its place. This is mostly the work of the editor, but it figures in the director's and the screenwriter's efforts as well.

A film cannot record all of reality. It cannot duplicate natural continuity, for it reduces what it sees to two dimensions. Moreover it must, one way or another, alter time. The earliest filmmakers came as close as one might to copying natural continuity by setting the camera at one end of a room and recording everything that happened at the other end without ever turning it off until the full action was over. "One shot-one action" may be a scheme that nearly catches natural continuity, but it is also a surefire way to create tedium. As soon as the idea emerged that a camera might be stopped and then started at another angle, a source of tension and interest had been found. That new found interest has greater value than the natural continuity that was lost. To replace the lost continuity, a "seeming" continuity must be created.

The secret for this lies in the screen's capacity to allow for flexibility of time and space. Since we grant that the screen is not reality itself, we are willing to accept jumps in time and space so long as we are left with a bridge to connect the shots. Then our imagination can readily fill in activity that is not actually there.

Suppose, for example, that our film is to incorporate a train trip from New York to Chicago. We cannot afford the seventeen hours or so that the trip would actually take. Instead, we may assimilate a series of selected representative moments in the course of the journey. As film watchers, we are so cooperative on this score that we can imagine the entire seventeen hours by way of one or two minutes' worth of shots. The script might read like this:

FADE IN

1. EXT., GRAND CENTRAL STATION—DAY

After a general establishing shot of the outside of the station in broad daylight, with traffic passing back and forth in front of it, we cut to a shot of the entrance. A Checker Cab drives up to the entrance. We see RON pay the driver, climb out of the cab, and walk toward the station, carrying a suitcase.

2. INT., GRAND CENTRAL STATION—DAY

RON appears in the doorway and makes his way through the crowds, where he is then lost to view. We see a sign saying "Twentieth Century Limited. Chicago. Leaving 1:00 p.m." RON passes the sign and we see him move down the length of the train until he pauses, then places his suitcase up on the platform of one car, and climbs aboard.

3. EXT., TWENTIETH CENTURY LIMITED—DAY

The train pulls out of the station, and, in a series of shots, we see it gain speed, pass out of populated areas and into the countryside. Daylight is seen to fade into twilight and night.

4. INT., TWENTIETH CENTURY LIMITED—NIGHT

A PORTER concludes making up berths for the night. RON settles in with a book.

5. EXT., TWENTIETH CENTURY LIMITED—NIGHT

In a series of shots, we witness the train's progress through the night. DISSOLVE.

6. INT., LASALLE STREET STATION—DAY

The train pulls into the station. RON emerges with other passengers. We see him making his way through the station passing a newspaper vendor holding up a copy of *The Chicago Sun Times.*

We have managed to get Ron from New York to Chicago in six swift scenes—and probably not too many more shots. That is the essence of continuity. In this case, it corresponds to a straight narrative structure, using a chronological sequence with one event leading to another.

Several conventions, understandings with the audience, help reinforce continuity. First is the "establishing shot," a shot that creates the locale as context for succeeding shots. Our trip to Chicago began with such a shot showing the exterior of Grand Central Station, and we understand that the shots that followed take place there. Occasionally, in longer scenes, reestablishing shots might be needed as reminders. A second convention is the "cut-away shot," a view of something or someone within the context but not focal. These are often reestablishing shots, as in the cut-aways of the Twentieth Century Limited roaring down the tracks. They might also be reaction shots of other characters in a scene or of objects that help tell the story. A third convention is the use of differing devices linking shots in such ways as to suggest something about their relation one to another, as in cuts, fades, and dissolves. A straight cut suggests a continuing action, without significant interruption. A fade suggests passage of time, as one scene fades from view and a new one fades in. A dissolve, in which one scene fades out *as* a new one fades in, usually implies simultaneity, as if one scene were progressing along with the last one, overlapping in action.

Obviously, montage, the assembling of shots into a film, depends upon the audience's capacity to make associations. In the case of Ron's train ride, the associations are fairly straightforward, but montage may work well with more subjective or emotional associations. This is true, for example, of the "Old Paddington" scene quoted above, in which some connections are made by way of the association of ideas in the mind of Sam. There the Principal's office clearly has an objective reality, but some shots will be dictated by Sam's emotional reaction prompted by his fear of Old Paddington: the door looms, the door handle takes on significance, the clock ticks more loudly, breathing is loud, and the paddle in Mr. Marsh's hand seems to assume larger proportions than it would normally have. This subjective linking of shots is called "classical montage" and it gives us the chance to enter another mind, to sense things in ways that go beyond objective reality.

This sort of montage can be pushed to an extreme, called "thematic cutting," using associations that have no grounding in physical reality nor even in subjective reality, but rather in thematic parallels. One image may elicit the next as commentary, completely apart from the supposed setting of the scene. This was a favorite device of the Russian pioneers of montage—Eisenstein and Pudovkin. For example, action may be commented upon by images of animals: a scene of indulgent plutocrats devouring food at a banquet might have interspersed shots of pigs at a trough, or a scene of relatives at a graveside hunched over in supposed grief might be accompanied by visions of vultures. Symbols and metaphors lend themselves to this sort of construction. It is difficult if not impossible to build a whole movie on this basis, for the result would almost certainly be heavy-handed and didactic. Nevertheless, it can be a valuable device from time to time.

Thematic cutting suggests some useful conventions and structural devices, such as parallel action, leitmotifs, flashbacks and flash forwards. Any time we cut to an apparently unrelated image, we are challenging the viewer to find the connection, the common ground the two images might share. Two actions might go forward simultaneously, involving two completely different sets of characters. As we cut back and forth from one to the other, the contrasts between them may provide dramatic tension. This is parallel action—two or more actions going forward simultaneously. Many films seek to create a kaleidoscopic picture of a place or time. A collection of vignettes in parallel action may serve well, as in such films as *American Graffiti* or *Nashville*. Leitmotifs are images that make symbolic comment on the action. Interspersing images of rolling black clouds in an otherwise happy scene may suggest an ominousness to which the characters are tragically oblivious. If a character encounters a child swinging in a park, the swing itself may trigger a flashback to another time when a swing happened to be present. Because flashbacks of this sort have become overworked, they are rarely used today, but they do illustrate the possibilities of montage.

The actual montage of a film is not the business of the screenwriter. The director plans for it, and it is actually the work of the editor, who has such power that a film can become an altogether different experience depending on how it is assembled in the editing room. Nevertheless, the patterns of montage are richly suggestive of ways to construct a screenplay and develop effects within and between scenes.

Camera Consciousness

Since the camera serves as intermediary between the action of a film and the audience, it is strongly associated with audience awareness of the characters, their actions and the world. In short, our consciousness is the camera's consciousness.

At first glance, this may not make much sense. A camera, after all, is a machine. It records reality. Whatever is in front of it when it is properly operated is put on film. Still, there are many ways in which the camera "sees" reality; in any event, it is not reality it records, but an image of it. The art of filmmaking lies in controlling that image. Well controlled, the image produces varying degrees of identification with the human subjects and varying attitudes toward them. This is what is meant by camera consciousness.

Now, where does the screenwriter, who is not the filmmaker after all, enter into all of this? The fact that the camera is always present means that screenwriting takes on some of the quality of prose fiction with the camera telling us the story. Tone and attitude will be determined by the camera, and it needs to be vividly there in the screenplay before the director can plan good camera work. Much as the playwright needs to envision a relationship between the spectacle and the spectator in the theatre, the screenwriter must imagine the journey the audience will make inside the magic one-eyed box of a movie theatre. The character of that journey is determined by tone more than any other single factor; tone, in turn, is a function of narrative voice.

As in prose fiction, there are four basic voices: omniscient, objective, third-person and first-person. The omniscient camera has the capability of moving into and out of characters' minds, of moving readily through time and space, and of being generally ubiquitous. The objective camera is a straightforward recording camera. It respects the normal limitations of observation. We see the world through its lens much as we do the real world through our eyes. It closes gaps in time and space, but it does so by the most natural means, never allowing the camera's presence to intrude on our consciousness. The third-person camera is an objective camera that "cares" about a particular character. It follows that character at all times, featuring him in most scenes. It may even turn subjective from time to time, but as soon as it does, it becomes a first-person camera, revealing dreams, reveries, and memories within the character's mind. The first-person camera, in other words, sees things as the character sees them, inward thoughts as well as the outward world. The first-person voice can be accomplished without resorting to the tedium of continual Point-of-View shots (POV's) by using other devices such as the "voice-over," background narration in which the first-person voice is literally a voice.

Despite the close parallel between camera consciousness and narrative voice, there is an important difference. In the case of a short story or a novel, we remain very aware of ourselves as apart from the story's narrator. In watching a film, we tend to merge with the camera and in a sense we become one with it. So closely do we identify with the camera, we become narrator. This means that the narrative voice can and does alter with comparative ease. An objective camera can turn subjective or omniscient at any moment. Such shifts would be jarring in prose fiction, but we accept them readily in film.

There is little use in getting terribly engrossed in the varieties of voices the camera can assume. The screenwriter's business is chiefly one of putting down stories that can be made visible. Beyond that, camera play is a secondary matter to be determined by the director. Still, opportunities exist that the screenwriter should keep in mind and bring to bear in composing the screenplay when they would genuinely serve the play's action.

Sources of Dramatic Tension on Screen

The sources of dramatic tension deriving from the imagined lives of the characters are as useful to the screenwriter as they are to the playwright. These include conflict between characters, tension between one motivation and another, contrast between the characters' present life and their past. These are sources cultivated by playwrights over the centuries, well before the invention of cinema or television. They function equally well in these new media. The screen offers some sources all its own. Since the director controls the medium by controlling the camera, the actual manipulation of the medium's tension belongs to him. But the basis for the tension lies in the screenplay. So the screenwriter does well to provide for them by envisioning the play on screen.

One of the screen's sources of tension lies in the potential contrast between voices. Since the screen allows for alternation of voice (omniscient, objective, third-person and first-person), it allows for tension to be built on contrasts and ironies in the alternation. For example, a boastful voice-over narration might accompany an objective camera revealing the shallowness of the boasts. *Citizen Kane* employs five narrators to recount, one after another, five phases of Kane's life. Another film, *Rashomon*, by Japanese director Akira Kurosawa, presents three different versions of the same story, each told as a first-person narrative by a different participant in the story. Such shifts would have to be developed within the screenplay itself. Subtler variations in voice could also be used, as in the case of the two characters despairing of ever reaching their destination in *African Queen* set against the omniscient camera's high angle view of the goal just beyond the trees. That too had to be scripted.

A second source of tension is found in the fact that the story must be told on both the video and audio tracks of the film. These are really separate. Each has to be produced its own way, edited its own way, and finally brought together. Even when projected, one appears as images on screen, the other as sounds through speakers. So it is possible for the play to develop dramatic interest by throwing what we see against what we hear. Ironic voice-over illustrates this tension. So would a scene of soft tenderness accompanied by harsh music or vice versa. Internal voices expressing fear or disdain might undercut a scene of elaborate courtesy. Bob Fosse's movie version of *Cabaret* played on this tension, throwing the atmosphere and especially the music of the cabaret into sharp contrast with the bitter and violent reality of emerging Nazi Germany. This is a tension that the stage version scarcely touches. Bob Fosse used a similar technique in *All That Jazz*, using the sound of a heart beat in the background of an otherwise normal scene, prefiguring the heart attack.

A third source of tension is found in the camera's ability to jump over space, making it possible for the camera to tell us things that are happening in more than one locale. This device, known as "parallel action," develops tensions by contrast between one episode and another occurring simultaneously. The tension can be all the greater if the audience can relish the anticipation of the two lines of action dovetailing in a scene of high conflict. Using this source requires a firm dramatic grounding. Without it, parallel action can become annoying, especially if done for obvious convenience. It produces the "meanwhile-back-at-the-ranch" syndrome so typical of bad cowboy movies. Alfred Hitchcock, however, used this sort of tension very effectively in many of his films.

Jumping over time can also produce dramatic excitement. It is associated with flash forwards and flashbacks. Again, the device needs to have an integral motivation to work, and should not be exploited for mere convenience. Because the flashback has become so overworked, only the most compelling reasons can justify its use. Certainly, flashing back just to deliver a piece of news smacks of phony contrivance. Nevertheless, some films have made good use of time jumps. *The Pawnbroker* is one, for its present objective reality prompts the central character to relive his experiences in a concentration camp. Because the whole movie is about his internal struggle with guilt associated with that past life, the flashbacks have an integral function for the whole play. Woody Allen's *Interiors* also makes effective use of such devices, as does Ingmar Bergman's *Wild Strawberries*.

Tension may be drawn between what is on-screen and what is off-screen. The actual framing of shots is the director's business, but the potential for this tension may come from the screenwriter. If done with attention to the dramatic impact of the play as a whole, suggestions are likely to be used by the director. Such tensions can have such dramatic power that they clinch a scene that would otherwise be either too long or too explicit. No one who has ever seen Alfred Hitchcock's *Psycho* can forget the bloodied water swirling around the shower drain. This is a powerful instance of on-screen and off-screen tension.

Taken altogether, a screenplay is composed of a series of scenes. As they succeed each other, they may provide ample contrast one to the other. The making of a film depends heavily on the creation of a sense of rhythm. Only the director and the editor can really create that rhythm. But the screenwriter provides opportunities by devising tensions that operate in time—between scenes or between whole sequences. One scene might assume a leisurely air, with a quiet, loping movement, succeeded then by a scene of staccato, nervous frenzy. One can sense failure in a screenplay if the scenes appear to be all nearly the same length. Variety of scene length—long ones alternating with brief ones, occasionally even a one-shot scene—can reinforce interest.

Any number of contrasts are available between scenes, between on- and off-screen, between now and then or here and there, between audio and visual elements, or between voices. Any of them may be tapped. The diagram on page 194 illustrates the several basic tensions the screen media afford. The screenwriter does not control all of these, but he does provide the basis on which they may operate. The structure of a good film derives from an integration of the medium's potentials with the dramatic effects. Thus the screenwriter does himself and everyone else a service by being alert to these possible sources of tension.

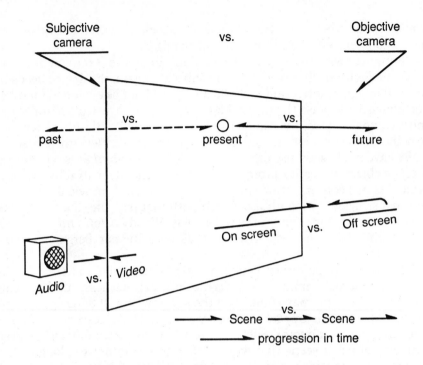

The Screenwriting Process

Despite this bewildering array of choices, the process of screenwriting can go forward with clarity if one maintains focus on dramatic action. As soon as attention wanders to indulgent uses of the camera, clever flashbacks, cute POV shots, the screenplay is lost. If any of these devices belong, they will grow naturally from the laying out of the action. Consequently, the process of screenwriting is predicated on a series of steps that control action.

The steps themselves derive from two fundamental premises:

1. Charting a screenplay is a collaborative enterprise.
2. The screenwriter's special charge is to lay down the central thread of action.

The first premise highlights collaboration; it is the nature of the medium that charting the film is the business of both the screenwriter and the director who must create a storyboard out of the screenplay. Moreover, both the film and the television industries resort to collaboration from the moment a proposal for a screenplay is made. In the jargon of the industry, at that moment the idea becomes a "property." The property may barely have an existence; it may be nothing more than a sentence or even a phrase, but it must be a phrase that shows such promise as to inspire an exchange of money. At each further stage of the screenplay's development, the screenwriter may be contracted to proceed to the next step—and money changes hands. And at each step, consultation takes place. Script conferences are held to permit the director, the producer, and other interested parties to influence the shaping of the script. Once the screenplay is completed, the director develops the shooting script, involving still more collaboration.

The second premise, the laying down of a central thread of action, focuses energies on composing the screenplay. Camera activity and editing are responsibilities belonging to others. While you need to bear in mind the potentials of the screen and the nature of its experience, your responsibility is to create an action of sufficient interest to bind together a succession of images to make a movie. The standard process entails a series of steps that progressively elaborate the central action and that keep the screenwriter ever mindful of it.

The steps begin with the *premise,* move on to the *synopsis,* then to the *outline,* the *treatment,* and finally the *screenplay.* These documents help plan *what* is to be filmed: the story, the characters, the locales, the situations—in short, the drama. They are followed by the *shooting script* and the *storyboard* which plan *how* it is to be filmed.

None of the steps preparatory to the screenplay is absolutely essential. A seasoned screenwriter might very well do without one or another, or shortcut through them, just as a playwright might not write a formal scenario. Nevertheless, both kinds of dramatic writers must plan somehow. Knowing the standard steps helps clarify the kind of planning called for; it also corresponds to the demands of the industry.

The premise is a simple statement of the film's dramatic situation. It may be as elaborate as Price's proposition (see Chapter 5) or as simple as the statement "It's *High Noon* in outer space," which is the premise writer-director Peter Hyams sold for the movie *Outland* (according to Michael Straczynski in *The Complete Book of Scriptwriting*). If the proposed movie is not to be merely derivative of another movie, novel, or play, then its premise needs to be more fully stated. The "what if" principle discussed in Chapter 5 can serve for screenplays as well as for stage plays. The movie *Tootsie* is based on a clear "what if" premise: "What if a young actor, unable to find work, were to land a lucrative role in a soap opera by disguising himself as a woman?" Or the premise for *E.T.:* "What if a charming extra-terrestrial creature, stranded on earth, were to make friends with a boy?" Or *North by Northwest:* "What if a sophisticated businessman were abducted by enemy agents, implicated in the murder of a diplomat, then pursued by both the abductors and the police?" Any of these could be expanded into the three-part proposition proposed by William Price.

"What if" premises are easier to state for plays that depend heavily upon situation and strong plots. Inasmuch as films create drama out of images, however, some rely more heavily on atmosphere and character than plot. Simple "what if" statements can be framed for such films, but they may not be revealing of film's intrinsic interest. Movies such as *Interiors, The Pawnbroker, Last Year at Marienbad,* or *Scenes of a Marriage* are of this sort. Nevertheless, a premise can be stated for any of these. Stating one may be useful to focus the film's action, so long as the statement catches the basic tension that will drive the film, as for example the tension between the pawnbroker's present life and his past: "What if a pawnbroker were haunted by guilt associated with his past in a concentration camp?" In itself it is not very revealing, but it does make clear where the tension is placed and that it will require rich characterization of the man and of the two contrasting realms.

The synopsis will reveal much more of a script's promise. A synopsis may be as brief as a paragraph (much like those found in television guides) to a few pages in length. It serves to trace the action, to give clues as to characters and their personalities, and to locate the action in time and space.

The outline elaborates the idea further, expanding the synopsis into sequences of action. As we have seen, a film breaks down into shots, scenes, and sequences. A sequence is a series of scenes which play upon one tension or complication. As soon as a new tension or complication arises, a new sequence begins. It is an organic unit of the screenplay which the form does not reinforce as do curtains or blackouts for stage plays. Sequences are most useful in planning a screenplay, for they reinforce the unity of action and test for a strong forward momentum to compel a spectator to watch. An outline, generally six to ten pages long, consists of a condensed narrative of the play, told in the present tense, as if we were watching it happening now. Outlines have their uses in the business of selling ideas. Some producers who do not have the time or inclination to read entire screenplays, and who do not trust synopses, may buy a property on the basis of a good outline.

The treatment is considerably more complex than other formats, and more necessary. It is essentially a short story or novella written in its own curious pattern. It tells the story in the present tense and often in the first person plural. These conventions remind us that we are describing action that is to appear to be happening *now* as *we* observe it on screen. It breaks down the action one step further—into scenes. Accordingly, the treatment indicates scene breaks with such terms as FADE IN, CUT TO, DISSOLVE.

A good treatment calls for a craft of its own. Writing treatments well does not guarantee one can write a screenplay well. Nevertheless, it is a craft worth learning, for good treatments can both sell an idea and maintain the dramatic unity of the screenplay. They channel your creative energies where they matter most—to the film's dramatic action. Another convention of treatment writing strengthens this focus: the avoidance of both dialogue and descriptions of camera activity. Unless a particular line of dialogue is crucial, it should not appear in the treatment. The treatment will serve you best by describing dialogue as action—which of course it must be. Otherwise, you may become so intrigued in making your characters talk that you forget the line of action to which they should be contributing. By the same token, unless the action calls for some unusual camera activity at a crucial point, all description of the camera should be omitted. There is no point in confusing the issue by introducing the camera into the action. The two things that matter are the forward action and that spirit of instantaneous observation evoked by the present tense and the first-person-plural observer.

One device that can aid the development of the treatment is the use of note cards to keep track of each scene that is to make up the screenplay. The first card for each scene should bear the appropriate label establishing the scene as an interior (INT) or exterior (EXT) scene, its locale, and the time of day (NIGHT or DAY). The rest of that card and the cards that follow describe the scene's action. Some scenes are very brief, easily contained on one note card; others are complex and pivotal to the whole play, and so require several note cards to complete. Indeed there should be variety of this sort. By this method, you have the opportunity to lay out the whole play before you like a solitaire game; you can organize it, reorganize it, and examine it for over- or under-development. The order in which the scenes are to occur can be written in pencil at the left of the label, so that a card may be easily placed in a new position if called for. A typical note card might look like this:

---

1 EXT COUNTRY ROAD—NIGHT

A bus rumbles along an otherwise deserted road. It comes to a stop. A woman gets off carrying a large shoulder bag. She looks around suspiciously, waits until the bus is gone, and then climbs the hill across the road. When she arrives at the top, she again looks around, removes a bundle from her bag, and places it in the hollow of a tree. She takes out a flashlight, turns and flashes it seven times across the valley.

Many other subsequent cards will describe the action set off by the woman's seven flashes. The seven flashes could, and probably should, set off a chain reaction, full of subterfuge, wild chases, and extravagant complication. Hopefully the cards can keep it all straight. Once the layout of cards seems promising, the treatment can be written.

Let's take the story of the seven flashes and begin a treatment based on it. The opening, in proper format, might read like this:

SEVEN FLASHES TO MAYHEM
Written by George Spelvin
5/15/83

FADE IN:

We see a lonely country road at night. A bus hoves into view over the crest of a hill, approaches us, and comes to a stop. The door swings open and a woman, STELLA, emerges. She wears a trench coat and scarf, and she carries a large shoulder bag. She steps away from the bus and waits for it to leave. The bus takes off, and she looks around furtively. Then she crosses the road and climbs the hill opposite. At the top, she takes a bundle out of her shoulder bag, looks around again and places the bundle in the hollow of a tree. Then, she takes out a flashlight, carefully aims it across the valley, and flashes it seven times.

CUT TO a terrace on which a man, BENNY, stands watching the flashing light through binoculars. He is ecstatic. He flashes his flashlight seven times in return. He descends the stairs from the terrace and takes off at a run.

CUT BACK TO the hilltop, where we watch STELLA make her way down the hill's other side. At the bottom she pulls away some tree branches and reveals a bicycle, which she mounts and rides off. FADE OUT.

We are now inside a bar, crowded and full of smoke, BENNY bursts into the bar. He spots two men at a corner booth, and goes to them. He tells them the news of the seven flashes. After some discussion, they (HARRY and MORRIS) get up. Leaving BENNY behind, they go out the door.

CUT TO a view of HARRY and MORRIS getting into a small car and leaving the bar parking lot.

CUT BACK TO the interior of the bar, where a young woman, FRIEDA, has been listening to all of this and now goes to the phone booth and makes a call.

CUT TO a dapper, fat gentleman seated in the back of a limousine listening intently to his telephone. He hangs up, knocks on the divider window, and the chauffeur drives off. We see the limousine approach a country intersection just as the small car carrying HARRY and MORRIS passes through. The limousine turns the corner, following the small car. It gathers speed and we see the two of them disappear into the night.

The story can go on from there. In a matter of some forty to fifty pages, we may have told the whole story of the bundle hidden in the tree. We can then transform the treatment into a screenplay. There through dialogue and more detailed action, we can come to know these characters and the potentials they offer.

The Screenplay

The screenwriter's last step is the script itself—the screenplay. Now we have the chance to give the dramatic action ample description. The focus of attention remains on the action, including the dialogue. The director's shooting script and storyboard will take care of camera angles and shot selection.

One difficulty with this last step is the sense that the story has been told already enough times, dampening any enthusiasm you might once have had for it. If one must write the story as a premise, a synopsis, an outline, and a treatment, surely a fifth writing is asking too much. This reworking of the material can sap one's interest. The fact is that there will undoubtedly be at least four rewrites yet to do on the screenplay itself. One might take some solace from the fact that writing the treatment probably saves at least one and probably two full rewrites. The mapping out of action through the treatment assures a strong structure, one that can be easily changed and improved without having to redo the whole script. Two things are worth remembering: one is the old adage that "plays are not written; they are rewritten," and the other is the fact that you do not know your characters or the dramatic impact they can make until you give yourself the chance to explore them in a full screenplay. In the treatment, they behave only insofar as they can help tell the story. They have not been talking or indulging their habits. The locales have assumed no particular character, the atmosphere is only vaguely suggested, and the uses of objects and things has not been specified. Writing the screenplay is your chance to find out about these things. A great deal of creativity is still required.

Still, there is no law that says that you may not write parts of your screenplay or even the whole thing prior to writing the treatment. Some screenwriters do exactly that. They omit writing the treatment in any presentable way until after they have finished the script. Then as both a means of assessing the play for revision and an instrument for selling the property they write a treatment. As with the playwright's scenario, the treatment must suit the creative temperament of the writer. It clearly has its uses. But if it is to fulfill them, it must not stunt the creative exploration every writer must make. If writing a full treatment does that to you, move on to the script and keep a treatment going at its side.

Fleshing out our story of the "Seven Flashes," we might arrive at a script that would look something like this.

SEVEN FLASHES TO MAYHEM

FADE IN

EXT., A COUNTRY ROAD—NIGHT

We see a lonely country road at night, accompanied by the sounds of crickets and an occasional whippoorwill. Looking up the road, we see a play of headlights over the crest of a hill. Then, a bus hoves into view. As it approaches, it slows down and comes to a stop. Its door swings open, and a woman, STELLA, emerges. She appears to be in her thirties. She is tired and nervous. She wears a trench coat and a scarf and carries a large shoulder bag. She steps away from the bus. The door swings shut and the bus takes off. She looks around furtively. Then she crosses the road and begins to ascend the hill opposite. We watch her progress through thickets and underbrush. When she emerges at the top, she stops and again looks carefully. Satisfied no one is watching, she goes to a large tree, kneels beside it and pulls a bundle from her bag. Glancing around one last time, she places it in the hollow of the tree. She rises, turns away from the tree. She checks her watch. She takes a flashlight from her bag and, aiming it carefully across the valley, she flashes it seven times.

EXT., TERRACE–NIGHT

A very young man, BENNY, also dressed in a trench coat, stands on the terrace watching the flashes through binoculars. He is earnest and intent. As he watches, he becomes more and more excited, repeating the number of each flash:

> BENNY
> . . . five . . . six . . . seven.

He waits a moment to be sure there are no more flashes. Then he produces his own flashlight, and gives it the same seven flashes back in the direction of STELLA. Then he turns excitedly, remembers his binoculars, puts them and the flashlight in a pouch, and, with studied nonchalance, descends the stairs from the terrace onto the street. Once there, he looks around surreptitiously, and then takes off at a run.

EXT., HILLSIDE–NIGHT

We cut back to STELLA, who is now replacing her flashlight in her bag. She turns and descends the other side of the hill. At the bottom, she pulls away some freshly cut tree branches to reveal a bicycle. She pulls it out, mounts it precariously, and takes off at a wobble down a country lane in the direction she had come on the bus. She is clearly unaccustomed to such an instrument.

INT., BAR–NIGHT

The bar is crowded and full of smoke. People are everywhere. We pick out a face or two here and there. Suddenly, BENNY bursts into the room. He is wild and out of breath, but he checks himself at once, remembering to look casual. He does his level best at this. He casts his eyes about the room, and spots two men, HARRY and MORRIS, in a corner booth. With studied ease, BENNY sticks his hands in his pockets and saunters in their direction. They meanwhile appear completely absorbed in conversation. He arrives, looks everywhere except at the two men, and then asks:

> BENNY
> Ahem. Mind if I join you gentlemen?

                    HARRY
Come off it, Benny. You want to sit
down, then sit down, fer crissakes.

BENNY gets a chair and sits at the end of the table. He pushes his hat
back on his head and leans in.

                    BENNY
It's happened. I got the signal.

                    HARRY
What's happened? What are you sput-
tering about?

                    BENNY
The signal! The signal! Seven flashes!

                    MORRIS
Seven flashes? You saw seven flashes?

                    BENNY
Yes! I tell you, it's happened. I saw the
seven flashes just now from the hillside. You know what that means.
You guys gotta get movin'.

                    HARRY
I don't believe it.

                    MORRIS
Why not?

                    HARRY
Hell, it's been two weeks. It's too late
now. No one would expect us to wait
two weeks. That's ridiculous. It's
gotta be some kinda hoax.

                    BENNY
Gee, I been up on that terrace every
night these last fourteen, fifteen days.
I ain't never come down with news
until I had some to bring.

                    HARRY
I'm not talking about you, Benny.

                    MORRIS
Look, Harry. You know this signal's
supposed to be seven flashes from the
hillside at quarter after ten at night.
Benny's got a signal from the hillside
must a been quarter past ten. Who
else would do it? What choice do we
have? If we don't do our bit, the whole
thing's a washout. Come on. Get your
coat. Let's go.

> HARRY
>
> Somebody's sending us on a wild goose chase. Somebody heard about this, bought a flashlight, and flashed it at Benny seven times. Have another beer, whyuncha?

> MORRIS
>
> (With heavy meaning.) Get up, Harry.

> BENNY
>
> Yeah!

MORRIS is up and on his way out. HARRY sits. He watches MORRIS go, looks at BENNY, then at the exit, and finally with impatience, back at BENNY again. He stands up, pulls his coat off the tree, and stomps out. The camera follows him and catches a woman watching all of this intently. Then we return to BENNY, who turns to the bar rail, looking as if he were planning to spend the rest of the evening.

EXT., PARKING LOT—NIGHT

MORRIS is already in the driver's seat of a tiny Fiat 500. He is drumming his fingers on the steering wheel. HARRY moves through the shadows.

> HARRY
>
> Hey, Morris. That you?

> MORRIS
>
> Of course it's me. Who'd you expect? Get in here.

HARRY opens the passenger door, and with great difficulty (as he is a big man) he manages to fold himself into the Fiat. He slams the door shut. We see the car ease out of the parking lot and out onto the road. Once there, MORRIS puts the accelerator to the floor, and the little car takes off.

INT., BAR—NIGHT

BENNY has settled down to a mug of beer, but behind him we again see that same woman who had listened so intently. This is FRIEDA. She studies BENNY and considers her next move. She turns abruptly and goes to the phone booth. The glass door closes, and we see her deposit a coin, dial and talk, but we cannot hear a word.

INT., LIMOUSINE—NIGHT

Settled comfortably in the back of his limousine and talking on the phone is a dapper, fat man. ALEXANDER ORNOVSKY. He is nicely wrapped in a camelhair coat and he sports a thick, black beard. We view him through the divider window, so we can hear him no better than we heard FRIEDA. Suddenly he hangs up, leans forward, and taps on the window. We pull back enough to see the CHAUFFEUR acknowledge him, put the car in gear, and pull out.

EXT., ROAD–NIGHT

We see the limousine moving slowly and quietly toward an intersection.

INT., FIAT–NIGHT

MORRIS is driving the car through the night at its top speed. HARRY beside him is putting a stick of gum in his mouth.

EXT., ROAD–NIGHT

Returning to the view of the intersection, we see the Fiat race through. The limousine then whips around the corner in pursuit. We see the two cars drive off into the distance.

And so on. The script will continue recording the snowballing mayhem occasioned by the seven flashes of Stella's flashlight over the next hundred and twenty pages or so, sufficient for a feature length film.

This is not innovative screenwriting, but it does serve to give an idea of the nature and layout of a screenplay and how it relates to the treatment. Worth noting is the much heavier reliance it employs on description and action, as opposed to dialogue, which usually takes up the bulk of the copy for a stage play.

Exercises

1. Write out a scene in each of the three media—the novel, the stage play, and the screenplay. Concentrate on taking full advantage of the qualities each medium offers.

2. Write a brief screenplay based on a short story. Select one that appeals to you and lends itself to a treatment in images (or write your own short story). Keep the dialogue to a minimum. Write in the present tense, describing *what* we see as the action unfolds. Concern yourself chiefly with the essential line of action.

3. Examine as many screenplays as you can find, especially those for finished films so that you can compare the screenwriter's work with the final product.

4. Watch a movie closely. If possible, find a way to view it on video cassette so that you might stop it to make notes or back it up to study it more closely. On the basis of this examination, write a master scene script (the term for the screenwriter's product) as it might have looked when turned over to the director to make into a shooting script.

5. Select a location you feel lends itself to visual and dramatic interest. Build a story around it in a film treatment.

9

The Jumping Box:
Television

On the surface, television does not appear to be a distinct medium. Since it uses a screen for a play of images, it should operate under the same conditions as the cinema. It does not; the television viewing experience is very different from that of cinema. Its technology also differs strongly. And television, as a social and economic institution, dictates some very particular conditions. All three factors impose conditions that markedly alter the work of the screenwriter. Ironically, despite the fact that television is a screen medium, it has almost as much in common with the stage as it does with film.

Television is a new medium; it has been with us for scarcely more than a generation. In the course of its short life, it has already undergone revolutionary changes, and right now it is experiencing a new revolution as cable and new recording devices emerge. This makes it difficult to generalize about the demands of television writing. What is true today may not be true tomorrow. And what is true in one country is not in another. All is in a state of flux, the more so since television is more directly affected by the social circumstance in which it operates than either film or theatre.

Rapid change characterizes the medium because television has the power to reach millions of viewers at once. It cannot play the same material over and over, but must be constantly renewing itself. Hours of programming time need to be filled. Television has always had a voracious appetite for material—not all of it is dramatic material. Sports, newscasts, documentaries, and game shows take up a lot of time. Yet even these formats tend to dramatize their material, as Martin Esslin notes in *The Age of Television*.

Esslin points out that television generally is characterized by the dramatic. The act of taping and placing within a frame even the most "real" events transforms them. Transforming calls for controlling and that control is likely to be fundamentally dramatic.

Nevertheless, putting aside sports events, newscasts, talk shows, and game shows, many hours remain specifically dedicated to drama in the strictest sense: plays that deal with fictional characters in fictional worlds. There has never been a time when society required more material from its dramatists than now and television is responsible.

Consider these facts. More than ninety-seven percent of all American homes are furnished with at least one television set and two-thirds have more than one. Indeed, there are more television sets than there are bathtubs. Each set is turned on for an average of nearly seven hours a day. The average viewer spends nearly three hours before the box daily; that is twenty hours a week and about a thousand hours a year. Thus, in the course of a year, the average viewer has spent the equivalent of forty-three days watching television. During a lifetime of seventy-two years, he will have spent better than eight of those years at the television. This is a staggering thought. The most inveterate playgoer could not hope to match it. A highly successful television play might reasonably attract some twenty million viewers, all watching it simultaneously throughout the country. This gives us some appreciation of the enormity of television's power to reach an audience. A long-run hit play on Broadway may be lucky to play before as many as a million viewers before its closing. Even a smash hit movie would require months to match the number of viewers a single big television show reaches in one night.

Whatever your attitude toward television may be, its pervasive power cannot be denied. A dramatist seeking a livelihood might well look into it: if you can't beat it, join it. Before you do, however, you owe it to yourself to give it some serious scrutiny. It poses some unique conditions for the writer—some more intriguing than others. It is powerful, novel, fascinating, frenetic, demanding, whimsical, commercial, and often inane. But there it is, begging to be exploited. And exploited it is, for a multitude of purposes. Its potential as a medium has yet to be fully realized. In the meantime, it pays writers more handsomely than any other form of writing and provides challenges uniquely its own.

The Television Experience

If the cinema may be described as a traveling box transporting us now here, now there, television is something more like a jumping box. The television set is literally a box which seems to contain its own worlds within itself. It leaves its spectators in their stationary positions while it appears to jump about, encasing now this vision, now that. It is the most frenetic of all dramatic media. Much of this is due to the jumping sensation it produces, but other factors enter in as well.

For example, containing its own worlds within the box, television does not involve or engage its audience with anything like the power of the theatre or even cinema. This helps to account for the fact that many movies that are highly effective in the movie house go dead on the television screen. Movies are created for a large gathered audience in a darkened theatre, all of its members mutually involved in the spectacle, their everyday lives suspended for the time being. When such a movie is diminished to the proportions of a television screen and encased in its box sitting in the familiar and still visible surroundings of one's home, the intensity of engagement also diminishes. We sit back and let the box jump about picking up varying images without our having the sense of joining in the journey.

Our relationship to fellow viewers (if indeed there are any) is vastly different from that in the theatre or movie house. Since the familiar surroundings do not fade from view, and since our fellow viewers tend to be our friends and relations, there is none of that concentrated, sustained attention found in darkened, anonymous theatres. Television viewers remain aware of each other. They will carry on other activities while watching television; they may even leave the room, switch channels, turn off the sound for a while, or make wry, witty remarks about the show in progress. Finally, of course, television viewers are free to turn off the machine at a moment's notice. It is a freedom unavailable to the movie-goer and the theatre-goer, who must resort to the awkward act of walking out to accomplish the same thing.

All these factors (the jumping box syndrome, the simultaneous awareness of our personal reality and television's reality, and the ease with which it can be cancelled) combine to make it a medium frantic for attention. Terence in ancient Rome complained of a similar situation, for his audiences were always rushing out of the theatre to investigate shouts from the chariot race next door at the Ludi Romani. Television has to seize and maintain attention and commercial sponsors will underwrite only shows that promise to do that. This accounts for the favoring of on-the-spot news, sports events, and game shows—all of which have the appeal of immediacy. Even soap operas, which are a form of drama, must strive to appear to be happening now, every afternoon, as ongoing lives. Applied to the work of the dramatic writer, this condition calls for forceful manipulation of material to capture and keep attention.

Television does nevertheless have certain powers of its own to enhance audience involvement. First, the movement and glow of the television screen creates a mesmerizing effect. In a dimly lit, familiar room, that glow calls attention to itself, augmented because it presents unfamiliar images—and moving ones at that. It may be true that one can turn it off any moment, but the mesmerizing effect checks the will to do so. We would have to overcome the inertia of sitting in a comfortable chair allowing the glow to play on our consciousness. This is the first source of the pop terms "idiot box" and "boob tube." It has the power to make us lethargic, hypnotized idiots.

Beyond this, television does indeed have its own immediacy—some genuine, some mere conditioning. What is genuine is its capacity to transmit images of events that are happening now somewhere else. That sense of suddenly "being there" on the spot works a wonderful magic. On the instant, with the help of satellites, we can watch something happen halfway around the world. The fact that television can do this clouds our ability to distinguish between what might really be happening and what we see on the screen. This is conditioning. In the early days of television, most dramas were "live." They actually were taking place the moment we saw them. But even now, when relatively few shows are live, we still carry the impression of that immediacy. To reinforce that impression, television resorted to such devices as "canned laughter," and when that grew too transparent, to "taping before a live audience." These are perhaps spurious, but they are still effective ways of underscoring the seeming immediacy of television. Finally, the fact that shows are broadcast in particular time slots, not to be repeated again (except in summer reruns and occasionally in afternoon reruns years later) lends a kind of urgency to television watching. We do not want to miss certain shows. Nowadays, however, as recording devices creep into homes, that urgency is quietly being undermined.

The Television Image

Like cinema, television is an image medium. The glowing screen constantly shifts patterns of light and dark and color to shape the images we recognize. But the way these images are created and the images themselves are quite different. The image is not projected by light passed through a film onto a screen, but rather assembled by the television camera, broadcast, and reassembled by electronic signals within the picture tube. Whether the original image be a live performance, a videotape, or a film, the image on the screen has relatively low resolution, making detail much less vivid than it is on the movie screen. Television has used each of the three sources listed. In its early days, the so-called Golden Age of Television during the fifties, television drama relied chiefly on live performance. It had a marvelous sense of immediacy, rendering television drama more like stage drama than cinema. The immediacy, the spontaneity, and the confined space of action were all theatrical rather than cinematic qualities. Kinescope, the early form of recording for television, was very awkward; it was not until the invention of videotape that it became feasible to prerecord television drama. The advantage of controlling the finished product seemed to outweigh the benefits of the immediacy of live performance. And so, more and more shows became taped, some with canned laughter or before live audiences. Film, an alternative to videotape as a source of television screen image, provides greater depth of field and generally a better picture. For those shows that depend on location shooting, film has proven preferable, even if it is more expensive. Even then, however, the television image retains its low resolution. And this has its effects on how the medium may be used dramatically, effects which the dramatist needs to take into account.

The television image is flatter and conveys much less detail than the film image. The resulting conditions are:

1. Where the cinema may resort to a rich and varied play of imagery, television must focus predominantly on the actor. Objects may still possess dramatic power, but, all things being equal, the television camera can more readily follow the expression given by actors than anything else.

2. As a result, television tends to resort to the close-up more frequently than film, especially close-ups of the face. Long shots are simply not as effective on television.

3. Another result is that television drama tends to rely more heavily on dialogue than does cinema. The television image, being less defined than the film image, requires somewhat more reinforcement from dialogue. Indeed, some television drama, especially "soaps," are like radio drama in that they can be followed without much visual attention.

Studio vs. Location Drama

As a matter of both tradition and convenience, two types of production methods have emerged for television drama. The first (and original) method is studio production, which entails settings constructed in a studio, multiple cameras, and editing in the control room. A variation is the use of multiple cameras and multiple video tape recorders (VTR), and editing later. Both are studio formats. The second method is location production, which entails moving out to actual places, usually recording it on film, and editing later. Each poses its own requirements and advantages. The screenwriter must adjust to the appropriate method of production.

The location method corresponds to the pattern employed in cinema; even the format for the written script corresponds. In writing for location shooting, the screenwriter should bear in mind all those factors discussed in the last chapter. In addition, the factors that bear upon the television image should influence the choices the screenwriter makes. By and large, this method is in fact used with actual filming, hence the use of the cinematic format for the written script. On occasion, however, location shooting is done by videotape—making the world a studio, using an elaborately outfitted van as the control room. This has the effect of a kind of *cinéma vérité* or the feeling of immediacy we associate with the newscasts. To gain the sense of events happening as we watch, hand-held cameras on location are used in certain shows as in some docudramas. Scripting for location videotaping follows the pattern of studio drama.

Studio drama, however, is the special province of television. It was once the format of early movies, but the cinema has by and large abandoned the old movie studios. Television, however, has retained the pattern, especially for certain episodic shows. Sitcoms and soap operas are both usually studio dramas. As these are both episodic series, they depend on the sensation of "returned visits" — the feeling of dropping in on familiar folks once a day or once a week. There is a kind of reassurance that they are all still there in the same old place. Commercial sponsors like to encourage that sensation, for if a habit of "dropping in" can develop, the commercial messages are guaranteed an audience. Since the episodes use a basic cast of characters and a basic setting, they are more efficiently produced in a studio.

Typically, studio drama uses between one and three settings, specially designed and built in the studio. Each setting consists of three walls; the fourth wall is omitted to give free access to the area for the three cameras that move about the studio floor. *All in the Family*, for example, made use of such a setting: it was a composite of the living room, dining room, kitchen, and front porch of the Bunkers' house. Occasionally, other settings were added: Kelsey's Bar, the loading dock, an office, a waiting room. For a period, another standard setting was added — a composite of the living room and kitchen of Gloria and Michael's house. All these settings consisted of three walls each. The wall behind the television set in Bunkers' house, for example, was never seen — it never existed. Page 211 shows a rough diagram of the setting for Bunkers' house placed in the studio with the control room, where the images produced by three cameras in two runs of the show were edited later to produce the master images recorded on tape.

Both location and studio drama are subject to the rigorous "act structure" of American commercial television. The institution of American television owes its existence to the large businesses capable of paying the costs of television time and production. Under this system, a television show may occupy its time on screen only if it relinquishes time for the commercial message. It is the message that counts. The content of the show should be consistent with the impression the sponsor seeks to create. Half-hour shows become "two-act" plays, frequently beginning with a "teaser" of one to two minutes, followed by an ad, then Act I (between ten and fifteen minutes), another ad, then Act II, another ad, and finally, a "tag" — a one- to two-minute capstone vignette to conclude the show. The hour show is, accordingly, a four-act structure, sometimes with a teaser at the outset — usually a montage of shots from the show that is to follow. Finally, the special and the "made-for-TV-movie" follow a six-act structure over their two-hour duration.

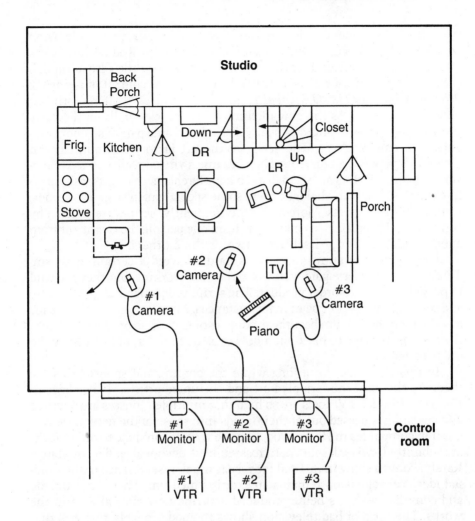

If it were not for this structure and the peculiarities of the television image, writing for the television movie would be no different from writing for cinema. If it were not for the fact that the studio drama depends on an image, it would be much like writing for the stage because it employs the theatrical conventions of a confined space, division of time into acts, an emphasis on the actor, and a reliance on dialogue. Television writing, therefore, tends to move in the direction of one or the other of its sister dramatic media.

The Television Industry

Perhaps the most startling conditions for the television screenwriter stem from the nature of the whole television enterprise. It is indeed an industry—which has taken a while to develop. In the early years, television writers such as Reginald Rose, Paddy Chayevsky, or Rod Serling had a greater creative control over their scripts than is now the case, although they did face a curious censorship and the ultimate control of sponsors. Programs such as *The U.S. Steel Hour* or *Playhouse 90* offered original new plays weekly. As the new medium matured, especially in the early sixties, this pattern changed radically. Writers became part of an enormous entertainment machine. The scene of the art factory in Kaufman and Connelly's play *Beggar on Horseback* became a virtual reality in the television industry. Writers are specialists in an interchangeable-parts, assembly-line process. Some are dialogue men, some specialists in suspense scenes, some one-liner experts. More and more frequently, scripts are written by committee. The initial idea may come from one person, the treatment from another, and the script itself from two or three others.

Under these circumstances, it is hard to avoid a certain cynicism. Television writers are paid well when they are working, but they are paid to provide a made-to-order product. The script is described as "property"—and so should the writer be in many instances. Most writers contribute for a while then move on to become producers or executive producers, where they no longer have to hack out a new episode to order, but can issue the order instead.

In this structure, for a long while the commercial sponsor was the "heavy"—the one who "crippled art and corrupted artists." Nowadays, in the age of film-for-TV, costs are so high that multiple sponsors are required and control has passed out of their hands into those of the networks. Production companies in Hollywood, like the writers, produce to order. Ideas are submitted, twisted, split apart, reassembled, devoured, and regurgitated. Rarely would a show in its final form bear much resemblance to the original idea. Yet television remains an exciting medium. There are valuable and convincing shows being produced and fine new ones always in the works. The ratio of bad television shows to good probably matches that of productions on the stages of Elizabethan England. It may well be, as Paddy Chayevsky is supposed to have remarked, that this form of drama, so derided in our time, will be regarded in the future as "our theatre."

The organizational structure is itself in a state of perpetual flux. Revolutionary changes are in the offing. For the present, the nature of the business is dictated largely by the three networks, with some variety offered by Public Broadcasting System. Cable television, video cassettes and video discs, high frequency channels—all pose a considerable threat to the current three-network structure of American television. The future of television is quite extraordinary to contemplate because the medium is still young. The one thing it has clearly demonstrated is its power and its intriguing uses for drama.

What follows is an account of the basic forms that have emerged in American television. Although these, too, are in constant flux with new forms being added, others being altered or dropped, some description is, nevertheless, possible.

Forms of Television Drama

Television writing is the most restrictive kind of dramatic writing because the forms are rigidly and thoroughly predetermined. While there are particular forms, such as act structures, teasers, and tags, each continuing show has its own set of strictures. To write for any of them, a writer needs to be familiar with the strictures of the show, the form, and the appropriate teaser-act-tag pattern.

Television drama may be divided into three general categories:

1. Episodic series.
2. Anthologies.
3. Specials.

Each of these has several sub-forms.

The first category, episodic series, includes all those shows that appear on a regular schedule, presenting each time a new episode, among a familiar group of characters in familiar surroundings. Most of them are either half-hour or hour shows. A variation on this pattern is the "mini-series," which usually uses several consecutive evenings and episodes of up to three hours each. Anthologies, once very popular, are now on the wane. Some are single shows appearing once a week, each time with an independent play such as *Twilight Zone* or *Police Story*. Others are collections of two to four episodes within a single showing—episodes that might have nothing to do with each other or are unified by theme (as in *Love American Style*) or place (as in *Love Boat*). The category of specials includes all those single plays that appear once, preempting regular programming. They are usually two hours in length and include most "made-for-TV" movies. The *NBC Movie of the Week*, appearing regularly, would however be an anthology show.

Of these three categories, the one that is thoroughly peculiar to television is the first—the episodic series. Because it also contains the greatest number of sub-forms, it deserves more extended treatment.

Episodic Series

Episodic series may be subdivided into five forms: the sitcom, action-adventure drama, episodic drama, soap opera, and the mini-series.

The sitcom

"Sitcom," a composite of "situation-comedy," is a term born of the television age. Almost all of them are half-hour shows presenting a familiar group of characters (one of whom dominates the series) in a variety of situations. The group is most often a family or at least a group always engaged in a mutual enterprise (as in *The Mary Tyler Moore Show.*) Early sitcoms dealt almost exclusively with good middle-class families, as in *Leave It to Beaver* and *Father Knows Best.* Many of the more recent sitcoms, however, present either a broken family or one that is not so solid or middle-class: *One Day at a Time, Gloria, Archie Bunker's Place, The Jeffersons.* A sitcom requires that its characters be engaged mutually in some ongoing enterprise; if that is not a family, it may be a military mobile hospital unit (*M*A*S*H*), a police station (*Barney Miller*), a taxi garage (*Taxi*), or a diner (*Alice*).

Most sitcoms are studio dramas, "pre-recorded before a studio audience." This means that they utilize a restricted number of sets—usually two or three. One or two are standard, ongoing sets; a third and perhaps still another might be "satellite sets," used occasionally but not regularly. The standard, ongoing set is often a multiple set. *Archie Bunker's Place,* for example, uses a set that includes three adjacent locales: the kitchen, the bar, and the office, built in such a way as to allow the camera's movements between them. Similarly, *The Jeffersons* uses a set that incorporates the kitchen, living room, and outside hallway of the Jeffersons' highrise apartment. Satellite sets are locations used occasionally, such as Snyder's apartment in *One Day at a Time* or Alice's apartment in *Alice.* Sitcoms can also provide for a special setting, intended for a single episode only: we might find Alice at the bank or Archie at a lawyer's office. Some sitcoms, however, focus only on the standard setting: *Barney Miller,* for example, never leaves the precinct office. *M*A*S*H* presents an unusual combination of types. It is not a studio drama, although it does have standard setting in the form of the compound, which includes the "Swamp," the Colonel's office tent, the VIP tent, the mess tent, the showers. Being a location drama, *M*A*S*H* also portrays events out on the road, in villages, and elsewhere.

Usually a nucleus of four to seven characters—"running characters"—appear in almost every episode. One of these characters tends to dominate the series as the central character, although some episodes might focus on another. In its last season, *M*A*S*H* had seven running characters: Hawkeye Pierce (the central character), B. J. Hunnicutt (the sidekick), Major Charles Emerson Winchester III, Colonel Sherman Potter, Margaret "Hotlips" Hoolihan, Corporal Maxwell Q. Klinger, and Father John Patrick Mulcahy. These, in fact, come close to corresponding to the stock characters of the Commedia dell'Arte, a ripe treasure trove of material for sitcoms: Hawkeye is a Harlequin figure and B. J. a Brighella, another *zanni* type; Winchester is a Dottore and Potter a Pantalone; and Margaret is a wench-type *zanni*. Other sitcoms more commonly employ somewhat smaller groups of running characters. There are, for example, four running characters in *Alice* and *One Day at a Time*.

Beyond the nucleus of running characters several others may make occasional appearances: the retired inspector on *Barney Miller*, the English neighbor on *The Jeffersons*, and Sydney the psychiatrist on *M*A*S*H*. Finally, most shows allow for the introduction of "program-specific" characters, those who appear in a single episode, never to appear again. Naturally, they need to be written into the episode at the beginning and out by its end, so that no one expects to see them next week. *Barney Miller* relies heavily on these transient, program-specific characters.

In many respects, a single episode of a sitcom is like a one-act stage play. There are, however, some important differences. First of all, the characters need no full introduction; they need only be reestablished at the outset of each episode. The sitcom may use jumps from setting to setting and from time to time without breaking dramatic momentum—a luxury not available to the stage playwright. There is correspondingly less sense of unity to an episode of a sitcom. In fact, many make deliberate use of a sub-plot or a double plot or even a multiple plot. For example, *One Day at a Time* frequently uses a sub-plot which involves a minor issue, while the main plot takes care of a major issue; *M*A*S*H* typically employs a double plot—two stories happening simultaneously; and finally *Barney Miller* uses a multiple plot, each associated with a different "visitor" to the police office. In any case, the sitcom usually ends in a dovetailing scene that resolves all plots.

Since each episode tends to have a wrap-up, there is rarely any continuity from show to show. Sitcoms do not have memories; what happens in one episode is generally forgotten and the next episode starts afresh. One cannot, however, kill off a running character or send him off on a new career in another city without people remembering it.

Sitcoms aspire to a comic tone, but increasingly they are taking on a sentimental edge, allowing a certain seriousness to creep into the human relationships. Issues facing the characters are sometimes quite serious, although they do not pose a dire threat. To do so would vitiate the comic effect. It might also militate against the comforting reassurance sitcoms strive for—that they will all be back next week, just as usual.

Action-adventure series

These evolved out of the Saturday morning movie serials, most of which were westerns. Many early television action-adventure series were also westerns, shows such as *Gunsmoke*, *Have Gun, Will Travel*, and *Bonanza*. Those that were not westerns were usually cops-and-robbers shows such as *Dragnet*. Over the years, the action-adventure show has assumed a greater variety and, in certain cases, considerable subtlety. Although relatively empty and inane shows continue, some newer shows deal with issues that have implications beyond the show and provide moments of sentiment and humor that are relatively rich. Indicative of this new variety are the settings of such shows and the occupations of the central characters: hospitals and doctors, morgues and forensic physicians, law offices and lawyers, newspaper offices and editors. Many of course center on private investigators and take the world as their settings, unifying it only by the vehicles used: Rockford's Pontiac, Magnum's Ferrari, or Columbo's Peugeot. These are exclusively location dramas, although some have a standard setting as well (the newsroom for *The Lou Grant Show* or the laboratory for *Quincy*). They are also generally one-hour shows, structured in four acts. Most of them use a montage teaser and some also add a tag scene. The fact that there are several sophisticated and subtle shows in this category does not prevent the more simplistic ones from continuing; witness *The Dukes of Hazzard*, *The Hulk*, and *The A-Team*.

Sophisticated or simplistic, the action in these shows pivots on a strong central character, patterned heavily on the star actor who often contributes more than a little of his or her personality to the fictional role. One is sometimes unsure which name belongs to the actor and which to the role: Lou Grant/Ed Asner, Jim Rockford/James Garner, Thomas Magnum/Tom Selleck. With such heavy reliance on the appeal of personality, there is scarcely a scene in a typical episode that does not include the star actor. There also tend to be fewer running characters than in sitcoms. Beyond the star, there are several in the *Lou Grant Show*, only four in *Magnum, P.I.*, three in *Quincy*, two in *Rockford Files*, and one in *Columbo*. A recent trend is to feature two star actors or actresses, and so split the central character in two: *MacMillan and Wife*, *Hart to Hart*, *Cagney and Lacey*, *Simon and Simon*. Even then there are few running characters and most of the characters in action-adventure series are "program-specific."

In keeping with that same spirit, the episodes are self-contained. Again, these are shows without memory; what happened last week does not affect this week. There are occasions when the producer and the network will agree to make a two-part episode, playing over two weeks, but most episodes have a fresh beginning each week. Storylines sometimes are single plots, but there are also shows that favor sub-plots, double plots, and multiple plots. They range from *Quincy* which uses a single plot to *CHiPs* which interweaves multiple plots. Except in relatively loose structures (such as *CHiPs*), there is always the endeavor to bring all the strands together in a single climactic scene, typically occurring fifty minutes into the show, early in the fourth act.

Recently, a variation on the action-adventure series has begun to develop: a sort of slice-of-life, *cinéma vérité* version of adventure and intense living. *Hill Street Blues* and *St. Elsewhere* are representative. In these, there is no single dominating figure, but a group. Plots are not strongly unified because they aim to convey the sensation of life lived at the crossroads of human suffering—a police station in the one case, a hospital in the other. Nevertheless, these shows continue the appeal of action and adventure.

Episodic drama

Episodic television drama is a form to itself, characterized by the portrayal of everyday life and the quiet struggles against crises by people like ourselves. It tends to the sentimental, but often mixes in a liberal dash of humor. Episodic drama borrows some of its features from other forms: the serious tone of action-adventure series and soap operas; a group as an ensemble of running characters as in sitcoms. The characters are not laughable nor are their situations, but by the same token they are not characters who daily face great challenges with almost superhuman strength, as do the central characters of many action-adventure shows. They are little people leading everyday lives. Some of the best of these dramas are *The Waltons, Little House on the Prairie,* and *Paper Chase.*

Episodic drama comes in the form of one-hour, four-act shows and they tend to have memory. What happens in one episode does have an effect on the next. Since they depict the trials and tribulations of a group struggling to maintain or improve their lives, the shows themselves become a kind of ongoing chronicle. The degree to which one show builds on the last is always optional, since a television audience cannot retain a memory vivid enough to build one show on another in a detailed way. Succeeding shows play off the preceding one to the extent that it pleases the writers and producers.

Episodic drama tends to distribute emphasis more evenly among the running characters than do sitcoms, and certainly more than the action-adventure series. The form concentrates on a close-knit group, and, even if one tends generally to predominate, any member may take focus for one episode. With the whole group at the disposal of the writers and a full hour to explore interactions, the use of double plots is not unusual. The two plots have to be tied together well, since the concerns of any one member of the group cannot but affect the others.

Most television episodic dramas are location dramas, using one basic multiple setting as a home base, but expanding to many other indoor and outdoor locations selected for particular episodes.

Soap operas

Soap operas ("soaps" for short) get their name from their initial sponsors in the days of radio dramas, manufacturers of soap who still do sponsor most such shows. In fact, Procter and Gamble maintains its own production company. Although they are a variation on television episodic drama, they have a few peculiarities all their own.

First of all, most soap operas are daily series, occupying a half-hour slot each afternoon. Recently some have expanded to an hour and a few have taken to weekly evening slots. They are all studio dramas, using a multitude of sets and occasionally inserting brief outdoor scenes. Since the shows rely heavily on close-up shots, the settings do not have to be elaborate; many are created by simply redecorating a previous setting. The cast of running characters tends to be large. The show typically does not concentrate on a close-knit group but on a wide assortment of characters—relatives, friends, lovers, colleagues, acquaintances, and some characters who do not even know some others. Finally, soap operas have memory. Each episode is a continuation of the previous one, an installment in the "ongoing lives" of the characters. With so many characters, usually at least a dozen, many strands of action are created and the soap may concentrate on any one of them at a moment's notice.

The main endeavor of a soap is to engage the audience empathetically in the action. It does not so much try to reflect life as to be life. It engages by creating dire and constantly impending crises. These are not the everyday sort of crises faced by the little ordinary people of the episodic dramas, but life-shattering crises of the very rich, very powerful, or very beautiful people. They are crises that threaten to overthrow a whole way of life. They "impend" for a long time and sometimes they run out of steam or prove less dire than originally thought. One can look in on the same character a few weeks later and they do not seem any the worse for it all. Moreover, the appeal to empathy is made by creating the impression of a continuous life being lived, day after day. At a certain hour every weekday afternoon, you may look in on these people struggling to maintain their lives—perhaps for years to come. Soaps are the most durable of all television series. Finally, the spirit of crisis is maintained in soaps by a combination of chance and wickedness. Some characters allow too much of their lives to be governed by chance, a vacuum which the wicked characters are delighted to rush into and fill.

In accordance with these qualities, the soap is structured in what seems a leisurely manner. The individual episode does not matter so much as the week: the entire week is the fundamental unit of a soap opera. All action builds toward its climax on Friday in order to attract the audience back on Monday after a weekend lull. Each soap opera series has its "bible," a master plan for the entire season. Like the chapter of a novel, the week is the important segment of the bible for a soap. The soap takes many other characteristics from narrative forms. It is open-ended, with an emphasis on a leisurely interweaving of different strands of narrative. The scenes tend to be explorations of nuances of feelings and emotions rather than dramatic scenes of contrast, tension, or conflict—although some scenes will take on those qualities. Finally, the structure of an individual episode is based on what might be called the "meanwhile" principle: scenes are usually encounters between two people who explore their relationship for approximately two to three minutes, then we shift to another duo, then another, and meanwhile the first scene has been continuing and we may return to it. Often four to six such scenes may go on simultaneously; our jumping box shifts from one to another; meanwhile life goes on.

Soaps are not convincing dramas; they are frequently irritatingly maudlin, unrealistic, and indulgent. On the other hand, they do not have to be bad drama. A chemistry of interaction among writers, producers, directors, and especially actors can make a soap genuinely engaging for a time. Soaps have a rich sense of immediacy; they work the close-up to its fullest advantage in developing very rich and subtle human relationships; and they take advantage of serialization to create the feeling of ongoing life—an opportunity simply not available to the stage or cinema. In short, this is one form of television drama that genuinely and peculiarly belongs to that medium. Recently, the soap has been elevated to prime time, location drama of hour-long, weekly installments with shows such as *Dallas* and *Dynasty*. They retain the loosely-knit groups of running characters, the dire ongoing crises, multiple strands of plot, and the "meanwhile" principle of their daytime sisters. On the other hand, as location shows taped weekly, they lose some of the immediacy and ongoing life that studio, daytime shows have.

The mini-series

The mini-series is a relatively new television form, inspired by the several limited series of the British Broadcasting Corporation shown on public television stations: first *Forsythe Saga*, then *Upstairs, Downstairs, Duchess of Duke Street*, and others. Despite its prefix, the mini-series is the longest form of dramatic writing produced in America. One mini-series may last from six to fifteen hours or longer. Because the productions cannot be watched in one sitting, they are spread out over several days and so qualify as episodic drama. Typically each episode is two to three hours in length with five or six episodes required to complete the series.

Since a mini-series is finite, its episodes are more carefully structured in terms of the whole series' experience than the soap opera episode. Each episode is akin to a novel chapter and, in fact, most mini-series are based on novels. Those that are not are based on history. Mini-series are the specials of specials demanding weighty and important subjects: adaptations of classic and best-seller novels or treatments of momentous historic incidents. Ideally, in fact, they are both. In keeping with the mini-series' pretentions to higher things, the characters do not face issues of import only to themselves (as most characters do in soaps). Mini-series concern issues of world consequence involving whole societies and a cavalcade of years. Frequently, they follow the pattern of pitting particular people against the backdrop of sweeping historic upheaval and change. Such is the case in *Roots*, the story of generations of American blacks from the times of slavery to our own day; *Holocaust*, the story of a German family set against the backdrop of Nazi Germany; or *The Winds of War*, the story of an American family dispersed in Europe at the outset of the Second World War.

Little more can be said about the mini-series; writing for them is essentially a matter of adapting material to the television medium from a novel, from history, or from both. They are location dramas shot as movies and borrowing prestige from their source—an important book or a striking period in history. They do not usually carry an inherent structure. Spanning fifteen to twenty hours, they sometimes seem to ignore the dictates of economy (dramatic and financial). This is due in some measure to the fashionable nature of the form, regarded as worthy, even demanding, of the nation's attention. On the other hand, the freer form can allow a greater integrity for the plays written for mini-series.

Episodic series in these various forms (sitcom, action-adventure series, episodic drama, soap opera, and mini-series) form the peculiar province of television, which is, after all, the only dramatic medium (aside from radio) that can reasonably expect to pull an audience back for another installment in an ongoing series. The cinema attempts to do it, more or less futilely, with such movies as *Godfather II*, *Jaws II*, *The Empire Strikes Back*, *Return of the Jedi*. The theatre long ago gave up the effort as a bad job. But television, that box in the home, uses the "same time, same station" appeal with considerable success in resummoning audiences. Episodic drama, then, is the special province of television, complemented by the anthology and the special.

The Anthology and the Special

The forms for the anthology and the special are neither as rigorous nor as predetermined as the form for various types of episodic drama. Fewer general statements apply across the board for either form. For that reason, they are more rewarding and interesting for the writer.

The anthology was one of the early forms of television drama. From the outset, shows such as *Playhouse 90* and *U.S. Steel Hour* specialized in presenting, week after week, original television plays, each one an independent, self-contained piece. At a regularly scheduled time a new, one-hour play would take place—hence the term "anthology." Some, of course, were anthologies of one, two, or three short pieces within the hour. Weekly plays might be unified by type, as the mysteries featured on the *Alfred Hitchcock Hour* or the tales of the eerie and of science fiction found on *The Twilight Zone*. Short plays might be unified by setting where all the dramas take place, as in *Fantasy Island* or *Love Boat*. We have, then, three types of anthologies: those that feature one original drama per week (such as public television's *American Playhouse*); those that collect two or three shorter pieces per installment, usually all of a type (*The Twilight Zone*); and those that interweave plots of different plays within a set format (*Love Boat*). Unfortunately for the writer, this form, once one of the best outlets for original television writing, has declined from its former glory.

A variation on the anthology is found in variety shows, which often feature individual skits within their formats. Some call for the use of particular running characters, as in *The Carol Burnett Show*, while others incorporate skits that are independent one from another, as in *Saturday Night Live*. Most have a predetermined tone and form.

The final form, the special, takes its name from the treatment it receives; it is advertised for days or weeks in advance and it preempts regular programming. In one way the special is the opposite of the series because it happens only once and is completed in one installment. In other ways, specials are similar to mini-series. They are most often adaptations of classic or popular fiction, or derivations from history. Increasingly, however, special "made-for-TV-movies" use original material. In any case, almost all specials are commissioned. They are almost exclusively location dramas, recorded on film. As such, they follow all the patterns of cinema writing, except that one must bear in mind the conditions of television screen and the restrictions imposed by television time. They are, accordingly, six-act plays intended for two-hour time slots. Very special specials are nine-act, three-hour shows.

A relatively new variation on the special has evolved as the docudrama—a form unique to the television medium. Docudramas deal with recent history, sometimes so recent as to be just yesterday. They capitalize on that immediacy television may tap, the sense of being there the moment something important happens, anywhere in the world. We have become accustomed to feeling as though we were there on the spot during the battles of Vietnam, during the Watergate hearings, during the holding of hostages in Iran, or the great earthquake of Mexico City. It is a simple step to contrive the spectacle *for* the camera instead of contriving to have the camera there at the time of the real incident. The resulting docudramas attempt to dramatize events that are fully documented as having happened at a certain time at a certain place. Although some extreme versions dramatize what never took place (as *The Trial of Lee Harvey Oswald*) they generally seek to create the impression that the show constitutes documentary evidence that what is shown is what happened. Every effort is made to give the impression, at least, that what appears on the screen is being recorded at the precise time it happens. Docudramas had their beginnings with the *You Are There* series of the fifties. They took a new impetus at the time of the Watergate hearings which made life into television drama on the spot. And it was very popular drama. The form may be illustrated by such specials as *The Pueblo Incident*, *The Missiles of October*, *The Kent State Massacre*, *Raid on Entebbe*, and many others. The marriage of Lady Diana and Prince Charles produced two docudramas almost immediately, probably among the fastest translations of fact into fiction ever recorded.

Docudrama has an interesting potential and an equally curious danger. Based on actual fact and using a medium of recorded fact that television is taken to be, docudramas can be a powerful form for illuminating the forces that operate around us. Well-dramatized, they can offer considerable human insight into national and world developments. At the same time, the form is capable of presenting misleading or even bogus facts, and of resorting to sheer sensationalism. Docudramas easily lend themselves to falsehoods and libel especially since the medium encourages dealing with up-to-date material. In the wrong hands, they can be dangerous.

The various types of episodic drama, the anthologies, and the specials are the basic forms currently in use for television. New forms will be appearing, some supplanting the present ones; some present ones will undergo evolution. Since the television market is predominately episodic shows, with original material by and large restricted to the occasional anthology, special, or mini-series, almost all writing for the medium is commissioned. This does not mean that free-lancing cannot be successfully done; it does mean that most writing must be done to order. Free-lancing must be done with a sharp eye on the market, speculating on where the main chances might be found. To have any success at all, one must study the market through trade papers and journals, be there on the spot to hear what is happening where. In addition, it is important to study the television plays themselves. In all this, one must make a special effort to maintain the writing discipline and one's own style. In this connection, it is helpful to examine briefly the process of television writing.

Process of Television Writing

In general, developing a television screenplay is the same as writing a cinema screenplay. Differences are occasioned by two factors: the nature of the television industry and the special case of television studio drama. Because the episodic forms, especially the sitcom and the soap opera, are most closely tied to television as a medium and as industry, the process of television writing can be illustrated by following the development of a sitcom episode.

A sitcom series begins life as a pilot. Someone—a writer, a producer, a vice president—has an idea for a continuing series. The idea strikes enough people in the production team as promising and money is put behind it to make an initial episode to test the possibilities. This is a pilot. At the moment of decision there may be nothing more than a brief description, a basic premise, or a situation. At the other extreme, there may be a full "bible." A bible for a sitcom or a soap opera is a basic sourcebook for the series. It contains descriptions and backgrounds for each of the running characters, an account of the basic premise for the series and the kinds of situations it would entail, studio settings that will be standard, the number of settings that may be program-specific, and any location shooting that may be interspersed. On this basis the pilot script is written, although on occasion, the pilot script is written first, the bible afterward. It is not uncommon for the person hired to write the pilot and the bible to become the head writer if the series is funded. He or she may then participate in the hiring of other writers, in all story conferences, and in the rewriting of scripts. The head writer for the soaps is a powerful and well-paid individual, controlling the soap's plot through a season and hiring and coordinating the dialogue writers.

Once the pilot is completed and the series optioned, experienced screenwriters are brought in to view the pilot and discuss the show. They receive the show's bible, other pointers, and an invitation to make their own presentations to the producer and head writer. A presentation is the writer's oral description of a proposed episode. In preparation for it, the writer may have worked out many details in written form, but for various reasons, both professional and legal, the industry wants the initial presentation to be oral. It is a traditional ritual to be learned by all television writers. It has even assumed jargon labels, such as "pitching an idea," "spitballing it," or "being good in a room." Not all writers are persuasive talkers, but the art of presentation is worth cultivating in the television industry.

This initial story conference requires that the writer be both knowledgeable about his own idea and flexible about other ideas. On the first score, a well-prepared synopsis will tell a great deal about how each running character will be used, how the standard settings will be used, what other settings or locations will be needed, what other program-specific characters might appear. On the other, story conferences are frequently brainstorming sessions in which a welter of ideas jostle each other. The writer needs to keep a sense of balance. Some ideas may be very useful and worth incorporating; others are distracting and irrelevant. One needs to develop a knack for making such distinctions quickly. The conference may result in a contract, and on-the-spot performance is a factor in that decision.

The contract most often is a "step contract," applying only to the first step—the submission of a treatment. The next step, a first draft, calls for another contract, which might well be issued to another writer altogether. The treatment is essentially the same as that required for a movie script. It is a narrative account of the plot, written in the present tense in terms of what we actually see in action. It contains little or no dialogue; no subjective, inner-mind sequences, unless they are to assume visual form; and no "purple passages" of elegant prose. A straightforward account of objective, observable action, it makes clear the number and order of scenes. Some writers find it expedient to work this all out on index cards, so that scenes may be shuffled, rearranged, or discarded easily. The treatment must clearly indicate the act break, allowing for a "hook" or moment to create curiosity and anticipation strong enough to endure the commercial between Acts I and II. Once satisfactory, the treatment is typed up, coming to about ten pages for a typical half-hour sitcom.

Once the treatment is submitted, one of three things will happen. The producer may decide to reject the idea altogether; the treatment may be accepted and the writer cut off, with a new contract for a first draft issued to someone else; or a contract will be issued to the writer. In any case, the writer receives payment for the treatment. If he is to continue, a second story conference is held. Suggestions are aired, revisions considered, new possibilities pursued, and notes taken. The writer is sent away to work on a draft. When that draft is finished, and the writer paid, he again faces the chance of being cut off. If not, he might find himself working with other writers, including the head writer, or he might continue alone. Finally, a draft is approved, and the writer turns the work over to the director.

As the sitcom is a studio drama, it is taken almost at once into rehearsal and shooting. Many changes are still possible as the director works with the actors and the cameras, so the writer is often requested to be on hand for any exigencies. The written format for studio drama is distinct, allowing considerable open space on the page for revisions. There is no time for rewriting and retyping the script at this point, so the changes are made while the play is being shot.

Television Writing: A Sample

The following opening scene from an episode in the sitcom series *The Jeffersons* serves to illustrate a number of things. First it demonstrates the format for television writing for studio drama. Then it reestablishes the running characters at the outset of the episode. Here the characters include George and Louise (Weezy as George likes to call her) Jefferson; Florence Johnston, their maid; Tom and Helen Willis, their "salt and pepper" neighbors; and Ralph, the doorman. The episode is written around the maid Florence and is designed to feature a special guest star in the singer Gladys Knight. Third, the opening scene reestablishes the basic situation, the "movin' on up" atmosphere of the Jefferson's household. Finally, the script reprinted here shows the act break—the span from the close of the first commercials to the appearance of the second set. By that time the focus and direction of the episode are clear.

This particular episode, entitled "The Good Life" and broadcast March 1, 1983, concentrates on Florence's attempt to pamper herself and really live well for one day. The script was written by Michael Moye, who was hired as a screenwriter by Norman Lear after winning the Norman Lear Award with his play *Tilt*, which he wrote as a student at Lenior Ryne College in North Carolina. The play was produced by his college, and entered in the Playwriting Awards Competition of the American College Theatre Festival, where it won the Lear Award. In the script, O.S. means "off-screen" and SFX means sound effects.

#0915

ACT I, sc. 1
(Florence,
Louise (O.S.)

THE JEFFERSONS
"The Good Life"
#0915
ACT ONE

FADE IN:

INT. JEFFERSON KITCHEN—DAY

(FLORENCE IS ON HER HANDS AND KNEES IN FRONT OF THE REFRIGERATOR SCRUBBING THE KITCHEN FLOOR. AFTER A FEW BEATS, SHE BEGINS TO SING SARCASTICALLY IN SYNCOPATED RHYTHM WITH HER SCRUBBING MOVEMENTS.)

FLORENCE

"Oh, the good life

Full of fun, seems to be the ideal

Oh, the good life"

(FLORENCE THEN BEGINS TO HUM THE REST)

SFX: DOORBELL

INT. JEFFERSON LIVING ROOM—CONTINUOUS

(Louise, Tom,
Florence (O.S.)
Helen)

(LOUISE GOES TO THE DOOR, OPENS IT TO AN EXCITED TOM WILLIS.)

LOUISE

Oh, hi, Tom.

#0915

TOM

Louise, don't move.

(CALLS OFF.)

Are you ready, sweetheart?

HELEN (O.S.)

Ready.

(TOM—*UNFORTUNATELY*—BEGINS TO SING)

TOM

"DID YOU EVER SEE A DREAM

WALKING, WELL, I DID . . ."

(HELEN SWEEPS INTO THE ROOM PAST LOUISE. SHE
HAS BEEN BEAUTIFULLY MADE UP AND HER HAIR
STYLISHLY COIFFURED . . . LOUISE REACTS AS TOM
CONTINUES SINGING. HELEN ENTERS.)

"DID YOU EVER SEE A DREAM

TALKING, WELL, I DID . . ."

LOUISE

Oh, Helen, you look . . .

TOM

(CONTINUING)

"DID YOU EVER HAVE A DREAM

THRILL YOU . . ."

#0915

HELEN

Tom, please. I'm being complimented.

TOM

Oh, I'm sorry, my angel.

LOUISE

Helen, I—I don't know what to say.
You look beautiful. Absolutely
beautiful.

HELEN

Thank you, Louise.

(CROSSES TO SOFA)

LOUISE

What happened?

(HELEN REACTS)

I don't mean "what happened" as in
you don't normally look good. I
meant "what happened" as in . . . uh
. . . you . . . uh . . .

HELEN

I think I understand.

#0915

LOUISE

Good. I didn't want to lay it on too
thick.

HELEN

(BUBBLING OVER)

Oh, Louise, Tom and I are spending
one of the most exciting days of our
whole lives . . .

TOM

Yes, You see, I . . .

HELEN

Tom just signed a new writer and as
a present, he got *me* a gift certificate
to one of New York's most fashionable beauty salons.

CUT TO:
(Florence,
Helen (O.S.)

INT. JEFFERSON KITCHEN — CONTINUOUS
(FLORENCE STILL ON HER HANDS AND KNEES, SCRUB-
BING, PAUSES TO LISTEN)

HELEN (CON'T)

I'm telling you it's like something
you'd see in a movie! Honestly. I just
couldn't get over it. Those people

#0915

treated me just like I was royalty.

(FLORENCE REACTS AS SHE SCRUBS HARDER.)

And Louise. It's not just a beauty
salon. They can make you over from
head to foot. Of course, I went with
the "works."

(FLORENCE LOOKS UP AND SIGHS THEN RESUMES
WORK.)

They have a chic international
clientele. But the thing that I really
really couldn't get over was the
number of celebrities in that place.

(FLORENCE REACTS NOW GENUINELY INTERESTED, AS
WE)

CUT TO:
(Helen, Tom,
Florence, Louise,
George, Ralph)

INT. LIVING ROOM—CONTINUOUS
(HELEN IS LOOKING AT HERSELF IN THE MIRROR)

HELEN

You really ought to give it a try,

Louise.

(CROSSING TO LOUISE.)

By the way, do you have a hand
mirror?

#0915

LOUISE

(HANDS MIRROR TO HELEN)

> Oh, well I don't think that salon is for
> me, Helen. I feel uncomfortable in
> ritzy places like that.

HELEN

(LOOKING IN THE HANDMIRROR)

> So did I, at first. But as you can see,
> I bore up well under the strain.

TOM

(RISES AND ESCORTS HER TO THE COUCH)

> Uh, sweetheart. Why don't you just
> sit down and give your face a rest
> while I tell Louise about my day.

(TO LOUISE)

> You see, I signed up this new writer,
> she is . . .

(FLORENCE ENTERS.)

FLORENCE

> Mrs. Jefferson, I'm through scrubbing
> the kitchen floor.

#0915

(TOM REACTS)

LOUISE

Oh, good, Florence, Thank you. Did

you hear about Tom and Helen?

FLORENCE

Yeah. Sounds like you've had a pretty

good day, Mr. Willis.

TOM

Well, actually, it was a super day.

Wait'll I tell you about it.

FLORENCE

And you, too, Miss Willis. Congratu-

lations. You look lovely.

(NO REPLY AS HELEN CONTINUES TO GAZE AT
HERSELF IN THE HANDMIRROR.)

Mrs. Willis?

TOM

Helen!

HELEN

Hmmm? Oh. I'm so sorry.

(GIVES THE MIRROR TO LOUISE)

#0915

I shouldn't have started this. It's a bad

habit.

LOUISE

Did you actually meet a lot of

celebrities in that new salon?

(AS SHE REPLIES, HELEN SEARCHES IN HER PURSE,
FINDS HER COMPACT AND CONTINUES TO ADMIRE
HERSELF)

HELEN

Well, I didn't actually *meet* them, but

I really did see a lot of them. I got my

hair trimmed right next to Liza

Minnelli.

FLORENCE

You didn't!

HELEN

(THEN WORRIED)

Oh, Tom, do my pores look

unusually large today?

TOM

No dear, you're looking into the

magnification mirror.

#0915

LOUISE

(TAKING THE COMPACT)

Give me that!

FLORENCE

(CROSSES TO HELEN AND SITS NEXT TO HER)

You mean, you actually sat next to
Liza Minnelli?

TOM

That reminds me. About my new
writer, she . . .

FLORENCE

(TO HELEN)

Child, what's the name of that salon?

(TOM REACTS)

HELEN

It's called Hollenbeck-Kroft. It's very
exclusive.

FLORENCE

(PONDERING)

Oh.

(GEORGE EXCITEDLY ENTERS THE ROOM)

#0915

GEORGE

Weezy! Guess what happened?

LOUISE

Wait a minute, George. Do you want

to hear about Tom and Helen?

GEORGE

(JOYOUS)

No!

(THE WILLISES REACT)

My stock split three for one!

FLORENCE

What's that mean?

GEORGE

(CROSSING TO FLORENCE)

It means that I made more in five

minutes than you can make in five

lifetimes! Ain't that great?

FLORENCE

I'm all aglow.

#0915

GEORGE

(TO LOUISE)

> You know what else this means?
> Remember that ring you wanted?
> It's yours.

LOUISE

Oh, George, thank you. That's

wonderful.

(GEORGE CROSSES AROUND LOUISE)

HELEN

Well, I'd say, it's been a pretty special

day for all of us. Tom's new client

TOM

Yes, you see . . .

HELEN

(PLOUGHING AHEAD)

> George's stock, Louise's ring, my
> new face, and Florence's . . . Oh
> Florence . . .

(AWKWARD PAUSE)

#0915

FLORENCE

Oh, that's okay. Listen it's been a good
day for all of you and I'm happy for
every single one of you.

(RISES)

Of course, I could've done without
hearing about all of it in one day. But
I am happy for all of you.

SFX: DOORBELL
(GEORGE CROSSES TO DOOR)

LOUISE

(CROSSING TO FLORENCE)

Oh, come now, Florence, plenty of
special things have happened to you,
haven't they, George?

GEORGE

(AT DOOR)

I can't think of none.

(GEORGE OPENS THE DOOR TO RALPH WHO IS
HOLDING A SMALL PACKAGE)

RALPH

Hello, there, Mr. Jefferson, sir.

#0915

RALPH (CON'T)

I have a special delivery package,

for Florence.

FLORENCE

(CROSSING)

For me?

(GEORGE GOES TO BEDROOM)

LOUISE

(CROSSING TO FLORENCE)

There. You see, Florence? All you

needed was a little patience and good

things were bound to happen to you.

What is it?

FLORENCE

My new vacuum cleaner bags.

LOUISE

(COVERING)

Oh.

(BEAT)

Well, there's a good side to *that*.

#0915

(TAKES PACKAGE)

> See? These bags hold two gallons
>
> more soot than the old bags.

(FLORENCE STARES AT HER. LOUISE MEEKLY POINTS TO
BOX LABELS.)

> It says right here. Oh . . . Helen.
>
> Would you like a cup of coffee?

(HELEN LOOKS INTO MIRROR)

HELEN

> Love some.

LOUISE

> I'll go polish you a cup.

(LOUISE EXITS TO KITCHEN)

RALPH

> Not been a good day, huh, Florence?

FLORENCE

> Oh, no. It's been a terrific day. For
>
> everybody else.

RALPH

> Oh, I understand. It's the plight of the
>
> working class. Doomed to spend a
>
> lifetime watching our superiors bask

#0915

at the end of the rainbow. It's tough.
But I guess the best we can do is use
each other to lean upon until we
finally reach our own greater and just
rewards.

FLORENCE

Well, I guess you're right. Would you
like to come in for some coffee?

RALPH

Oh, I'm sorry but I can't. You see, I
helped fund a little expedition that
brought up a Spanish galleon last
night. So I have to jet down to Key
West for the opening of the treasure
chest. You know how it is.

FLORENCE

Goodbye, Ralph.

(RALPH LOOKS DISAPPOINTED)

TOM

(CROSSING TO RALPH)

Oh, Ralphy. Would you like to make
an extra five bucks?

#0915

RALPH

Passionately, sir.

TOM

Good. Because all you have to do is hear me out.

(HANDS RALPH THE MONEY)

I'm going to tell you about my new client . . .

(THEY EXIT)

FLORENCE

Now that is the last straw. I mean it's one thing for all of y'all to have a special day, but when *Ralph's* on top of the world, it's time for me to come out fighting. Mrs. Willis.

(HELEN IN THE MEANTIME IS ADMIRING HERSELF IN THE CANDY DISH)

Mrs. Willis!

HELEN

Hmm?

#0915

FLORENCE

You know what I'm going to do? I'm
going down to that beauty salon you
went to. I'm gonna sit back and let
folks wait on *me* for a change.

(GEORGE ENTERS)

So, how much does it cost to get "the
works?"

HELEN

(UNEASILY)

Three hundred dollars.

(BEAT)

But, it's worth it.

FLORENCE

Oh, well, what the heck. I've got two
hundred dollars saved. I'm gonna
blow it. I can at least get two-thirds
of "the works."

(FLORENCE STARTS OFF TO HER ROOM)

GEORGE

Uh, Florence . . .

#0915

(LOUISE ENTERS FROM THE KITCHEN AND GIVES
COFFEE TO HELEN)

FLORENCE

Mr. Jefferson, you can stand there and

insult me all you want. I'm going.

GEORGE

I know.

(SOTTO TO FLORENCE)

No, no, no. I just want to give you a

hundred dollars so you can get the

whole treatment.

(GEORGE HANDS HER THE MONEY)

FLORENCE

A hundred dollars?

GEORGE

Shhh! Shhh!

FLORENCE

Oh, Mr. Jefferson, thanks. Thanks a

lot. You know this might turn out to

be a special day for me after all.

(SHE EXITS TO BEDROOM)

#0915

LOUISE

(CROSSING TO GEORGE)

Oh, George, I'm so proud of you.

That's one of the best things you've

ever done for Florence.

GEORGE

Look I just *had* to, Weez. I can't

imagine one-third of that face

running around New York City

unmasked.

(GEORGE LAUGHS. LOUISE REACTS. HELEN IS STARING
INTO A COASTER AS WE)

FADE OUT.

This is the end of Act I. By this point the focus has clearly been placed on Florence for the episode. We know now that the remainder of the episode will deal with her efforts to make this her special day. Act II begins with a montage of quick shots of Florence at Hollenbeck-Kroft, the luxurious beauty salon, managing by a series of circumstances to avoid seeing Gladys Knight who is there with her. She finally engages her in conversation at a time when they both are wearing an avocado pack liberally applied to their faces. Florence's unassuming frankness and good feeling endear her to Gladys Knight. In the last scene, set back at the Jefferson apartment, Gladys Knight comes to call on Florence, who finally recognizes her for the first time.

Exercises

1. Select a television series with which you are already reasonably familiar. Watch an episode keeping notes on the material that the series' "bible" would contain:

locations, standard characters, plots and subplots, policy on program-specific characters. On the basis of this, do the following:

a. Write a treatment for a new episode.

b. Compose at least one act in standard script form based on the treatment.

2. Compose a "bible" as a presentation to a network proposing a new series. Make sure that it has potential for constant variation through shifts of locations or characters, so that the piece clearly lends itself to a succession of episodes and yet maintains a unity of its own.

3. Suppose you are hired to adapt a short story for an anthology series. Select a story that seems appropriate to the television medium and compose at least a portion of the screenplay you would submit.

PART IV

Final Stages
of Creation

10

Toward the "Final Draft"

The myth of the "final draft" can stultify efforts to revise a script more surely than any other single factor. That myth says that there is such a thing as a perfected script, one which cannot be changed without doing damage to the work. Despite the awesome masterpieces from the pens of great masters such as Sophocles, Shakespeare, Molière, Ibsen, or Chekhov, none of them ever produced a final draft, except in the sense that they never will produce another. Shakespeare in particular did not "finish" any of his plays until forced to by the numerous pirated editions of his works. Impure as it is, drama depends on the continual flux of both the forces embedded in the play and those which surround it whenever and wherever it is performed. Only our reverence makes the old masterpieces fixed documents. Even at that, each time we encounter a genuinely exciting new production of any of these works, we rediscover them by finding new values and effects in them. The same is true of any really good new play; it is so full of possibilities that only some can actually be realized.

This does not mean that a dramatist should leave things alone after the first draft and go on to other things. Improvement is possible even if perfection is not. The first draft only hints at the play: effects are still rough; the piece is out of proportion; it contains moments of sheer bordeom. In short, the play has yet to be released from the tangle of ill-conceived, hasty structures that seemed so fine initially.

Some of us are prone to another myth that stops revision dead in its tracks, namely that the play is the product of pure intuition and inspiration. Writing the play is an act of ritual sacrifice, calling for blood, sweat, and tears; surely any alteration is a desecration. This sounds silly, but there is something very real about it. While writing the first draft, your discoveries are fresh, the characters and their situations are alive, and the whole play reverberates in your mind. You are immersed in the play, feverishly living it as you write it. This is nothing mystical; it is simply the fervor of artistic creation. But it is not an altogether reliable state of mind. Inspiration alone does not create a work of art. It requires as well a detached contemplation of the work as a whole and calculated judgments about what works and what does not. That is the business of revision. At this point, aesthetic distance takes over from empathy. You have been inside the play; now you must stand outside. It is from the outside that the audience will encounter it, and if you hope they will enter in, you have to make it accessible.

Respecting the Will of the Play

We have spoken before of "the will of the play," referring to the play's apparent drive to assume a particular form given the forces that operate within it. This, too, is nothing mystical. Unless the play is absolutely incoherent, it demonstrates an implicit form. So, although neither plays nor their characters really have wills of their own, they do incline in certain directions. This is due to the fact that a play is a composite of many factors; some work in conjunction with others so convincingly they call for combination of some elements and deletion of other "inoperative" elements.

Thus, respecting the will of the play means discovering what the play is really about. It requires sorting out the elements that support it, weeding out those that do not, strengthening those that are weak, and providing those that are missing. Respecting the will of the play also means granting the play its integrity. To be sure, you wrote it, but once the first draft is done, the play begins to move away from you. Some day, hopefully, it will live on its own through various actors and you will be superfluous. The play's growing up and going out to seek its fortune begins with the second draft. In literal terms, all that you have imagined to be part of the play may not actually be there. The effect of the parts that are there may be entirely different from what you felt it would be. So you have to find out what this play really is as distinct from what you thought, and probably hoped, it was. This produces surprises—some of them actually pleasant, others much less so—but it must be done.

The painter, who steps away from the canvas from time to time to assess the contribution of the latest strokes to the overall effect, has an advantage over the dramatist. In fact, he has three advantages. First, he can check the overall effect any time he pleases, while the dramatist must wait until the whole draft is complete. Second, he can do so at a glance, while the dramatist has to read through the whole draft. And third, he can check the effect in the chosen medium, pigment on canvas, while the dramatist can only guess at the appearance of his work on stage or screen. This means that the dramatist must equip himself with some special tools of analysis. This is a creative sort of analysis, one that some non-dramatists cultivate so well that they become "play doctors" for dramatists unversed in this special art. How much better if one can do it for oneself!

Some practical considerations contribute to the success of analyzing one's own work. First of all, the detachment necessary for sound analysis can only come with a certain lapse of time. It cannot happen while you are in the midst of writing nor immediately after the first draft. You have to let the reverberations die down. You can never approach the play as a completely fresh experience, but you must do everything in your power to simulate that condition. So, a first practical rule is to avoid serious revision for two to three weeks after completion of the first draft. Only then can you begin to regard the play as its own experience.

A second consideration is the value of the comments of others: let others read your material and comment on it. This is not so easily done. Choosing and persuading the most appropriate people for the task is downright difficult. The best people are not always anxious to do it. Friends and relations are certainly the most willing; they would just love to read the latest work of their favorite son, nephew, friend, lover. That is exactly why their reactions are the least useful to you. What you most want is fresh but informed and detached reactions. Criticism has its uses, but because it is rooted in another person's perspective, it may or may not be appropriate. Descriptions of the play and what it does are more useful because they tell you how close to or wide of the mark you may be. Both responses are most valuable coming from someone who is knowledgeable about drama and interested in new work. Such people are often professionals in the theatre or cinema world, and you should be prepared to pay for their services.

The third and last practical consideration is that you need a means to examine the work as a totality without having to read it over and over or search through it endlessly. If you have not drafted a scenario or treatment for the play prior to writing the first draft, now is the time to do so. If you have already a scenario or treatment, chances are that the draft departed from the plan in several instances. At any rate, you need a capsule summary of the play as it exists now. By describing the essence of the play and paring away all the overlay of wit, charm, joy, and sheer beauty of the full play, you expose the play's structural weaknesses to the cruel light of day. That light allows serious analysis to begin.

Play Analysis for the Dramatist

Analysis begins by recognizing a basic truth about any play: it is deliberately not actuality. A play separates itself from the life around it in order to reflect on some facet of that life. It can only dramatize by first separating itself from life. Life does not seek to inform, delight, compel, and fascinate us. Drama does. So, how a play differs from life is a leading indicator of what it is all about. Analysis concerns these four factors: medium, audience, context, and agent. A play occupies its medium, the stage or the screen, in its own way; it also confronts its audience in its own way; it carefully isolates the time and place of the play's action, and it characterizes the agents of its action. All four matters must be treated with consistency, especially with respect to the overall effect the play is to produce. That consistency is hard to maintain in the first draft. Only after a full draft exists, concretely characterizing the people, places, and actions that make up the play, can you know what patterns might give it fullest coherence and power. A finished first draft is your first chance to discover that consistency. The following questions may help find it:

1. *Where is the play's crux and what forces lead to it?* Since every play is an energy system of forces aligned in a basic polarity to produce tension, both the polarity and the tension should be clear. The crux is the one moment in the play when that clarity should be inescapable. It is the snapping of the play's basic tension. If that moment is vague, over-extended, or omitted, the whole play suffers. The crux may be so muted that one is not aware that the tension has snapped until later, on reflection, but provided it occurs at a precise moment, it passes the test. A play in its first draft may not polarize its forces clearly or may never snap the tension. It is the first thing to look for, because it affects everything else.

2. *Who is the play's central character?* The question is sometimes phrased simply as, "Whose play is it?" Now, as we have seen, it is possible to write a play that has no central character, but then the driving force is embodied in something other than a character, which functions as a character. So the question remains relevant. Unless there is some point of identification (sympathetic or otherwise) for the audience, they cannot relate to the play except as an abstraction. A play in its first draft may exhibit an uncertainty about where that point of identification belongs. It may seem to be a play about one character at one point, then about another, and then suddenly perhaps about no one in particular. That sort of fuzziness needs clearing up.

3. *Where in the play do characters appear?* Drama consists of encounters and relies on pivotal choices about who encounters whom, when. A useful device here is a "character distribution chart" which costume designers always draft to understand the comings and goings of the costumes. The chart shows who appears in each French scene and it can help the dramatist know what encounters occur when. You may discover that two characters who could guarantee dramatic action if they were to encounter one another never meet. Or you may find that a certain group of characters meet too often or spend too much time together, creating scenes that are predictable and dull.

4. *Why is the play set where it is?* The setting or settings of a stage play, the locations of a screenplay, may seem at first a static, settled matter. In fact, they are potential sources of tension, contrast, and interest. They can make dynamic contributions to the play's action. Indeed, if the setting is genuinely neutral, it is probably a mistake. If the setting is irrelevant to the action, you have not only overlooked a valuable source of tension, but also ensured that the play on stage or screen will exhibit dreary emptiness. Beyond the question of the contributions of scenery or locations to the look of a play, the placement of its action—in a certain city, in a certain room, indoors or outdoors, in the daytime or at night—all bear on the drama. It should matter that an action is here rather than there; there should be a reason *this* action occurs in *this* place.

5. *Why does the action occur at this time?* Why now? Since drama trades upon immediacy, something must be at stake in a play. What happens matters to both the characters and the audience, even if for differing reasons. A frequent problem with a first draft is choosing too broad a time span, and so incorporating events that serve only informational purposes— events that were better heard about than seen. Less frequently, the first draft keeps offstage or out-of-sight events that do indeed matter, while presenting those that do not. Generally, if the present time contains no impending concern, the audience can anticipate nothing, and the drama withers. Three points in the developing action of the play are worth examining: the point of attack, the crux, and the dénouement. Consider if the time span were different, would any of these points assume greater strength?

6. *How does the play use its medium?* An effective play derives its effects from the material at hand, that of the chosen medium—the screen or the stage. The screenplay makes deliberate use of images and their juxtapositions, moving bodies, and a moving camera. The stage play uses the confines of the stage, the implied extension of the world offstage, the double presence of actors and characters, and the encounter of audience and actors as people. The play that ignores its medium will be empty and flat.

7. *How does the play confront its audience?* A play's ultimate and most important encounter occurs between the play and its audience. How that encounter is characterized can make a world of difference: a dull play can suddenly become exciting, new values can be tapped, and a play may even assume new meanings. Remember that the audience is in a sense a character in your play. Give them a character. This is done through tone, the attitude you ask them to take toward your material. If treating material comically leaves it flat, try a serious tone or vice versa. Sometimes, a simple adjustment here can save a play that otherwise seemed doomed.

8. *What is the play about?* This is the big question. Knowing the answer can save you a lot of grief. There are so many pressures exerted on a playwright or screenwriter to make changes, for good reasons and for bad, by producers, directors, actors, agents, and anyone else involved, that one needs confidence in one's material. Deciding whether to make a change and, if so, how to do it requires that you know what your play is about. Asking what a play is about, it should be added, is not the same as asking what it means. What a play means is probably not a matter about which the dramatist should bother his head. Its meaning is inherent in the issues, the tone, the emphases, in all the decisions made writing the play. To express that meaning now in expository prose may be of no help in the revision process. It might even hurt it. But to be able to say what the play is about, what facet of human experience it explores, can help because it lays down the parameters of the play. It tells you what is relevant and what is not. The question boils down to what in the play is crucial to its experience and what is ancillary. Knowing that, you would also know what changes might enhance the play's overall effect and what might detract from it. If you know that your play is about "the way we perceive time," or about "the effects of unrelieved guilt," or about "the absurdity of bureaucratic posturing," then you know what matters to the play.

Answering these eight questions could be a dry and academic exercise. They are intended as guideposts; they are the issues you need to face in the revision process. Do not let them discourage you. For some you will have ready answers; for others you may have to wrestle in the back of your mind. Now, what makes the analysis creative is that you can answer any question indirectly by imagining the scene, the setting, the characters, the issues all framed in other ways. If you have doubts that this is the right point of attack, for example, apply the "What if?" test to it and place it at another point in the play's story. If you question the selection of the setting, what if you were to use this or that setting in its stead? If the tone is uncertain, try another one. Would another character take focus more convincingly?

Revising a play requires several drafts. The second draft is usually the most drastically changed, provided it is based on a thorough analysis. It then is usually followed by two or three more drafts, each of which polishes the play's finer points. This is the standard pattern, but it is by no means universal. Other developments usually interfere. It may be that the analysis of the first draft persuades you that this play is a loss, not worth working on further. You may be right, and your honesty with yourself will save you considerable trouble. You may also be wrong. In that case, throwing away the script is the worst thing you can do. Later you may discover the key to making it work, if only you still had it. In any event, it is always a bad idea to throw away your creative work, for some portions of it may prove useful in another context, and even if not, you can always learn from it. Another possible result of the analysis of the first draft is salvaging the play by testing for new values and writing quite a different play.

Testing for New Values

Contemplating and analyzing the first draft may do nothing to clarify what is to be done in the second, except that you remain convinced that there is something at the core of the play that still fascinates you and so still demands that you struggle with it. Testing for new values in the script beyond those that surfaced in the first draft can be very useful. This amounts to reshaping the play's basic premise or drastically altering one of the fundamental givens of the play—its major character, its context, its style, the tone of the play.

This is a time to return to the record book. Not only may there be some lost ideas there, but the major revisions you are now contemplating need to be tested in writing. New scenes, character descriptions, snatches of dialogue, and scenarios or treatments are called for. The experiments may be disjointed; they are, nevertheless, ones that you can use to teach yourself more about the possibilities inherent in your play. Suppose, now, that you were to move the play from a bar in an industrial Northern city to a cafe in a Southern town. Suppose you were to add a character, keep a piece of knowledge from another character, alter a scene to give it a comic edge, open the play to the audience in a different way. All these need to be tested in written form before they can become part of a full draft of the play.

No play is so perfect that it cannot profit from such experimentation. Perhaps the most valuable attitudes a dramatist can cultivate are willingness to experiment and reluctance to put the play aside until one knows where the most tempting possibilities lead. The first draft has its fascinations and its blind spots for its dramatist. Until the fascinations are put into perspective and the blind spots eliminated, the play is not playable. For example, the play may be written out of a compulsion to feature a certain flamboyant character, which is all well and good, except that a play is always more than a character, even a play with a cast of one. The character needs a setting, a point in his life that matters, a way of encountering that life and this audience that makes him fully interesting. Another play may be written out of fascination with a particular image: a person wound up in a sheet, a setting in the form of a magnificent cathedral, a character with a penchant for snipping out newspaper articles, a character hobbling about on crutches clutching a whisky bottle. All of these are valid, theatrical images, but they are incomplete. The first draft may not have completed all the facets needed to make it a play. Further experimenting may show the way to the full play, which the second draft will then round out.

Punishing the Characters

Another common shortcoming of a first draft consists of characters who are too comfortable. This is understandable; you tend to grow fond of your own characters as you work with them. So, you protect them, shield them from danger, and generally give them a good life. Perhaps they will reward you by being witty or charming or endearing. Still, the essence of drama lies in tension. Characters who are comfortable will produce nothing much more than boredom. A good, engaging character requires circumstances that make him squirm. He needs to be at odds with himself, with other characters, or with his situation.

If your play seems flat and unvaried, it may be that the characters are simply too comfortable. Put them to the test: put them in upsetting, troublesome, or demanding circumstances. Push your characters. Force them to make decisions. Drama lies in such spectacle. Once challenged, they will begin to behave dramatically. The play itself will assume vibrancy. This applies equally to comedy as to tragedy or serious drama. Even the characters in Oscar Wilde's glib high comedies are made to suffer. Jack Worthing, for example, is *earnestly* seeking to prove himself Ernest in *The Importance of Being Earnest*. Anton Chekhov remarked to a dramatist after reading his play:

> Now about your play. You undertook to depict a man who has not a grief in the world, and then you took fright. The problem seems to me to be clear. Only he has no grief who is indifferent. . . . Those unmoved dullards who will suffer no pain even when you burn them with red hot irons cannot be discussed at all.

Chekhov's letters are a refreshing set of reflections, well worth looking into. At any rate, you yourself can discover your characters' full dramatic potentials only by putting them to the test. Make them suffer and see what reaction will come of it. Action and reaction make up drama. If the actions are not powerful enough to produce reactions or the characters too bland, the play cannot happen.

Polishing

The question of the play's overall shape and effect should be resolved by the second draft, and certainly by its third. The play now has an appropriate setting in time and space, its forces are well-marshalled, the action has direction and momentum, the crux is clear. Now, with some satisfaction, you can turn to polishing the play.

Polishing involves fine tuning the various elements and sharpening the effects they produce. It may require cutting, adding, shifting, and rearranging. Strangely enough, some of these minor changes can produce vastly enhanced effects. In some instances, a simple gesture may replace a long speech. The gesture not only serves the interests of economy, but also produces a stronger effect by being more pointed and emphatic. On other occasions, a brief exchange of dialogue may assume a new, longer life by the insertion of an ironic undercurrent. Rhythm becomes important now. The time spent on one issue rather than another may need adjustment. Many special techniques discussed earlier, especially in Chapter 7 on the dramatic script, find new application now in revising a script. Some deserve reiteration now.

First, the major concern is that one single action bind together the whole play. A play requires a strong sense of forward movement and that can come only of a single driving action. This is the overriding consideration. Other techniques are ways of providing or testing for the presence of that single action.

The "but/therefore" principle tests for sufficient contrast in the succession of events that make up a play. If events flow too directly, linked one to another by a series of "ands," the revision ought to seek ways of throwing them into contrast through "buts" and "therefores."

The "second dialogue" also works to insure a sense of tension and interest by providing another level of interaction besides the overt one. It often works by incorporating a "third factor," an outside reference point beyond the two characters engaged in an action. Often a scene that is blatant and without energy may assume interest by adding a third factor. Although drama plays directly on our senses, it can suggest inner life through the use of bouncing boards—of objects and even of other characters who reflect the deeper concerns. These are third factors.

Ironies may also be of use in polishing the script, producing a pleasant, controlled ambiguity that intrigues an audience. If one character knows something other characters want to know or the characters know something we very much want to know, a palpable tension is created. Polishing can vary these levels of knowledge and produce some engaging ironies.

Finally, one can pose any of the three clipped questions: "What if?" "Why now?" and "So what?" The first two should have been thoroughly tested in the analysis phase of revision, but, on a minor scale, they serve even now in polishing the script. The "now" of the play may be enriched. Some new twist of the condition of action, the "what if," may cause a new dimension to spring to life. The third question, "So what?" may serve the polishing phase very well, especially in demanding clarity about what matters in the play as a whole.

These special techniques for polishing should not produce cataclysmic changes that revamp the whole script. If that happens when you thought you were polishing, it suggests that the play was foundering, destined to sink anyway. Hopefully you can salvage another play from its hull.

As the polishing phase progresses, you become more and more detached from the play, more able to judge it objectively, and yet also more weary of it. It leads sometimes to such disinterest that you can no longer be sure why you wrote the play in the first place. As soon as this attitude sets in, you would be well advised to leave the play alone. Any further tinkering is likely to destroy something valuable. You have now arrived at the "final draft." If you can anticipate a production, you can cling to the reassurance that in the rehearsal process, the play's life and its interest for you will rekindle. Then you can revise some more.

11

The Script Out in the World

Provided you have faith in it, a completed script needs to go out into the world. As with parents and children, it is bad for a dramatist and his play to remain together at home too long. This applies to any professional artist and his work of art; the whole point in art is sharing the work with others. The painter who piles paintings in a studio, the poet who stuffs poems into a desk drawer, the composer who crams compositions into a piano bench commit a sin against their art, pardoned only if releasing these works on the world could be construed as a worse sin. In many cases it certainly would be. For just such a reason, many fine artists have a trunk full of works they do not wish anyone to see. The amateur may well keep his art at home, too, for he derives satisfaction chiefly from the doing of art, not from sharing (selling) it. But, if you are serious about writing, have done all you can with a script you believe in, get it out of the house.

This journey out into the world is more important for a play than for any other type of art work, for it is a phase of its development. A painting does not alter by going on exhibit. A novel or a poem may receive some further polish in the editorial process, but both are published substantially as they left their author's desk. A play, however, is not a play until it is performed. Although a musical composition is also incomplete until performed, even here there is a difference. The musical score rarely needs to undergo any significant change in the process of rehearsal. Scoring music is much more precise and dependable than scripting a play. In contrast, the stage and the screen pose too many uncertain variables and they depend on too diverse a set of arts and artists for a script fully to account for the outcomes. In planning and rehearsing a play, new dimensions inevitably appear—as well as faults and flaws which could not be clearly foreseen. Drama thus depends heavily on the creative collaboration of its several artists and the script may change enormously as a result. In short, the play's journey into the world is very much a part of its very creation. Your work is scarcely complete with the "final draft."

More will be said about this creative collaboration later. But first, before any of this wild, exhilarating and painful business can begin, the play has to get off your desk and out into the world. That calls for marketing the script.

Marketing the Script

Technically, "marketing" means "selling," but the term is used here in the broad sense of convincing someone to produce a play, whether money changes hands or not. Ultimately, we indeed aim to have money change from someone's hands into ours; meanwhile, there is an advantage, especially early in a career, in seeing the play on stage or on screen and knowing how it works. What was the "final draft" can now be revised after all.

Until recently, advice to an unknown dramatist seeking a production of a play was severely limited: look into the "amateur theatricals"—the college and community theatres in one's area. It is still good advice; in fact better than ever. Interest in new plays is growing on all levels. The timidity that prompts people to let others find interesting new plays and test them out first is fortunately fading. It is no longer surprising to find a community theatre offering a new play; some even have resident playwrights. Colleges and universities with reasonably adventurous drama programs have long been producing workshop performances of plays in progress. There is now much more of that and a more frequent incidence of full-scale productions for the subscription season. This growth has been spurred by a changing general climate and by the specific encouragement of the Playwriting Awards program of the American College Theatre Festival, the ingenious idea of screenwriter Michael Kanin. Designed specifically for student playwrights, the program has fostered an interest among college theatres in producing new plays by others as well. In larger cities, regional theatres, both professional and semi-professional, often sponsor play readings, workshop productions, and studio productions of new work—sometimes including one in the subscription season. The Actors Theatre of Louisville, one of the most prestigious, sponsors a New Play Festival every spring. Another example of the ferment in new plays is the creation of the Atlanta New Play Project, where the city's theatres have banded together to present a summer festival of new plays.

Another growing opportunity for the dramatist is the professional workshop. Most workshops are invitational, based on competition and awarding stipends to the participating playwrights. The revelations that can come of working with professional actors and directors on rehearsed script-in-hand performances speeds a play on to its fullest realization and simultaneously makes it known to those who might take it to its next step, a professional full production. Probably the most successful of these and certainly the inspiration behind many others is the O'Neill Theatre Center in Waterford, Connecticut, founded in 1965 by Charles White and for many years now under the artistic direction of Lloyd Richards. The playwright or screenwriter spends several weeks in a summer residency working with the director and the actors and with his script. An enviable record of successful plays and television pieces has emerged. In New York City, a number of such enterprises have long been in operation, the oldest and best known being the New Dramatists.

Screenwriting presents a special case. Producing a stage play can be done with the proverbial "two boards and a passion," but producing a screenplay requires elaborate equipment and technical expertise—both costly. Nevertheless, one can learn something of the behavior of a movie or videotape on one's own initiatives. Super eight movie cameras and editing equipment are now available at reasonable cost. Recent developments in videotape, VTR cameras, editing equipment, and cassette recorders make it possible to experiment with videotape; no doubt such equipment will gradually become more and more accessible. Still, one needs other people, capable of contributing talent and expertise, and these may not be available at affordable prices. Film and television programs in colleges and universities often conduct production programs. The aspiring screenwriter, however, need not restrict himself to screen experiments; any experience in dramatic writing and production will be helpful. Several production companies and studios conduct apprenticeship programs and they are constantly in need of new talent and in search of it. Such programs are worth looking into.

A vast array of contests are organized for both stage and screen media. Some are for treatments or even completed screenplays, others for stage plays. The former tend to offer an award of a standard screenplay contract with an established production company or film studio. The latter usually carry a cash award, production of the play, and expenses to travel to the producing theatre for rehearsals and the opening performance of the play. There are so many of these contests that entering them could become almost a full-time occupation.

This is not the place to catalogue all opportunities; there are too many and they change yearly, happily with new projects always appearing. Various organizations and publications can offer help in obtaining information on current opportunities. First among these are professional writers' unions: the Dramatists Guild for playwrights and the Writers Guild of America for screenwriters. Although they are unions, both allow associate memberships for nonprofessionals and access to their publications and some services. The *Dramatists Quarterly* and the *WGA Newsletter* are both treasure troves of information. The Theatre Communications Group, another valuable organization, produces an annual publication, *The Dramatists Sourcebook,* one of the best compendia of information for playwrights and screenwriters available. The TCG also conducts the Plays-in-Progress program, which selects and distributes a restricted collection of worthwhile new plays to participating producing groups. Two other publications worth consulting are *Simon's Directory of Theatrical Services and Information* and the September issue of the magazine *The Writer* which lists contests and producing groups interested in new plays. The American Theatre Association sponsors two significant programs, the Playwrights Program and the American College Theatre Festival. The former develops workshop productions of new plays for the organization's yearly conventions, while the latter sponsors the Playwriting Awards program encouraging college productions of student-written new plays through a wide assortment of awards and regional festivals of college productions and playwrights' workshops, all culminating in the national festival at the Kennedy Center in Washington, D.C., featuring at least the best new play of the season.

One fact of the dramatist's life should now be clear: the necessity to promote one's own work. No play in its "final draft" should be left sitting on your desk. It should always be on someone else's desk, someone in a position to do something for it. Find out who these people are and keep your most worthwhile plays in circulation. A single stage play may be copied and sent out to several different people, although as soon as it is selected for production by one of them, the others should be notified, for they often wish to offer a premiere of a play. Since production of a screenplay virtually nullifies any other production and since the film and television world is relatively limited, you ought to restrict the number of people looking at your material. If too many are looking at it at the same time, there is a chance for confusion and misunderstandings, especially if you cannot remember who they are.

With a playable play ready for potential producers, you might take this series of steps. First, make up multiple copies in correctly typed format. No one receiving an incorrectly typed manuscript will be impressed with its author's professionalism. The first copies are destined for the copyright office, for you do not want your uncopyrighted material circulating. Unpublished dramatic material for stage may be copyrighted since it is intended for public consumption and so may be produced by any theatre group that chooses to do so. For the appropriate forms and a quotation of the current registration fee, write to:

Register of Copyright
Copyright Office
Library of Congress
Washington, D.C. 20540

Screenplays, on the other hand, are normally registered with the Writers Guild of America, west. Write to them at 8955 Beverly Boulevard, Los Angeles, California 90048. Your script should now have the notation "Copyright, 1983 by yourself" (your name) or "Registered, WGAw." If for any reason you are in a hurry, you may use the shortcut of sending yourself a copy of the script by registered mail and leaving it sealed once you receive it, as evidence that the play existed in your name as of the date of mailing.

Next, do research on where to send the script. Some theatres and film production companies will accept unsolicited manuscripts, others will not. In any case, it is wise to send a letter of inquiry first. Do not overlook workshop or contest opportunities. Then send the scripts out, each accompanied by a specially addressed cover letter dealing with the nature of your script and how it suits the needs of the company insofar as you know them. The letter should be brief and to the point. Enclose in the package a "SASE" (self-addressed, stamped envelope), for the play's eventual return. Duplicating and postage costs can add up quickly. This means you do not want to send the script where it is likely to have no appeal and you want to do what you can to have the script returned. Be prepared nevertheless to lose a few. You may also wish to include a self-addressed, stamped postcard acknowledging receipt of your script. Keep a good record of where your scripts are. Then you must accept the fact that you may not hear any response for some time.

In light of that, it is best to get busy on your other writing. There is nothing more that you can do for that play, so you would do yourself a service to get it off your mind. When it comes back with a rejection notice, send it out again. Still do not bother your head about it. There are any number of reasons for script rejection that do not touch upon its quality. If it does not suit one company at this time, it may suit another. In the interest of self-preservation, most groups do not send any detailed commentary; for the same reason, you should not dwell on the rejections. Let them pile up in the back of your mind while you work on other plays. After a while, that pile may tell you that that play has no future; until then, keep sending it out.

Film and television industries have some practices that vary from those of the theatre. Since both distribute widely and dedicate themselves to a single production of any screenplay, the screenplay is regarded as a one-shot deal. Once produced by any company, it is of no use to anyone else. A stage play can play only to a very limited audience in any one production, so if it is good, it continues to be of use to other companies. As a result of this difference, television and film production companies have their own way of doing things. They do not want to hear ideas because too many people have the notion that they could sue a company for producing an idea they once had. Consequently, these companies require a query letter which asks permission to submit a script, but does not describe it beyond its title and its type or genre. These companies also require you to fill out a release in connection with your submission. The release is a legal statement that frees the company from liability in the event they should ever produce a piece that seems based on the same general idea as your material. It cannot free them from obvious plagiarism. The form is standard and available from the Writers Guild. Some companies, however, have their own form, which you should request. Your query should also offer to submit your material in the form of a synopsis, outline, treatment, or full screenplay. You should be prepared to submit it in any of these forms: after all, if they buy the treatment, their next step is to hire someone to write the screenplay; they may as well know that a screenplay already exists—yours. If you are then invited to submit, package it all up and mark the envelope "Release Form Enclosed" (as the package will probably be returned unopened otherwise) and send it off.

Although self-promotion may not be palatable to you, it must be done. The world is full of people of negligible talent who are nevertheless successful because they seek out and maintain appropriate contacts and know when and where to promote their own work. Conversely, some very talented people have never succeeded at all for having withdrawn from the fray. Self-promotion, at least, is something anyone can do; writing good plays is not. You may get to the point where it is appropriate to obtain an agent who will take some of the burden of promotion off your shoulders, but it is a responsibility you can never avoid. Even established playwrights and screenwriters must continue to develop contacts and search out opportunities.

The Deal

In the midst of all this, it is possible that you will receive a contract. At this point, we are talking about money changing hands. Money always puts a new light on things. Certainly, it is pleasant that someone will actually pay you to do what you like to do anyway—to write. At the same time, paying you is a way of exerting control over you. Your work is wanted for someone else's purposes. So long as these purposes coincide reasonably well with your own, no harm is done. If enough money is involved, you may not worry about artistic control. Still, these contracts deserve scrutiny and you need some expert advice.

Since money is involved, you may be sure that there will be those ready at hand to proffer help. You may wish to turn to an attorney first for a legal opinion on the contract. You will shortly have to join the appropriate union, the Dramatists Guild or the Writers Guild, and they will, even beforehand, examine the contract. Both guilds are closed shops dedicated to looking after the best interests of writers. They do it well. They have established standard contracts and options that insure that the writer's rights are respected and that the work is not wrongfully exploited. They also stand for the collective interests of writers, offering many professional services and publications. All this is expensive, and so is the membership fee.

Another source of assistance at this time can be an agent. Any agent is apt to be interested in a writer who has just won a contract, since that suggests someone capable of turning out saleable material, from which a percentage might be earned. Many production companies, producers, and theatres will accept submissions only through agents. This leads to the famous adage, "You can't sell a script until you have an agent, and you can't get an agent until you've sold a script." This is not true, but there is enough truth in it to suggest a value in having an agent. A good agent has contacts in the production business, keeps abreast of developments, knows who is looking for what, where opportunities are found, how to critique a play, and generally how to look after the dramatists to whom he commits himself. A good agent makes sales of your work that you would probably never make otherwise. You must not begrudge such an agent his ten percent.

It pays to take care in selecting an agent. It can be done only slightly more casually than entering into matrimony. Writer and agent have a complex and personal relationship; although it may not last a lifetime, your career will be deeply affected. In addition to being your business representative, your agent is your personal critic, your artistic advisor, and sometimes confidant-confessor. He needs to be someone who takes interest in your work, but more than that, one who genuinely understands it. He may have to tell you some day that you are on a wrong track in your career. You do not have to believe him, but if you are persuaded at the outset that this agent does indeed understand what your work is all about, such advice is worth serious consideration. The agent may also from time to time have to see you through a fallow period, encourage you, make suggestions. All these depend on a close, comfortable relationship.

Do not take this to mean that, once you have signed on, your agent is simply going to take care of you. This is still essentially a business arrangement. The agent troubles himself most about those clients he most needs. You are still in charge of your life. The agent cannot take care of your personal needs as a writer. He cannot even do all the marketing of your scripts. You will need to continue to make your own contacts, press for productions of your material, and seek out opportunities. The fact that the agent takes ten percent of all sales whether he makes them or not should not deter you. After all, you keep ninety percent, and you have had another production. The greatest values in an agent are his managing your business affairs, negotiating your contracts, and making you known. Whatever he may be able to do beyond this is a bonus.

Both the Dramatists Guild and the Writers Guild of America will provide lists of approved agents. Some agents are willing to read unsolicited manuscripts, others are not. Few will read material that arrives unannounced. A letter of inquiry describing yourself and your work and requesting permission to submit should be sent first. If possible, it pays to have one or more letters of reference from professional people, actors, directors, designers, professors of drama. Do not be in a hurry to obtain an agent; a beginning dramatist does not need one. It is embarrassing to be told that your manuscript is very interesting and please send others, when the fact is you only have one. Do not in any event sign with an agent unless he is recognized by the appropriate guild and do not ever pay him in advance of doing work for you.

Contracts vary so greatly that it is difficult to generalize about them. They range from a simple letter of intent, such as an amateur theatre offering so much for each performance of one of your plays, to a complex legal document allowing so much advance money, another sum later, and a percentage of the box office, all contingent on this or that. Obviously, there are times when only legal counsel can see you through the maze.

In the professional theatre, it is common to take an option on a play—to purchase exclusive production rights to the play for a specified period of time, usually six months to a year. No one else may produce the work during that period, which the producer uses to secure the wherewithal to produce the play: the capital, a theatre, a director, perhaps a star actor or two, a designer. If at the end of the period the play is still not in production, the option must either be dropped or renegotiated. A professional resident company will normally issue a direct contract for the production and performance royalties for the play, since with resources already in place the option is usually not necessary.

The film production company or the television network often use "step contracts," calling for a piece of work in return for a set sum of money—with the minimum amount already set by the Writers Guild in negotiation with the industry. The steps include an outline, a treatment, a screenplay, and revisions. The contract is open for renewal at each step, so the company retains its freedom to hire whomever it pleases to accomplish the next step. Again, an attorney is advisable, for these are complex legal documents.

Through all this, it pays to remember that you remain the single most important promoter of your work. If you are unwilling to go to bat for yourself, you will not stimulate anyone else to do it—including your agent. Short of making a nuisance of yourself, you need to make and maintain contacts; make yourself and your work known to directors and producers; write letters; apply for grants, awards, and workshop opportunities; keep records of your finances, copyrights and scripts. Behind a majority of productions of new scripts is some form of personal contact; few of those contacts occurred because the world beat a path to the dramatist's door.

Creative Collaboration

Once "marketed," the script goes into production, ushering in a new phase of creative endeavor, vastly different from the work you have done up to now. It is no longer lonely. You are joined by scores of people. While it is nice to have company, especially of people dedicated to fulfilling the play your script describes, it is also confusing—even frightening.

In all its media, drama is a collaborative art. A fully realized play depends on a diversity of artists unmatched in any other art form. A glance at the credits as they pass by at the end of a film or at the program of a stage play provides some idea of the enormity of the collaboration that has taken place. The people on these lists are artists (such as directors, choreographers, conductors and musicians, costumers, scene designers, art directors, scene painters, light designers, sound designers, actors, singers, dancers) who join with technicians (technical directors, grips, electricians, light board operators, fly gallery operators, sound operators, wardrobe mistresses, dressers, cutters and drapers, make-up technicians) to realize a play. Somewhere back in the wings or lurking about the studio is the little dramatist. Once in a while, someone might remember who that person is and ask about the play. If you feel as do the characters in Jean-Paul Sartre's *No Exit* that "Hell is other people," getting involved in drama is tantamount to passing through the gates marked "Leave all hope ye who enter here."

Difficulties and frustrations attend this final phase of creation because drama happens to take people as its material. In this respect it is like no other art except dance. People are unpredictable; they can be sensitive, jealous, anxious, passionate; to try to make art out of them would seem the height of folly. Designer and theorist Edward Gordon Craig, who was fond of the idea of purity, hoped for a theatre that would escape this mayhem by submitting itself to a "super-director," capable of writing, directing, designing his plays to be enacted then by "super-marionettes" under his full control. William Gibson uses an analogy to capture the frightening uncertainty of using people to make art; he describes an incident following one of the early rehearsals for his play *Two for the Seesaw:*

> In the evening I visited a painter's studio, and envied her; she was working in a medium where she alone could ruin it. . . . When another artist asked what I had against actors, I said writing for them was like painting not in oils but in colored mice; after the painting was finished the mice began running around.

All these mice running around can drive you to distraction. Surely there must be ways of exerting control, and hopefully too, some compensation for putting up with it all.

As for compensation, a play makes up for its "impurity" by being capable (if well-controlled) of engaging an audience with a power and a vigor well beyond an equally good painting, sculpture, novel, poem, or symphony. It unveils a whole world. It delights our senses with a panoply of paint, fabric, light, sounds, words, and movements. It brings us face-to-face with issues that color our lives, issues pushed into such compelling relief that we glimpse the wonder, the joy, the absurdity, and the pain of that strange condition we share with the others in the audience: the human condition. Another compensation is that Gibson's "colored mice" can come up with astonishing insights, improvements, and enrichments of the play. As actors lay claim to their characters and begin to live their lives, dimensions you may never have dreamed of can emerge. The world that the designers have provided can usher in similar surprises. That is exciting and rewarding.

Jean Giraudoux, in his eloquent *Visitations*, speaks of two laws which govern the work of the dramatist. The first is that the characters, and the play itself, will wander off and become strangers to their creator. The play never again belongs to the playwright:

> From the first performance on, it belongs to the actors. The author wandering in the wings is a kind of ghost whom the stagehands detest if he listens in or is indiscreet. After the hundredth performance, particularly if it is a good play, it belongs to the public. In reality the only thing the playwright can call his own are his bad plays.

When he meets these characters again, "in Carcassonne or Los Angeles," they are total strangers to him. All this is happy and sad and a little awe-inspiring. The second law, a corollary of the first, is that despite this loss, the voice of the playwright remains as a force rallying a public to shared concerns. Giraudoux sees the dramatist as a visionary conducting rituals in the theatre that accomplish a communion among all who participate on a level richer, more varied, and more moving than can happen anywhere else. Giraudoux's vision of the dramatist as a spokesman-priest of an age and of the theatre as a house of communion may seem Romantic hyperbole. But the playwright's presence in a play is an undeniable force.

Here the matter of control enters. For both stage and screen, the director coordinates the production process. The director's special charge is the coordination of all artistic elements—an art in itself. He must have a vision of the fully realized play and use it to inspire, direct, balance, and judge the contributions of all other artists. It requires a firm hand, but also enough diplomacy and charisma to make everyone want to contribute fully and respect the contributions of others enough to make needed adjustments.

Where does the dramatist fit into this? Is he simply another one of these artists who is supposed to contribute his best and respect the rest? Yes and no. Yes, the dramatist must recognize that the control of the production lies with the director. The dramatist, and anyone else for that matter, would be making a serious mistake to deal with any of the artists except through the director. On the other hand, the dramatist does not operate in a way parallel to that of the other artists. There are important differences which are clearer if we examine them in connection with medium—first the screen media, then the stage.

The screenwriter's creative collaboration occurs almost exclusively during the pre-production phase. The pressures to revise are sometimes relentless, even during the time he is composing. All through the process of composing the screenplay he finds himself in a series of story conferences. Some pressures may not be particularly creative, since they may come from extrinsic considerations such as market analysis or the peculiar talents of the star actor for whom the film is being made. The screenwriter can respond to this and all pressure in any way he chooses: you can lead a horse to water, but you cannot make him drink. The screenwriter has to deal with the material as he sees fit, because, for the time being, he is doing the writing. Naturally, the studio or production company may accept the script and hire someone else to revise it. That is pressure, too. Under it, even some horses will drink.

Despite the concentration of pressure and forced collaboration, screenwriting has two advantages. First, the screenwriter's collaborators are usually a relatively small group of people with whom he deals directly and regularly. It includes those people who have a stake in the overall play, the producer, the director, his staff, sometimes the designers and editors. The group is usually maintained as a group, the "regulars" at the story conferences. So, the screenwriter can become attuned to their wishes, able to anticipate them and deal with them. The second advantage is that, once the script is purchased and production starts, the screenwriter does not face an onslaught of other people. In fact, he sometimes hears no more about it. The screenwriter does not face that adjustment of suddenly dealing with colored mice. From time to time during the shoot, he may receive a request for a revision, but he will receive it from the same people he has been dealing with all along. He does not undergo the mayhem of rehearsals nor advice from everyone when nothing seems to be working. The manipulation of images and the design of shots is the business of the shoot, and that is the director's business. Much "revision" can be done by devising shots another way. So the screenwriter is left in comparative peace.

The theatre production is a much more complicated process for the playwright. While the film director may take advantage of new values by altering camera angles and framing, in the theatre only the playwright can take full advantage, for these new values are apt to call for script changes. Words replace images as the chief vehicle, and the words belong to the script. The director needs the playwright to witness the possibilities and difficulties brought to light in the course of production conferences and rehearsals.

The playwright should be involved from the time of the initial planning. He can always shed some light on his intentions for the director and the designers, and it is likely that ideas from these people—specialists in making plays work on stage—may prompt changes, even restructuring, in the playscript. Both playwright Arthur Miller and designer Jo Mielziner have given accounts of how staging and scenic ideas for the play *Death of a Salesman* considerably altered the script. This sort of creative collaboration is the very life of the theatre. No playwright should cut himself off from it. In fact, you should look for it. Involve yourself in the production process and be alert to all the possibilities that present themselves. Do this, of course, without making a nuisance of yourself: after all, these people have work to do.

There is a certain etiquette to all of this. You need not be present for every rehearsal. You can understand that your presence is a little irritating: you do not appear to be doing anything useful and any actor would prefer to develop a character without the character's creator standing in judgment. On the other hand, you should be there often enough that you become a recognized human being doing something useful after all: examining how the script behaves as a play. Generally, everyone would profit most by having the playwright present for those rehearsals given over to running whole scenes, acts, or the total play. You need to concentrate on the shortcomings and missed chances the running of the play may reveal. You are not directly concerned with actors or designers—they are the director's business. If, however, the contribution of one of these artists is interfering with effects essential to the play, deal with the problem by consulting with the director. He may already be addressing the problem, and, if not, he will need to deal with it in his way, since other facets of the production may be affected. He may want you to talk directly with the actor or designer, but that is his decision, not yours. Remember that you have enough to worry about without worrying about the actors. When you wrote the play, you had to imagine people moving about the space of the stage. Now that they actually are, they will present you with quite enough food for thought. Even though the stage remains bare throughout much of the rehearsal process, you can still learn a great deal about your play, which consists chiefly of actions in words and movements—both of which you can witness. Each evening, you should work on any revisions that you found necessary. They should be talked through then with the director, and as soon as you both can do it, they should be in the hands of the actors. You need to be alert and take care of these matters early, for no director can assimilate significant changes in the last rehearsals.

The director and the playwright should know and trust one another enough to be able to introduce ideas, complaints, suggestions without worry about the other's feelings. That cannot be mandated, but at the very least they must concentrate professionally on the work before them in recognition of their mutual vested interests in it. Some theatres employ a "dramaturg" to work on the production with the playwright and the director. With no vested interests, this person can examine the behavior of the play on stage and make dispassionate judgments and recommendations for playwright and director alike. He is a sort of ombudsman for the play. As such, he also arbitrates any disputes that may erupt between playwright and director. If the dramaturg has a good eye, a keen mind for drama, and a sense of diplomacy, he can be enormously useful.

As rehearsals progress, something both sad and happy happens: the actors gradually take the play away from you. Their world begins to fill up with scenery under appropriate lights, they don the clothes of their characters, properties appear, sounds fill the air. The play is moving away from you on its own feet. It is a delight to see this happen because it suggests the play is rich with its own life, but of course it is a reminder of your uselessness. You become, in Giraudoux's words, a ghost wandering in the wings. In fact, everyone would appreciate it if you would go wander somewhere else.

Learning from Audiences

In a sense, your last collaborator is the audience. This is especially true of stage plays, where adjustment can yet be made once a trial or invited audience has participated in the play's experience. Stage audiences are much more active and demonstrative than cinema or television audiences, largely because they directly encounter the human beings who make the play happen. In cinema, you can join an audience and learn from them where and how your play works and what effects it creates, even if you cannot revise it then and there. The film is made; apply your lessons to the next screenplay. In the case of television, you have almost no direct feedback because the audience is scattered throughout the nation, most in the privacy of their homes.

Any dramatist hopes ultimately to affect an audience in a particular way. This aim has rarely been (or should have rarely been) at the forefront of your thought while you were composing the play, because, paradoxically, the more you think about effect for its own sake, the less able you are to create it. But now that the play has assumed a full life before an audience, you can afford to give attention to effect.

In the past Broadway plays were regularly given "out-of-town tryouts" before opening in New York. They would play before audiences in Philadelphia, New Haven, Boston, or elsewhere to audiences that "did not matter" quite as much as Broadway audiences. The audiences and critics in these towns were important instruments in the last phase of the play's creation—

provided they did not kill the play. Many a play died in out-of-town tryouts and never arrived on Broadway. The practice is no longer common. Now the play may have a showcase early in its life, a simple workshop production; then near the time of opening, it may play to one, two, or three invited audiences. Again the purpose is to test a play. A play is not complete until it encounters its audience. The addition of this last factor can make an enormous difference for better or for worse.

Now, as a playwright, you can approach these experiences in extreme ways. You can watch the audience every moment, react with paranoia every time they do not respond the way you think they should, and generally interfere with the open give and take that should happen between spectacle and spectator. At the other extreme, you can walk out of the theatre and stay out until the audience has gone home—which is probably more paranoid. W. S. Gilbert, of Gilbert and Sullivan fame, was in the habit of walking the streets during the premiere of any of his plays, returning to the theatre precisely at curtain time to be able to hear the audience's applause and take his bow if it was enthusiastic.

Somewhere between these two extremes is an appropriate attitude that will let you learn from your audiences. Bear in mind that they are encountering the play for the first time. They are neither as weary of it as you are nor as alive to its "deeper meanings." What should interest you most is how they become, or do not become, involved in the play. Knowing the play as well as you do, you know at what points crucial effects occur. You need to examine responses at these points. If the response is not what you expected, is it by any chance more appropriate? That may well happen, since you are apt to forget nuances you are tired of but which intrigue or delight your audience. If the response is what you expected, have you overlooked any element on stage that might enhance it? Generally, does the audience assume the character you intended for them? Remember, audiences tend to be perverse, and if they sense that they are to respond one way, they are apt to respond in the opposite. Have you tamed that impulse?

The interval between performance before an invited audience and the opening night is brief, one or two days. At this juncture, there can be no sweeping changes. Still one can make some last-minute improvements. The work by this time has usually become clouded by heavy anxiety emanating from everyone. Inevitably, it is focused upon you, the one who was responsible for the whole thing in the first place. If anyone can fix apparent flaws, it is you. In these last days the pressure to revise sometimes becomes unbearable. They come from every quarter: the director, the leading actors, the producers, the stage manager, and even the elevator boy all have opinions. If something is not going well (as it inevitably is not), the first place to look for a cure is in a script change. The agony of this pressure has been vividly chronicled in such essays as William Gibson's *The Seesaw Log*, an account of his involvement in the initial production of his play *Two for the Seesaw* and in Frank Gilroy's *About Those Roses*, a journal of the mounting of his play *The Subject Was Roses*. The only answer, short of (and perhaps including) an ulcer, is to know so well what matters in your play that no one could convince you to do anything to violate it.

You also may take comfort in the knowledge that you are allowed one more chance. Once the production is running, you are free to revise your script for future productions any way you please. If the play is at all successful, publication will be a next step, and here you are in full control of the text. The stage manager can be a great help to you here, since he possesses the one authoritative version of the script as presented in this production—the full record of the collaborative decisions taken so far. Publishing houses are generally not interested in publishing plays until after they have been thoroughly tested on stage. Once you are published, of course, you can anticipate several other productions.

As screenwriter, you are spared much of this. Revisions have been taking place all along; most were made before production ever started. Once shooting stops, editing starts. Few script changes are made at that phase: it is too late to accommodate any serious change, and those that are made can be done by the editor. And so, by the time the film is released, you have long been involved in some other enterprise. That makes it possible for you to join the audience and watch the film in a much fresher frame of mind than would otherwise be possible. You can see more clearly how your script has translated into a film. While there is nothing to be done with it now, it will tell you much about your writing to apply to future screenplays. True enough, many difficulties in translation are due to curious decisions made by the director, the editor, or other artists. If you can learn anything valuable from that it may be simply how to make such decisions so awkward that no one would make them. That is not altogether possible, but the screenwriter—and the playwright as well—must incorporate techniques in their crafts that guard against wrongheaded decisions of interpretive artists.

Bruised Egos and Misplaced Pride

Once your television play has been aired, your movie released, or your play premiered, another shock wave is due. It comes in the form of reviews. In fact it comes in multiple waves, first from the dailies, then the weeklies, and then the monthlies; the quarterlies might even add to the ripples. If your play is really successful, people will be condemning it for years to come.

As Larry Divine, critic for the *Detroit Free Press*, is fond of pointing out, there is no conspiracy of critics. They do not have periodic clandestine meetings and decide who to praise now and who to condemn. In fact, critics disagree famously. Nevertheless, the nature of our society and of the critic's business makes reviewing take on a certain sensationalism. Critics, especially those who write for the dailies, have to work under enormous pressure, too. There is little time to write reviews and the reviews are supposed to attract attention. Under this pressure, it is only human that reviewers tend to resort to displaying their own personalities, relying on stock responses and catch phrases, and either clever indictments or overdone paeons of praise. This is not intended as a sweeping castigation of critics, most of whom are honest, intelligent, and sensitive people. It is merely to indicate that certain conditions encourage reviews to take extreme and overly simplified stands. If you take them too seriously, they will bruise your ego or swell your head.

Criticism is a form of audience response. It can be enormously useful to you, for it is formalized, and, in the hands of an able, perceptive critic, it can make clear to you some things that had been mysteries despite your long association with your play. This side of criticism balances out the tendency toward sensationalism. In either case, a published review remains the work of a single audience member. It is ultimately that one person's well-informed or misguided opinion. It is also addressed to your play as performed by those artists involved; it is not addressed to you personally, however much you may feel it is. Over the long haul, these immediate responses will fade. If the play continues to attract attention, it will be attention based more and more on the play's own terms.

If the play is enormously successful, drawing great national and even international attention, you face another set of problems. You will find yourself labeled. The public is quick to categorize. It will expect you to produce another play, equally astonishing, and yet also just like the first. Becoming prominent can pose a serious threat to your artistic freedom. Many playwrights to whom this has happened have found it harder and harder to write anything fresh and interesting. It happened to Luigi Pirandello, who finally responded by writing a play about himself trapped in public expectation, the play *When One Is Somebody*. It happened to Tennessee Williams, who toward the end of his career found it virtually impossible to provide anything new.

Perhaps the only answer is a hard one. You must fall back on your own honest reaction to your work, to the world around you, and to the opinions of those whom you respect. And you must turn your attention to new endeavors, putting the old ones behind you. They are indeed the product of your most intense labor and feelings and thoughts, but they are over and done with. You are no longer the same person who composed those plays. Any attacks on them have little bearing on "the you" of today or the work you are doing now. It is poignant that the finest work Eugene O'Neill accomplished as a playwright came after the American theatre had turned its back on him; many of these plays of the late thirties and early forties were never produced in his lifetime. Still, the honesty and integrity of his last plays, such as *Long Day's Journey into Night* or *The Iceman Cometh*, have made them a lasting testament to his greatness as a playwright.

The irony here is that one who starts out seeing the world as a stage may end up forced onto it by his public. This need not rob you of the joy and satisfaction that composing drama can offer. If you are compelled to write for the stage or the screen, let nothing stop you. Filling the empty pages that become a script, you have your own private satisfaction in imagining these characters moving about in their world. To augment that satisfaction with the joy of seeing them spring to life on a stage or screen yields a personal pleasure that no one can take away from you. Relish that, and then move on to your next play.

Glossary

Some Terms Useful to Dramatists

Absurdism: Style of drama used almost exclusively on stage to confront audiences with the irrationality of life, often set against the desperate human desire for meaning. Typically, plays are structured with a crescendo of an uncontrolled element until the play seems to burst its seams, as in the accumulation of chairs in Eugène Ionesco's "The Chairs" or the multiplication of pieces of furniture in his "The New Tenant." Also called "Theatre of the Absurd."

Action: Action derives from the exchange of forces seeking to alter, avoid, or adapt. It is the very basis of drama. Behind it is motivation or purpose. Action renders the activities of a play coherent and meaningful.

Action-Adventure Series: A type of television series concentrating on the adventures of a strong, dominant central character or team of characters. Cowboys, policemen, detectives, emergency room doctors, city desk reporters, trial lawyers are favored central characters. Few continuing characters are involved. Episodes, usually one-hour shows, are self-contained, a new adventure launched with each new episode.

Actor: The primary purveyor of action in a play. The actor embodies character by lending his body and voice to the play on stage or his image to the play on screen. In both cases, the script must first of all be "actable," its effects such that actors may indeed project them.

Aesthetic Distance: The state of detached contemplation that alerts us to the unity and meaning of a work of art by reminding us that it is a human creation. It is a mental state for the audience counteracted by empathy, which works to involve the viewer in the work of art.

Agent: 1. A dramatist's representative in the market place. The agent seeks buyers for the writer's scripts, places him in jobs, and helps guide his career. His efforts are recompensed by 10 percent of the writer's earnings. 2. A character in a play who undertakes action.

Alienation Effect: The basic effect in Bertolt Brecht's idea of Epic Theatre by which the events of a play are deliberately "made strange" in order to keep the audience in a critical frame of mind, judging the actual world against the contrived world of the stage.

Allegory: The arrangement of symbols into a system that corresponds completely to another level of reality, as in the medieval morality play *Everyman* in which characters such as Everyman himself, Death, Good Works, and others represent the experience of death.

Allusive Realism: A style of drama using a basic Realism but alluding to outside forces at work, sometimes social or political, sometimes metaphysical. The effect is sometimes chilling and mysterious and sometimes cartoon-like. Examples: Slawomir Mrozek's *Tango*, David Rabe's *Sticks and Bones*, John Guare's *House of Blue Leaves* and Sam Shepard's *Buried Child*.

Antagonist: A character exerting a major force against the protagonist.

Anthology: A type of television program presenting self-contained plays. They may be grouped together by theme or genre or setting. Each show may feature a single play or a group of plays or an intertwined set of plots. Examples: *The Twilight Zone, American Playhouse, Love Boat.*

Apron: The extension of the stage forward of the proscenium arch. It may be employed as an acting area or as neutral ground separating the play from the audience.

Arena Stage: A theatrical configuration placing the stage in the middle of the audience. The seating surrounds the entire stage so that entrances require the actors to pass through the audience.

Auteur: A French word meaning author, used in cinema to refer to the writer-director-editor as the supreme film artist.

Avant Garde: French term meaning "forward guard." In art, it refers to the effort to explore new ground, the artists deliberately creating untraditional, even anti-traditional, art. Consequently, the avant garde tends to be both cliquish and renegade at the same time.

Bathos: An overdone appeal to emotional involvement in a character's suffering. The result is "corny."

Beat: A sequence of dramatic action during which one motivation dominates. When another motivation supplants it, a new beat begins. It is also called a "motivational unit." The idea originated with Konstantin Stanislavsky who used it as a means for the actor to analyze the shifting currents of a role. It is equally useful to the playwright in studying the interactions of characters.

Bible: The guide for a continuing television series, containing sketches of the characters, details of locations or settings, and a long-term projection of the story line. It is a crucial part of the development of scripts for soap operas.

Birdseye Shot: A shot recorded with the camera directly overhead.

Black Box: A type of theatre permitting a wide variety of configurations of the seating and acting areas. It is usually a rectangular or square room painted black to render it neutral. Moveable platforms for the seating and an overhead grid for the lights make it highly flexible.

Boom: A moveable platform for transporting a camera into the air and through space, usually used for moving shots. It is also called a "cherry picker."

But/Therefore Principle: Tying dramatic events together by ironic or causal links and so insuring a continuing tension. "Buts" and "therefores" are more compelling than "ands" in dramatic action. The idea is originally Marian Gallaway's.

Camera Angle: The degree of tilt of a camera focused on a subject. A high angle shot, for example, places the camera well above the subject and tilted down.

Catharsis: The release of tension in the final phase of a tragedy's action. It works upon the emotions of pity and fear, the one altruistic, the other self-centered. By focusing them on a worthy protagonist, the emotions are "purged" or "released." The term appears first in Aristotle's *Poetics* and scholars have puzzled ever since about its exact meaning.

Characterization: The differentiation of characters one from another. We recognize and understand characters by what they say, by what others say about them, and most of all by what they do. Characterization may also be thought of in terms of four levels: 1. physical (the character's appearance determined by age, sex, and size); 2. social (the character's place in society, his trade, and family relationship); 3. psychological (the drives and motivations); and 4. ethical (the moral standard and values of the character).

Climax: The point in the dramatic action when the last, crucial decision is made. It is the "beginning of the end," introducing the dénouement or resolution. It is synonymous with "crux."

Close-Up: A camera shot focusing on the face of an actor or on a detail. Abbreviated CU.

Comedy: A form of drama creating a spectacle out of the ludicrous, the incongruous, the inconsistent, and the absurd. It depends on deviations from the norm, and on the audience's feeling a certain detachment and superiority to the characters. There are many sub-forms of comedy: comedy of character, situation comedy, comedy of ideas, comedy of manners, and farce.

Commonplace Book: The writer's notebook for recording anything and everything that could conceivably be used in a future play and for experimenting with ideas, scenes, characters, and pieces of dialogue. It is the writer's sketchbook.

Complication: A moment in a play that severely alters the dramatic situation. Generally, complications come in one of two forms: as a discovery, when new information or understanding emerges, and as a reversal, when action produces unexpected results.

Conflict: Direct and active opposition of characters against one another or their environment. It is the most reliable way to create dramatic tension. Conflict may arise between characters, between motives in a single character, between characters and their environment, or between causes, ideologies, or beliefs.

Continuing Characters: Characters in a television episodic series who appear regularly from episode to episode.

Continuity: The internal logic of a film by which we recognize the context and links between shots. Since films are created by multiple shots, they require an orientation in space and time. One shot needs to connect with the next in such a way that we recognize where and when they occur.

Convention: A tacit agreement on the part of the spectator to accept certain artificial devices as referring to something real. An "aside," a line spoken to the audience and supposedly unheard by other characters, is a convention, as is a "Point of View" (POV) shot in film.

Cover Shot: A general shot of a scene's action used to provide an alternative in editing when the planned cutting fails to work.

Crisis: The moment when dramatic action reaches a point of decision, when tension attains its tautest development and something must happen to snap it. The crisis then leads on to the climax or crux.

Cross-Cutting: The device of cutting back and forth from one sequence of events in one location to another in another location, as if both were happening simultaneously. It is also called "parallel action."

Crux: The moment in the developing dramatic action when tension snaps, introducing the dénouement or resolution. It is synonymous with climax, but places emphasis on the release of tension rather than on decision.

Cut: A break in the action created by turning off the camera at the end of a shot.

Dénouement: The last phase of dramatic action, the resolution, restoring a kind of order to the situation now relieved of tension. The French word means literally "unraveling," suggesting the relaxation of tensions.

Depth of Field: In film, the depth of field is the distance in which objects remain in focus. Dramatic tension can be created by activity at differing planes in the depth of field.

Deus ex Machina: A sudden contrived resolution to a drama created by the intervention of an outside character powerful enough to resolve an insoluble situation. The day is saved by the arrival of an astonishing hero. The Latin phrase means literally "god out of the machine," referring to the ancient practice of lowering god-characters onto stage by means of a crane machine.

Dialogue: The interaction of character in the form of words.

Didacticism: Using art to instruct or teach a lesson. It tends to render all effects thin and one-dimensional.

Discovery: See "complication."

Dissolve: The passage from one shot to another by fading one image as the next gradually appears in its place.

Dolly: A shot in which the camera physically moves through space as it records action.

Dramatic Mode: The recreation of human life through spectacle and action. It may occur in a variety of media, most commonly stage, screen and radio.

Editing: The joining of one shot to another to create a film. It is also called cutting and montage.

Empathy: The audience's vicarious experience of the life of a character, sensing the same emotion the character undergoes. It may also describe the audience's involvement in the play as a whole. It is balanced by the contrary spirit of aesthetic distance. See also aesthetic distance and willing suspension of disbelief.

Environmental Theatre: A theatrical form calling for a constantly shifting arena of action, playing in the total environment of the locale.

Epic Theatre: A style of theatrical presentation using the stage as an arena for story-telling. The stage is treated frankly as a stage, its actors miming the story as something that once happened. The audience is continually reminded that the play is pretense, illusions being constantly shaped and shattered. The idea is closely associated with playwright Bertolt Brecht.

Episodic Series: A television continuing show, each episode using a group of characters and a set number of standard locales. Sitcoms, soap operas, adventure series are all types of episodic series.

Establishing Shot: A shot used at the outset of a scene to orient the audience to the location. An extreme long shot or a long shot is used for this purpose.

Exposition: Basic information about the characters, circumstances and prior events of a play. A certain amount of exposition is necessary for the audience to understand the present action of a play, but exposition usually occurs throughout a play.

Expressionism: A style of theatre and film consisting of distortion of objective reality in order to convey a personal, often dream-like vision. Examples: Georg Kaiser's *From Morn to Midnight*, Elmer Rice's *The Adding Machine*, and Robert Wiene's *The Cabinet of Dr. Caligari*.

Extreme High (or Low) Angle Shot: A shot taken with the camera high above the subject and tilted down (or well below and tilted up).

Extreme Long Shot: An exterior, panoramic shot taken at a considerable distance. It is often used as an establishing shot. Abbreviated XLS.

Extreme Close-Up: A very close shot of a small detail of an object or person blown up to occupy the entire screen. An extreme close-up of a person would consist of a particular feature, such as an eye, a mouth, an ear. Abbreviated XCU.

Eye-Level Shot: A shot taken with the camera at eye level.

Farce: An extreme form of comedy, consisting of physical bufoonery, mistaken identities, outrageous misunderstandings, and slapstick. Examples: Molière's *The Pranks of Scapin* and Philip King's *See How They Run.*

Fade: The gradual disappearance of a screen image into blackness (fade out), or the gradual emergence of an image out of blackness (fade in).

Feature Film: A full-length film designed to provide an evening's entertainment. Modern practice calls for feature films to last between ninety and a hundred and twenty minutes.

Flashback: A scene or sequence from the past inserted in the midst of present action. Essentially it is a screen device, but it can be used on stage. The flash forward is a device less commonly employed.

Form: Generally, the shape of a play or the pattern in which its material is arranged. "Structural form" refers to the way in which space and time are manipulated. This involves how stage space is isolated and defined and how time is divided and characterized. In film, similarly, patterns of framing and editing determine structural form. "Tonal form" refers to patterns traditionally associated with attitude or tone, producing such standard forms as tragedy, comedy, tragi-comedy, farce and melodrama.

French Scene: A sequence of action in a stage play involving the same group of characters. When one exits or a new character enters, the French scene ends and a new one begins. Breaking a play down into French scenes is a useful way to examine structure and the sources of tension or conflict. Thus, a dramatist's scenario is usually based on French scenes.

Full-Length Play: A stage play intended to provide an evening's entertainment, usually two to two-and-a-half hours in length. Modern full-length plays are usually structured into two or three acts, more and more commonly into two.

Genre: A recognized type of drama, based on material and treatment. Examples: Westerns, mysteries, musicals.

Hamartia: Aristotle's term for the composite qualities of a tragic protagonist, those that inspire awe as well as the fatal weakness (the tragic flaw) that contributes to a downfall.

Histrionic Sensibility: The awareness of the meaning of the actions of others. It is an innate faculty in humans, making it possible for us to sense another person's feelings by facial expression, "body language," vocal intonation and the general context. Naturally, it is crucial that the audience contribute histrionic sensibility to the dramatic experience. The term was coined by Francis Fergusson.

Hook: An astonishing or striking event at the outset of a play designed to seize and focus audience attention. The term is used predominantly in television, where the hook can keep the audience waiting through the opening commercial. Also called a "teaser."

Illusion of the First Time: The audience's sensation that the events they are witnessing are taking place now for the first time. It is a valuable effect attained only after considerable effort on the part of the writer, director and actors. Because of the immediacy of theatre, the illusion of the first time is most important there, but it bears on all dramatic media.

Improvisation: An acting technique calling for inventing lines and business on the basis of an agreed-upon situation. Actors use it to explore values and motivations in a character. The device is sometimes used to develop new plays.

Inner Life: The interior motivations and feelings of a character, sensed by the audience through histrionic sensibility. It can be a source of dramatic tension at odds with outward action, as in the plays of Tennessee Williams or Anton Chekhov.

Irony: A disparity between the overt meaning of a statement or action and its intended meaning, or between two interpretations of its meaning. It is a valuable source of dramatic tension.

Location: A "found" scene for a screenplay. A location is a place in the actual world selected as the setting of a film scene. Shooting on location is opposed to shooting in the studio or on the lot.

Locus: The figurative meeting point of the suggestions projected from the stage and the imagination of the audience. In Realistic plays, the locus is relatively close to the proscenium since the suggestions are fuller and the audience provides less imaginatively; in a Theatricalist play the locus is closer to the audience.

Long Shot: A shot taken with the camera at some distance from the subject, far enough to take in the whole subject and some of the context. Abbreviated LS.

Low Angle Shot: A shot taken with the camera well below the subject and tilted up.

Master Scene Script: The screenplay script as produced by the screenwriter, structured according to scenes. The director then writes out the shooting script based on the shots to be taken.

Medium: The context and materials used in an art form. In drama, that may consist of live actors moving in the space of a stage (the theatre medium) or of their images moving on a screen (television and film).

Medium Shot: A shot taken with the camera at a moderate distance from the subject. A medium shot of an actor includes approximately the body from the waist up. Abbreviated MS.

Melodrama: A form of drama characterized by the introduction of powerful, threatening forces in the form of calamities or unbridled evil, designed to arouse indignation and terror. Simplistic melodramas such as old Westerns use blatant villains, powerless heroines and dashing heroes. More subtle instances portray humanity at the mercy of uncontrolled social forces as in Friedrich Duerrenmatt's *The Physicists* or Charles Gordone's *No Place to Be Somebody.*

Mini-Series: A form of television drama presented in a limited number of episodes within a short time of one another. Typically, the episodes are two hours long and about five in number, adding up to a ten hour drama. Despite the term, mini-series are clearly the longest form of drama available. Examples: *Roots; Upstairs, Downstairs; The Winds of War.*

Modified Realism: A style of dramatic writing using a basic Realism, but modifying its usual objective nature by introducing elements of a more subjective, psychological nature. It is also called "Psychological Realism." Examples: Tennessee Williams' *The Glass Menagerie* or Arthur Miller's *Death of a Salesman.*

Moment: A sequence of dramatic action during which tension is drawn between the same poles. Once tension is redrawn, a new moment begins. Synonymous with "beat" except it is based on tension rather than motivation.

Montage: The joining together of shots to make a film. Also called "cutting" or "editing." The term is sometimes used to refer to a sequence of quick shots.

Multi-Cam: The technique of recording shots by two or more cameras from various viewpoints. It is used in studio drama most commonly.

Multi-Media: A theatrical presentation employing a variety of media: live actors, recorded sound, film clips, videos, slide projections, lighting effects.

Naturalism: A style of dramatic writing based on the idea of duplicating reality on stage to provide the chance to examine life closely and even scientifically. It depends, therefore, on reproducing exactly the details of objective reality. Examples: August Strindberg's "Miss Julie," Emile Zola's *Thérèse Raquin.*

Objective Camera: Use of the camera to record action in a direct, detached manner. It is one of the "voices" of the camera along with first person or subjective camera, third person, and omniscient.

Obligatory Scene: The scene in a play which the playwright is obliged to provide, having built up anticipation of some ultimate confrontation. Simplistically, this is the duel at high noon in the street in the old Westerns. The term was coined by Francisque Sarcey in describing the Well-Made Play. It has application beyond that formula in connection with the handling of tension in a play, which must sooner or later rise to a point of snapping.

Off-Screen: The unseen area beyond the frame of a shot. It can be a source of tension or anticipation, as someone or something may be forcing things to happen on screen and naturally arousing curiosity as it does so.

Off-Stage: The unseen area beyond the confines of the stage. It can figuratively embody extensions of the world portrayed on-stage and so be a source of tension or anticipation, much as off-screen can be.

Omniscient Camera: The use of a camera that appears capable of seeing anything and everything relevant to the story: it can see beyond the horizon, beyond this moment, into the minds of the characters, as well as normal objective reality. It is one of the "voices" of the camera, along with the objective camera, the third person camera, and the first person camera.

One-Act Play: A relatively brief stage play lasting under an hour and usually playing as one sequence of action. The form requires a considerable economy of effect, and frequently depends on creating an impression rather than a process of change in a character or a complex series of events. The one-act play on television is one lasting the time between commercials, usually used only in anthology series.

Option: The exclusive legal right of a producing company to produce a play within a specified period of time in exchange for a fee paid to the playwright.

Outline: A brief scene-by-scene narration of a projected screenplay. It is more elaborate than a premise, but briefer than a treatment.

Over-the-Shoulder Shot: A shot of one character taken over the shoulder of another, the shoulder thus providing part of the frame.

Pan: To turn the camera side to side on its pivot, thereby bringing off-screen areas onto screen.

Parallel Action: See "Cross Cutting."

Pilot: A sample television play produced as a test for a proposed series.

Plant: A detail appearing early in a script and later proving to be significant to the action. The device serves as preparation for dramatic surprises. A blatant example would be "the gun in the drawer." The device, however, can be handled subtly and effectively.

Plot: The central action of a play. It is not to be confused with the "story," which is simply a series of events. Plot assumes unity and momentum by purposive action moving forward against resistance.

Precipitating Context: The opening phase of dramatic action, during which the world of the play opens itself to us and introduces some force that launches action. The term was coined by Bernard Beckerman.

Presentationalism: Presenting dramatic action openly and directly to the audience, without attempting to develop a full illusion of a life being lived somewhere other than the stage. It stands at the opposite extreme from representationalism.

Probability: The internal logic in a play that renders its world and events believable on the play's own terms, whether possible in our world or not. Aristotle first described the concept, arguing that the playwright is obliged to make the world of play believable regardless of normal expectations. He also asserted that it is far better to have a probable impossibility on stage than an improbable possibility. In the case of Eugène Ionesco's

Rhinoceros, for example, the impossible transformation of people into rhinoceroses becomes very probable, even inevitable.

Property: 1. An object used in a drama. Floor properties include all manner of furniture; hand properties, objects brought on by the actors. The term is often shortened to "prop." They provide a useful way for a playwright to focus attention. 2. As a commercial term, property refers to the script itself, a product to be bought and sold.

Proposition: A way of expressing the plot of a play to test its structure. The process, described by W. T. Price, is based on the syllogism and moves from the condition of action (major premise) to the cause of action (minor premise) to the resulting action (conclusion).

Proscenium: The arch dividing the auditorium from the stage area. The proscenium theatre is the most formal type of theatre, depending on a full picture frame stage and a high degree of illusion and spectacle.

Protagonist: The central character of a play. The term derives from Greek, meaning the one who acts or suffers for the play, hence the character who moves the plot forward.

Raisonneur: French term for a character who speaks for the dramatist.

Realism: A style of drama which concentrates on presenting human life objectively, much as it appears to our eyes and ears. It attempts to catch the details and subtleties of the appearance of reality, and presents action as if transpiring in the real world rather than on stage or screen. For the stage, consequently, it uses the convention of the "fourth wall" as if one wall of a room had been removed for our glimpse of the life lived there. Nevertheless, Realism is not as closed to the audience as Naturalism, for its works by selective and somewhat more presentational means. Examples: Henrik Ibsen's *Doll's House* and Jason Miller's *That Championship Season*.

Record Book: A writer's notebook maintaining notes, ideas, sketches, and descriptions pertinent to a work in progress. It is the same idea as the commonplace book, but devoted to a current play as it is being written. It serves to keep track of ideas and possibilities as they occur.

Release Form: A legal form which screen producing companies require signed by those submitting unsolicited material. It frees the production company from any legal action on the ground of plagiarism.

Representationalism: A mode of stage presentation emphasizing illusion, giving the audience the sense that the stage action is being "represented" rather than "presented." Accordingly, it stands at the opposite pole from "presentationalism." Elements of both modes have to be present in stage drama, but styles may approach one extreme or the other, Naturalism being close to representationalism and Theatricalism close to presentationalism.

Resistance: The phase of dramatic action following the emergence of the driving force of a play as that force encounters obstacles and complications. It is the rising action of the play up to the point of crisis. The term used this way belongs to Bernard Beckerman.

Reversal: A form of complication occurring when action produces an unexpected result. See "complication."

Reverse Angle: A kind of shot taken from the opposite angle as the previous shot.

Rough Cut: The first edit of a film, done to test the edit prior to precise cutting and laboratory work.

Scenario: In stage plays, scenario refers to the outline or blueprint of the entire play. It is composed of a French scene breakdown of the play describing the action contained in each scene and indicating the function of each scene for the play as a whole. It serves to keep track of the play's essential structure, and as an easily altered scheme preparatory to re-writes. In the screen media, the term sometimes refers to the treatment and sometimes to a shot breakdown.

Scene: In stage plays, a scene is the action presented in one sequence from curtain up to curtain down, usually briefer and less complex than an act. In screenplays, scenes are those series of shots of action in one location and in one time span, introduced in manuscript by the notation of whether the scene is an exterior or interior place, what the place is, and the time of day.

Sequence: A term used in the screen media referring to a group of scenes that complete a major action. It is analogous to a chapter in a novel.

Shot: The action recorded during one run of the camera. The shot is the basic building block of a film. The shooting script developed by the director breaks the screenwriter's master scene script into shots. These shots are given to the editor at the end of the shoot for assembly into the finished film.

Sitcom: A television term, short for situation comedy, applied to comedy series with continuing characters. The series derives from a basic situation, elaborated in each episode.

Soap Opera: A form of television drama depicting a series of crises in the ongoing story of a large group of intertwined characters. The form tends to use brief scenes between two or three characters in rapid succession, relying heavily on close-ups to give the impression of a kind of never-ending life. These are usually daytime series, appearing each afternoon, but they also appear in evening slots, such as *Dallas* and *Dynasty*. Advertisers sponsoring these shows traditionally have been soap companies, hence the term.

Soliloquy: A speech spoken by an actor alone on stage to suggest an inner conflict of the character's mind. Unlike a monologue, it is a convention by which the audience translates the act of speaking into the act of thinking.

Special: A television program produced one time only as a special occasion, not intended to continue as a series.

Stage Directions: Indications of activity or special effects incorporated into the script for a stage play. These should be restricted to those that contribute to the dramatic action significantly. Stage directing is a task beyond the work of the playwright.

Step Contract: A type of contract issued in the screen industries providing employment for one step in the development of a piece. A screenwriter, for example, might be hired only for the treatment development, or for a single draft of the screenplay, and then be re-hired or dropped at the next step.

Storyboard: The screen director's layout of shots, rendered in the form of sketches of each shot with descriptions.

Studio Drama: Television plays taped in the studio, using multiple cameras, which can be simultaneously edited in the control room. The pattern is used for most soap operas and sitcoms.

Style: A characteristic mode of expression determined by the way in which the dramatist sees reality. There are both "personal styles" by which we recognize at once a play by Tennessee Williams or Jean Anouilh, and "established styles" which group playwrights together by shared devices, styles such as Realism, Epic Theatre, or Theatre of the Absurd.

Subjective Camera: Camera used to see reality or dreams as a character sees them. Also called "first person camera."

Subplot: An action accompanying the main action of a play, often involving some of the same characters and finally resolved by the same act at the crux of the play.

Symbol: The device of making a character, object or action refer to or represent something beyond the play. Symbols work best when well integrated into the play and working on a number of levels.

Symbolism: 1. A systematic use of symbols. 2. A style of drama depending on the creation of a dreamlike atmosphere and the use of implicit, instinctual symbols. Examples: Maurice Maeterlinck's *Pelléas and Mélisande* and Tennessee Williams' *Camino Real.*

Synopsis: A brief description of a proposed television or film play, usually only a paragraph long. Occasionally it is bought by the producing company which then hires a writer to develop it into an outline or treatment.

Tag: A last brief vignette, intended to encapsulate the entire preceding television episode, following the last commercial.

Take: A single attempt at a shot. Several takes are usually needed to get the shot desired.

Teaser: See "hook."

Theatre of Cruelty: An approach to theatrical presentation developed by Antonin Artaud and designed to create spectacles that create a vivid sense of human cruelty, both in the material represented and in the manner in which it is presented.

Theatricalism: 1. Use of the stage to present an elaborate spectacle. 2. A movement in the theatre emphasizing the fact of the theatre by reminding the audience of the contrivance of the actors and designers. Its intent is usually social protest, provoking the audience to recognize parallels between their world and the contrived world of the stage. The approach appears in many contemporary plays, the plays of Dario Fo, Bertolt Brecht, Friedrich Duerrenmatt, Jean Anouilh, and Tom Stoppard, for example.

Third Factor: An object or person who functions as a point of reference for two characters engaged in dramatic action. The device helps bring to the surface the feelings and motivations of the characters and to give variety to their interaction.

Thrust Stage: A type of theatre configuration in which the audience sits on three sides of a stage as if it were thrust into their midst. The background of the stage can then serve for scenic effects.

Tone: The attitude of the writer toward his material, an attitude which hopefully will be communicated and shared with the audience.

Tragedy: A form of drama which presents humanity facing the most dire circumstances. It is marked by a sense of awe, as characters valiantly deal with powerful forces and yet often are themselves marred by a flaw that leads to confrontation. Typically, the action ends with catastrophe. It is associated with the great plays of the Greek and Elizabethan periods, such as *Oedipus Rex* and *Hamlet*, but it also appears in the modern theatre, as in such plays as Ibsen's *The Master Builder*, Pirandello's *Henry IV*, or Duerrenmatt's *The Visit*.

Tragi-Comedy: A hybrid form of drama, mixing comedy and tragedy and creating a tone that is ambiguous or alternating. Plays dealing with serious and dire circumstances contain richly comic exchanges, and plays that are ultimately comic contain moments of serious implication. Most of the modern theatre is written in this form. Examples: Samuel Beckett's *Waiting for Godot*, Tom Stoppard's *Rosencrantz and Guildenstern Are Dead*, Harold Pinter's *The Birthday Party*.

Treatment: A scene-by-scene narrative version of a proposed film written in the present tense as a description of the experience of watching the film. For a feature length film, the treatment is in the neighborhood of forty pages. It serves to visualize the film's action and to coordinate its structure. It also serves as a product to be negotiated as one step in the series of commissions issued by a producing company.

Voice Over: The screen device of playing a narration over a series of shots.

Willing Suspension of Disbelief: Term coined by Samuel Johnson and associated strongly with the writings of Samuel Coleridge to refer to the state of mind of an audience. It is a sense of involvement in the play, countered by the awareness of its contrivance, a composite of empathy and aesthetic distance. The audience does not believe the illusion of the life portrayed on stage or screen, but does willingly suspend disbelief.

Zoom: An effect available with the zoom lens, which can adjust to enlarge an image by "zooming in" or diminish it by "zooming out." The effect is similar to moving the camera in, which also enlarges the image, but it carries no sense of the camera's motion, no sense that we are closer.

Bibliography

Some Books of Interest to Dramatists

Allen, Walter, ed. *Writers on Writing.* New York: E. P. Dutton, 1959.

Appia, Adolphe. *The Work of Living Art* and *Man Is the Measure of All Things.* Coral Gables, Florida: University of Miami Press, 1960.

Archer, William. *Playmaking: A Manual of Craftsmanship.* New York: Dover Publications, 1960.

Aristotle. *The Poetics,* Ingram Bywater, tr. New York: Random House, 1954.

Arnheim, Rudolf. *Film as Art.* Berkeley, California: University of California Press, 1957.

Artaud, Antonin. *The Theatre and Its Double.* New York: Grove Press, 1958.

Baker, George Pierce. *Dramatic Technique.* Boston: Houghton Mifflin Company, 1919.

Bazin, André. *What Is Cinema?,* Hugh Gray, tr. Berkeley, California: University of California Press, 1967.

Beckerman, Bernard. *The Dynamics of the Drama.* New York: Alfred A. Knopf, 1970.

Benedetti, Robert. *The Actor at Work.* Englewood Cliffs, New Jersey: Prentice-Hall, 1970.

Bentley, Eric. *The Life of the Drama.* New York: Atheneum, 1965.

Bentley, Eric. *The Playwright as Thinker.* New York: Meridian Books, 1955.

Bentley, Eric, ed. *The Theory of the Modern Stage.* Baltimore: Penguin Books, 1968.

Bentley, Eric. *What Is Theatre?* Boston: Beacon Cliffs, 1956.

Bergson, Henri. *Laughter: An Essay on the Meaning of the Comic.* London: Macmillan & Co., 1921.

Bluestone, George. *Novels into Film.* Baltimore: Johns Hopkins University Press, 1957.

Blumenberg, Richard M. *Critical Focus: An Introduction to Film.* Belmont, California: Wadsworth Publishing Co., 1975.

Boleslavsky, Richard. *Acting: The First Six Lessons.* New York: Theatre Arts Books, 1933.

Brecht, Bertolt. *Brecht on Theatre,* John Willet, tr. New York: Hill and Wang, 1964.

Brenner, Alfred. *The TV Scriptwriter's Handbook.* Cincinnati: Writer's Digest Books, 1980.

Brockett, Oscar G. *The Theatre: An Introduction.* New York: Holt, Rinehart and Winston, 1964.

Brockett, Oscar G., and Robert B. Findlay. *Century of Innovation: A History of European and American Drama Since 1870.* Englewood Cliffs, New Jersey: Prentice-Hall, 1973.

Brook, Peter. *The Empty Space.* New York: Avon Books, 1968.

Brustein, Robert. *The Theatre of Revolt.* Boston: Little, Brown and Company, 1964.

Busfield, Roger M., Jr. *The Playwright's Art: Stage, Radio, Television, Motion Pictures.* New York: Harper & Row, 1958.

Catron, Louis E. *Writing, Producing and Selling Your Play.* Englewood Cliffs, New Jersey: Prentice-Hall, 1984.

Chekhov, Anton. *Letters on the Short Story, the Drama and Other Literary Topics,* Louis Friedland, ed. New York: Minton, Balch and Company, 1924.

Chekhov, Anton. *The Life and Letters of Anton Chekhov,* S. S. Koteliansky and Philip Tomlinson, trs. and eds. London: Cassell and Company, 1925.

Chekhov, Anton. *The Personal Papers.* New York: Lear Publishers, 1948.

Chekhov, Michael. *To the Actor on the Technique of Acting.* New York: Harper & Row, 1953.

Clurman, Harold. *The Fervent Years.* New York: Hill and Wang, 1957.

Cole, Toby, ed. *Playwrights on Playwriting.* New York: Hill and Wang, 1960.

Cole, Toby, and Helen K. Chinoy, eds. *Directing the Play: A Source Book of Stagecraft.* Indianapolis: Bobbs-Merrill, 1953.

Cole, Toby, and Helen K. Chinoy, eds. *Actors on Acting: The Theories, Techniques, and Practices of the Great Actors of All Times as Told in Their Own Words.* New York: Holt, Rinehart and Winston, 1949.

Corrigan, Robert W., and James Rosenberg, eds. *The Context and Craft of the Drama.* San Francisco: Chandler Publishing Company, 1964.

Craig, Edward Gordon. *On the Art of Theatre.* Boston: Small, Maynard, 1924.

Driver, Tom F. *History of the Modern Theatre.* New York: Delacorte Press, 1970.

Eidsvik, Charles. *Cineliteracy.* New York: Random House, 1978.

Eisenstein, Sergei. *Film Form* and *The Film Sense,* Jay Leyda, tr. Cleveland: World Publishing Co., 1957.

Esslin, Martin. *Age of Television.* New York: W. M. Freeman, 1981.

Esslin, Martin. *An Anatomy of Drama.* New York: Hill and Wang, 1977.

Esslin, Martin. *The Theatre of the Absurd.* London: Penguin Books, 1980.

Fergusson, Francis. *The Idea of a Theatre.* Garden City, New York: Doubleday and Company, 1949.

Field, Syd. *Screenplay: The Foundations of Screenwriting.* New York: Dell Publishing Co., 1982.

Forster, E. M. *Aspects of the Novel.* New York: Harcourt, Brace, Jovanovich, 1927.

Frenz, Horst, ed. *American Playwrights on Drama.* New York: Hill and Wang, 1965.

Gallaway, Marian. *Constructing a Play.* Englewood Cliffs, New Jersey: Prentice-Hall, 1950.

Geduld, Harry M., ed. *Filmmakers on Filmmaking.* Bloomington: Indiana University Press, 1969.

Ghéon, Henri. *The Art of Theatre.* Adde M. Fiste, tr. New York: Hill and Wang, 1961.

Giannetti, Louis D. *Understanding Movies.* Englewood Cliffs, New Jersey: Prentice-Hall, 1976.

Gibson, William. *The Seesaw Log.* New York: Alfred A. Knopf, 1959.

Gibson, William. *Shakespeare's Game.* New York: Atheneum, 1978.

Gilroy, Frank. *About Those Roses.* New York: Random House, 1965.

Goffman, Erving. *The Presentation of Self in Everyday Life.* New York: Doubleday and Company, 1959.

Gorelik, Mordecai. *New Theatres for Old.* New York: Samuel French, 1940.

Granville-Barker, Harley. *On Dramatic Method.* New York: Hill and Wang, 1956.

Grebanier, Bernard. *Playwriting: How to Write for the Theatre.* New York: Thomas Y. Crowell, 1961.

Gross, Roger. *Understanding Playscripts.* Bowling Green, Ohio: Bowling Green University Press, 1974.

Guthrie, Edwin R. *The Psychology of Human Conflict: The Clash of Motives Within the Individual.* Boston: Beacon Press, 1962.

Hainaux, René, ed. *Stage Design Throughout the World Since 1935.* New York: Theatre Arts Books, 1956.

Hainaux, René, ed. *Stage Design Throughout the World Since 1960.* New York: Theatre Arts Books, 1973.

Huizinga, Johan. *Homo Ludens: A Study of the Play Element in Culture.* Boston: Beacon Press, 1950.

Ionesco, Eugène. *Notes and Counter Notes: Writings on the Theatre.* New York: Grove Press, 1964.

James, Henry. *The Art of the Novel.* New York: Charles Scribner's Sons, 1934.

James, Henry. *The Scenic Art.* New York: Hill and Wang, 1957.

Jones, Robert Edmond. *The Dramatic Imagination.* New York: Meredith Publishing Co., 1941.

Kerr, Walter. *How Not to Write a Play.* New York: Simon and Schuster, 1955.

Knight, Arthur. *The Liveliest Art.* New York: The Macmillan Company, 1957.

Koestler, Arthur. *The Act of Creation.* New York: Dell Publishing Company, 1964.

Kracauer, Siegfried. *Theory of Film.* New York: Oxford University Press, 1965.

Langer, Suzanne. *Feeling and Form: A Theory of Art.* New York: Charles Scribner's Sons, 1953.

Langer, Suzanne. *Problems of Art.* New York: Charles Scribner's Sons, 1957.

Lawson, John Howard. *Film: The Creative Process.* New York: Hill and Wang, 1967.

Lawson, John Howard. *Theory and Technique of Playwriting.* New York: Hill and Wang, 1960.

Lindsay, Vachel. *The Art of the Moving Picture.* New York: Liveright, 1970.

MacCann, Richard Dyer, ed. *Film: A Montage of Theories.* New York: E. P. Dutton and Co., 1966.

MacGowan, Kenneth. *A Primer of Playwriting.* New York: Random House, 1951.

MacGowan, Kenneth. *Behind the Screen.* New York: Delacorte Press, 1965.

MacGowan, Kenneth, and Robert Edmond Jones. *Continental Stagecraft.* New York: Harcourt, Brace, and World, 1922.

May, Rollo. *The Courage to Create.* New York: Norton, 1975.

Osborne, Elizabeth, ed. *The Dramatist's Sourcebook.* New York: Theatre Communications Group, 1983.

Pudovkin, V. I. *Film Technique* and *Film Acting,* Ivor Montagu, tr. New York: Grove Press, 1970.

Raphaelson, Samson. *The Human Nature of Playwriting.* New York: Macmillan, 1949.

Rowe, Kenneth Thorpe. *Write That Play!* New York: Funk and Wagnalls Company, 1939.

St. Denis, Michel. *The Rediscovery of Style.* New York: Theatre Arts Books, 1960.

Sarris, Andrew, ed. *Interviews with Film Directors.* New York: Bobbs-Merrill Co., 1967.

Shank, Theodore. *The Art of Dramatic Art.* Belmont, California: Dickenson Publishing Company, 1969.

Simon, Bernard, ed. *Simon's Directory of Theatrical Services and Information.* New York: Package Publicity Service.

Simonson, Lee. *The Stage Is Set.* New York: Dover Publications, 1932.

Smiley, Sam. *Playwriting: The Structure of Action.* Englewood Cliffs, New Jersey: Prentice-Hall, 1971.

Stanislavsky, Konstantin. *An Actor Prepares.* Elizabeth Reynolds Hapgood, tr. New York: Theatre Arts Books, 1936.

Styan, J. L. *Drama, Stage and Audience.* London: Cambridge University Press, 1975.

Styan, J. L. *The Elements of Drama.* New York: Funk and Wagnalls Co., 1960.

Styan, J. L. *The Dark Comedy: The Development of Modern Comic Tragedy.* Cambridge: Cambridge University Press, 1962.

Swain, Dwight V. *Film Scriptwriting.* New York: Hastings House, 1977.

Taylor, John Russell. *Cinema Eye, Cinema Ear.* New York: Hill and Wang, 1964.

Vale, Eugene. *The Technique of Screenplay Writing.* New York: Grosset and Dunlap, 1972.

Van Druten, John. *Playwright at Work.* New York: Harper, 1953.

Young, Stark. *The Theatre.* New York: Doubleday and Company, 1927.

Index